Fort Worth's Historic Congregations

CAMP MEETING TO CATHEDRAL

Fort Worth's Historic Congregations

To Zena —
Blessings!
Ann Arnold

Ann Arnold

FIRST EDITION
Copyright © 2004
Published in the United States of America
by Landa Press
P. O. Box 122336
Arlington, TX 76012

ALL RIGHTS RESERVED

Library of Congress Control Number: 2003114443

Library of Congress Cataloging-in-Publication Data

Arnold, Ann
    Campground to Cathedral:
Fort Worth's Historic Congregations

Includes bibliographical references, index and photos

ISBN 0-9721297-1-5

1 2 3 4 5 6 7 8 9 0
1. Title   2.Fort Worth   3.Churches   4. Religious Denominations
5.Historic Buildings

All inquiries for purchase or delivery of this book should be made to Landa
Press, P. O. Box 122336, Arlington, TX 76012; or call 817-451-0884.

Sketch on page ii, courtesy St. Andrew's Episcopal Church

Cover photo courtesy Joe Griffith, circa 1956 First Presbyterian Church archives

Cover and text design by Bill Maize; Duo Design Group

Unless the Lord builds the house,
they labor in vain who build it."

Psalm 127

Table of Contents

Acknowledgements

The history of a church includes names and dates of pastors, records of special events and dedications of buildings. These are facts a researcher is able to dig out of archives. But how inadequate! Unanswered are questions such as "What changes came in the minds of those listening to sermons? What comfort resulted from a visit to the sick or dying? What caused persons to dedicate themselves to a religious life?" Concerning these, written records are mostly silent, but we may have confidence they are penned in God's book.

The editor of *History of St. John's United Church of Christ* asked "Can one actually write the history of a congregation? The answer is no. The real history of any congregation lies in the loyalty, faith and devotion of its ministers and laymen and laywomen. This we cannot unearth for it is written on the tablet of the human heart." This expresses my feelings as I attempt to preserve a record of countless deeds of those who have gone before us.

How can one squeeze a hundred years' history into a few pages? How can one describe a $1,000,000 facility in a few sentences? Moreover, space limitation does not permit me to include the stories, or even the names, of those other than senior pastors who built sanctuaries and nurtured congregations. I ask your forgiveness for these omissions.

To the busy ministers, the church archivists and historians, and others who helped in this project, I am especially grateful. I am indebted to church librarians, and the wonderful staff of the the Fort Worth Public Library's Local History Department, the University of Texas at Arlington Special Collections Library, the Texas Christian University Mary Couts Burnett Library, Texas Wesleyan University West Library, and Southwestern Theological Seminary's William Fleming Library. Also Vickie Bryant, Arlington Bible College historian, Carol Roszell, archivist for the United Methodist Records and Archives Depository—Central Texas Conference, and the Catholic Diocese of Fort Worth Media liberian provided valuable denominational data. Fellow author Hollace Weiner gave cogent suggestions.

Clifford Gaskamp, AIA, of Southwest Architects, Inc. helped with descriptions of our many stately churches. Lastly, I would be remiss if I did not thank members of the Freelance Writers Network and eagle-eyed editor Robyn Conley for their instructive critique of the manuscript. To each of you, thanks.

In all my endeavors I thank God for my family and my church who support me with their love.

Introduction

"Goodbye, God, I'm going to Texas" was a popular, but inaccurate, saying in the nineteenth century. Some second generation Americans on the Atlantic seaboard viewed the vast expanse of prairie to the west, inhabited by Indians and a few Mexicans, as Godforsaken. Hardy pioneers, seeking a new home, saw it as the second Promised Land. On Sundays, inside log cabins, calloused hands held Bibles. Outside, hands held rifles, eyes alert for Indians who did not observe the Lord's day. "The sentries weren't posted for show. The unknown lay out there—perhaps not too far away—and it was no small comfort to the early settlers around Fort Worth to feel God was nearby."[1]

In the United States the early American religious experience was based on the immigration of people from many cultures and the faiths they brought with them. New England pilgrims came to establish a religion different from the Anglican Church, but it was not long before Anglicans were a factor in the Middle Colonies. Puritan reformer Roger Williams broke away and founded the Baptist movement in Rhode Island. Maryland's settlers brought Catholicism to the New World. Turmoil in Europe caused thousands to emigrate, pushing inward toward the Appalachian Mountains. Presbyterians and Methodists inhabited the valleys, carving out new settlements which were steeped in Old World religious values. Decades later Scandinavians plowed the flat prairies of Minnesota and the Dakotas on weekdays, and worshiped in Lutheran churches on Sundays. And in the cities of the Eastern seaboard, Jews plied their trades and read from the Torah on the Sabbath.

In this spiritual polyglot a new society emerged. Rather than a dominant state religion, Americans created a religious pluralism unique in history. Democratic theology replaced the orthodoxy of European and Colonial American churches. Even with this multiplicity of backgrounds, Robert S. Ellwood pointed out in *Many Peoples, Many Faiths*, that despite their differences, ". . . most groups have found themselves affirming common American ethical and social ideals—democracy, patriotism, social concern—together with their distinctive doctrines and worship."[2]

Moreover, the frontier churches served another role. They functioned as training schools for political democracy. According to the *Oxford History of the American West*, "The numerous church gatherings introduced citizens to basic democratic principles: the conduct of public meetings via accepted rules of order, the need to speak persuasively to the issue at hand, and (usually) the realization that the majority rules."[3] Such discussions also reinforced the virtue of listening, freedom of expression, respect for others' views, and the necessity for compromise, all essential components for survival on the frontier.

Catholic priests accompanied Spanish, and later Mexican, explorers and soldiers in their eighteenth and nineteenth century excursions into what would become the state of Texas. These padres established the first mission, La Bahia, as early as 1817. Within twenty years some Irish Catholics joined the Mexicans worshiping in San Antonio, Goliad, Refugio and San Patricio. By mid-century the Church estimated 10,000 Catholics in the new state, including those in Fort Worth.

The Methodist movement in Texas was born in Tennessee. In 1815, the Tennessee Conference met near Lebanon and voted to send missionary William Stevenson to the sparsely settled land bordering the Louisiana Purchase. He preached in Pecan Point in Red River County, and is believed to be the first Protestant to hold services in the area.

"As far back as 1830," in *Historic Churches of Texas* Frank Driskill and Noel Grisham wrote, "a few Baptist preachers had done sporadic work in Texas."[4] In 1837 Z. N. Morrel organized one of the first churches of that denomination at Washington-on-the-Brazos. From there Baptist missionaries and evangelists spread out to newly formed towns and villages throughout the state.

"The first Church of Christ was established in 1836 four miles from San Augustine,"[5] Driskill and Grisham noted. Close on the heels of these groups were the Episcopalians. Only two years after Sam Houston defeated Mexican dictator Santa Ana at the Battle of San Jacinto, the Foreign Committee of the General Convention of the Episcopal Church in the United States sent Caleb S. Ives as a foreign missionary to the Republic of Texas. He founded a church at Matagorda. He and others organized the Diocese of Texas there in 1849. Northern and Western Texas were established as missionary districts. In its first hundred years the Episcopalians counted 196 parishes and missions, with a membership exceeding 50,000.

On April 2, 1839 Houstonians established a Presbyterian church. The first Disciples of Christ congregation was founded in 1841 in Bowie County.

Stephen F. Austin's Central Texas colonies, under Mexican rule, were nominally Catholic, but the Anglo settlers refused to give up their Protestant beliefs. With only minimal objection from Mexico, they started churches keeping with those tenets. After the Texas declaration of independence from Mexico, the frontier opened up to mass migrations. By the 1850s, when Fort Worth's history began in earnest, homesteaders came from East and South Texas, and from all parts of the United States and Europe.

The end of the Civil War saw the rise of another dimension of the religious scene: freed slaves established their own houses of worship. The churches, mainly Baptist or Methodist, generally patterned the congregations after the white churches where slaves had been allowed to attend, albeit in separate sections of the sanctuary.

In 2003, sixteen pages of the *Greater Fort Worth Yellow Pages* are devoted to the advertising and listing of churches. One hundred and six denominations, ranging from Adventist to Word of God Fellowship, are represented. Listed elsewhere are Jewish and Muslim congregations. Settlers, immigrants and freed slaves brought the seeds of several denominations, and in time these seeds germinated to form Fort Worth's historic churches.

"What is it that makes a church great? Not soft seats and subdued lights, but strong courageous leadership—past and present. Not alone their tall towers with their bells, but the lofty vision of the people. Not the amount of money received, but the amount of service rendered in Christ's name. Not a large membership, but God's direction and power. Not what we have done in the past, but what we are doing now and will, under God's grace, do tomorrow."[6]

Chapter One

IN THE BEGINNING

For centuries Spain claimed almost all the territory west of the Mississippi River that would later become part of the United States. Unlike the English, the Spaniards had no desire to colonize the New World. Soldiers guarded explorers searching for gold, but they returned to Spain when their tour of duty was up. Priests who accompanied them attempted to Christianize the Indians, sometimes at sword point. A few missions were built, but the effort was half-hearted at best. The search for mineral riches proved as fruitless as true conversion of the native tribes, and Spain lost interest in their far flung empire except as a buffer protecting the enormous gold and silver riches of Mexico.

In the late 1700s Spanish military and political officers confronted two major problems—the continuing menace from hostile Indians and a newer, and greater challenge, the westward expansion of English-speaking Americans. This movement gained strength when Moses Austin secured a grant from Spain to colonize 300 families. His son, Stephen Fuller, advanced the elder Austin's work by bringing more Anglos to what was referred to after 1821 as the Republic of Mexico. Within ten years he issued land titles to 1,065 families and his several colonies counted 8,000 settlers along the lower Brazos River.

Other impresarios with similar grants brought even more Anglo-Americans. In the 1800s streams of migrants flowed into Texas. From 1820 to 1835 an estimated 38,000 settlers, for a small fee, received 4,000 acres per family. In their covered wagons loaded with furniture, staples and cooking pots, clothing and the family wash tub, they trekked overland to the newly opened territory. These immigrants homesteaded in the central and eastern parts of what we now call Texas.

They farmed much as they had in their previous locations. As the populace increased, small towns, more American than Mexican, sprang up. Following the 1836 rebellion against Mexico, and especially after the 1845 merger with the United States, more thousands poured into the new state.

Without the restrictions of Mexican *padres* and *soldados*, independent Texans openly practiced their Protestant beliefs, with the Methodists boasting more than half of the registered church members. Handley United Methodist Church historian Mrs. P. J. Brown wrote of these pioneer ministers, "They started preaching under trees, in homes, saloons, gambling halls and under arbors. Congregations might be small, even one or two people, but services were held, and the churches grew."[1]

Many came from what historian Frederick Jackson Turner labeled the Upland South. He noted "In spite of the influence of the backwoods in hampering religious organization, this upland society was a fertile field for tillage by such democratic and emotional sects as the Baptists, Methodists and the later Campbellites, as well as by Presbyterians."[2] They brought an attitude of mutual cooperation among neighbors and less reliance on formal governmental entities. This proved useful on the raw frontier and set the political stage for later migrations.

As conditions of famine and war in Europe worsened, Czechs, Germans, Irish, Norwegians and Swedes made the perilous voyage to start a new life. By 1850, about 33,000 Germans, one-fifth of the state's population, had settled in the Texas Hill Country and around San Antonio. Post-Civil War years brought numerous families from devastated southern plantations to farms and ranches in Texas. In addition to these farming families seeking relief from the tight economy, ". . . others came from Europe, including Belgians, Danes, and Greeks to become craftsmen (and) keepers of small shops."[3]

The newcomers pushed the frontier northward and westward. This expansion exacerbated an age-old problem: Indians. Caddos, Comanches, and Tonkawas fought those who encroached upon their historic hunting grounds. Pioneers fought just as hard to subdue the virgin prairie as part of their manifest destiny. The United States government ordered forts built along a line from South Texas to the Red River. One such military outpost was Fort Worth.

Oliver Knight in *Fort Worth: Outpost on the Trinity* described Major General William Jenkins Worth, as ". . . a hot tempered soldier risen from the ranks, whose talent as a tactician qualified him especially for such a potential trouble zone as the Southwest."[4] The veteran of the just completed war with Mexico faced a daunting task—secure the 500 mile line dividing east from west Texas, protect the settlers from the Indians, and conversely, protect the Indians from the settlers. He created the Rio Grande District along the international boundary and the Frontier District in what is now Central and North Texas. Worth ordered his second-in-command, William S. Harney, and Brevet Major Ripley Arnold to establish forts in the area.

Harney determined to establish a post on the West Fork of the Trinity River. William Tate Johnson, a former comrade-in-arms to Gen. Worth and who was familiar with the area, met with Arnold. Johnson suggested fifty acres at the juncture of the Clear Fork and West Fork of the Trinity. Arnold and his men encamped on the south bank of the river on June 6, 1849. He named the fort for Gen. Worth, who had died of cholera the previous month. Reporter Katie Casstevens noted, "Tradition has it that the first sermon preached in Fort Worth was in 1850 by a Baptist missionary, J. A. Freeman, at the invitation of Major Arnold, to the soldiers in the fort."[5]

Arnold's blue-uniformed mounted Second Dragoons fought Indian war parties when they raided settlements along the dividing line until he and his men were ordered westward to Fort Graham in January, 1852. Brevet Major Hamilton Merrill replaced Arnold. By September, 1853, Merrill and his troops turned the several barracks of Camp Worth over to the few civilians living there. Soldiers Abe Harris, Francis Knaar, and Louis Wetmore, their enlistments up, chose to stay in the area. Press Farmer, the fort sutler, moved his family from a tent pitched on the open prairie to the barracks. Instead of selling provisions to the soldiers, he now operated a general store. Julia K. Garrett in *Fort Worth: A Frontier Triumph* wrote, "In the score of cabins on the horizon north, south, east and west of the fort were spirited pioneer dwellers."[6] From 1854 until the Civil War, Fort Worth was a boom town.

E. M. Daggett, Carroll M. Peak, J. C. Terrell, and John Peter Smith—names now familiar as streets, schools or hospitals—chose to put down roots on the bluff overlooking the Trinity River. Daggett operated a dry goods store, Dr. Peak tended the sick, Terrell opened a law office, and John Peter Smith taught school. But, there were no clerics listed among the first Fort Towners.

While the popular vision of the frontier has been too often one of unrestrained bawdiness, there was in the early settlements a kernel of God-fearing men and women. True, in early Fort Worth, saloons outnumbered churches ten to one. Yet just as true, the leading townspeople brought with them deeply felt roots of religious denominations spawned from New England to the Appalachian Mountains. Those convictions would later flower in prairie congregations. "As a rule they were pious people, for I cannot recall an irreligious family,"[7] J. C. Terrell said of his early contemporaries.

The 1878-79 City Directory, the oldest one in existence, listed churches from seven denominations for white people and two for colored. But the first settlers' main concerns were building cabins, battling sometime hostile environments, sometime hostile Indians, and always the back-breaking labor of taming a wilderness. Food for the table outranked food for the soul. Psychoanalyst Abraham Maslow maintains once the basic needs for food, safety and shelter are fulfilled, the yearning emerges for belongingness, love and other higher needs. The camp meeting provided pioneers the opportunity to meet these essentials through worship—be they Baptist, Methodist, Presbyterian or other conviction.

"Loneliness and desolation were inevitable when settlement was sparse and widespread; they were the common laments of frontier women,"[8] Charles A. Johnson wrote in *The Frontier Camp Meeting*. The gatherings became an antidote to their loneliness and an opportunity to meet new friends and renew ties with old ones. Among the young people, it provided a chance to court and seek out prospective mates.

Homesteaders also needed a doctrine that would relieve the element of danger inherent in pioneer living and at the same time emphasize the presence of a caring God. Camp meeting preachers were acutely attuned to these needs, and consequently were the source of inspiration to which many turned. J. C. Terrell, in his book *Reminiscences of the Early Days*, noted that "as a general rule it is sinful to laugh at Divine services." Nevertheless, with good intentions, ". . . but at fearful risk of offending the 'cloth,' I would recall an amusing incident."[9] It seemed Brother Dehart (no first name given) was known for his powerful public prayers. He also was known for using ". . . mellifluous and sometimes unmeaning words; so that (if) they had the bigness and sound it was all right with him." Brother Dehart prayed:

"'Oh, thou all-sufficient, inefficient, self-sufficient being, O thou almighty, all-powerful, omnipotent, omniscient, omnipresent, eternal, petroleum, insignificant, Lord Jesus H. Christ—eh—Jehovah God—eh—' and the conclusion, after a long breath—'And O, Lord—eh—when thou are tired and done serving thyself with us on earth—eh—wilt thou take us into that upper and better kingdom, prepared—eh—from the foundation of the earth, for the devil and his angels!'"[10]

Brother Dehart's prayers probably fit in since, more so than in the East, many prairie denominations viewed emotion as well as intellect to be an important part of profound religious experiences. Camp meeting preachers believed the pathway to the intellect was through the feelings, and they used every tactic at their disposal to ensure that every hearer would be moved. Peculiarly susceptible to crowd suggestion, the secluded frontiersmen responded to warnings of hell-fire and damnation. Today churchgoers are more restrained, but in the nineteenth century public display of one's inner feelings was taken as an expression of one's convictions. Samuel E. Morrison and Henry S. Commanger captured the essence by quoting Abraham Lincoln—"When I see a man preach I like to see him act as if he were fighting bees."[11]

Johnson, in *The Frontier Camp Meeting*, described the brush arbor meeting as the most practical solution to the problem of carrying religious services to the sparsely populated areas. It was more than just a sharing of the Scriptures. "This socioreligious institution flourished on the American frontier side by side with the militia muster, with cabin raising and the political barbecue."[12]

Regarding politics, W. Eugene Hollon in *The Southwest: Old and New* recounted an imaginary, but realistic, conversation.

"Friend, we never see you at the meeting."

"I read my Bible at home."

"That's well, but . . . it would be better to attend meetings and if it is true what I hear that you intend running for Congress next year, if you do not mix with your Methodist friends, you will not be elected. . . ."[13]

Camp meetings were usually held in the summer, and audiences came in wagons and buggies from miles around. Sometimes more than half the population of the area attended. An August 1880 *Fort Worth Daily Democrat* story noted "Camp meetings are all the go now. From almost every nook and corner of the county comes news of soul-stirring sermons and many conversions."[14]

An appropriate site, usually in the form of a natural amphitheater, featured a pulpit set up on one end facing parallel rows of seats. Some pulpits were mere upraised platforms on logs, others were sturdy two-level affairs, often roofed to keep out the sun or the rare July rainstorm. The elevation allowed the preacher to be seen and heard by those unfortunate ones forced to sit on the ground.

The genesis of the camp meeting was the 1801 Cane Ridge assemblage in Kentucky. Presbyterian Reverend Barton W. Stone, joined by eighteen other ministers, both Baptist and Methodist, preached for six days. This ushered in a phenomenon known as the Second Great Awakening. It also gave rise to a new genre of clergy dubbed the circuit rider.

Pioneer Fannie Beck recalled, "We had no church buildings . . . and no regular church services. The Methodist circuit rider came about twice or three times a year, and sometimes a Baptist preacher or a Hard-shell Baptist visited the town and preached to us. Everybody turned out to these services, saint and sinner alike."[15] These circuit riders traveled over a thousand miles each year, and were paid the princely sum of $50.00 to $100.00 a year. Most were young and unmarried, as it was impossible to raise a family on such meager wages, and being gone for weeks at a time was hardly conducive to a stable home life.

Beck pointed out, "There were no denominational differences, no petty group prejudices, among those early congregations."[16] In fact, a Methodist circuit rider might preside at the funeral of a Lutheran, and the deceased buried in the village cemetery next to a Baptist or Presbyterian.

Historian Warren Thomas Smith wrote, "The circuit rider stands as one of the major contributors—an outstanding contribution—to American church history."[17] Astride his horse, he traveled from camp meeting to camp meeting, and preached the Gospel where no church existed. In Texas, early camp meetings were usually conducted by Methodists or Cumberland Presbyterians. The long-winded sermons, the colorful confessions of "sinners" and the melodious singing and shouting of the worshipers, filled the campground until late at night.

Pocket size song books, 2¾ by 4 inches, were common. The *Methodist Pocket Hymn Book*, revised and improved, was the 1830 official hymnal. Western poets John A. Granade and Caleb Jarvis Taylor's verses were put to music and widely used in camp meetings. A shortage of books, and the illiteracy of the populace led to the practice of "lining the hymn." In this procedure the leader sang a line and then the congregation repeated it. Charles A. Johnson attributed the remarkable growth of Methodism as much to its congregational singing as to its preaching. It was aptly named the "singing church."

Howard W. Peak, the first boy born in the old fort, became a traveling salesman when he grew up. He made his rounds throughout West Texas first on horseback, then by buggy. Before his death in 1928 he recalled the early days.

> "Religion at the time of which I speak (1850s) was very fervent, generally speaking, though in a manner dormant, for the want of means and opportunity through which to give it expression. Most of all the families who emigrated to this country were members of some church from the home town whence they came, but could not align themselves with their home church because there was not organization here at the time. Hence those inclined were compelled to attend any worship that might be offered, no matter what particular denomination offered and these were precious few."

He continued, "Now and then a circuit rider would drop in and preach Sunday and away again on his itinerary."[18]

Concerning the Civil War period, Peak paid tribute to the workers of every one of the pioneer churches who "struggled so arduously to upbuild and who worked under such adverse conditions, and who kept the religious fires kindled on the Western frontier."[19] In his seventies at the time of the interview, he told of the founding of the Fort Worth's First Christian Church. He also recalled the camp meetings.

"But the greatest of all the spiritual gatherings of my boyhood days were the old fashioned camp meetings. There, as the religious brethren and sisters, regardless of faiths, assembled under brush arbors and sitting on crude benches, with their feet in the straw, listening intently to the earnest and heartfelt exhortations from the zealous preachers and joining en masse in old time hymns of 'It's Old Time Religion,(sic)' and 'Am I a Soldier of the Cross?' and 'Come Thou Fount of Every Blessing'...."

(A photograph of such a brush arbor graces the "History Wall" at Hemphill Presbyterian Church.)

"Sometimes these protracted meetings would last for weeks and many were the conversions made and some wonderful confessions listened to from some convert who had formerly lived a wild and reckless life. There were no organs, violins, or saxophones in those days. They were considered sacrilegious by the early worshipers."[20]

Referring to camp meetings, Clyde A. Milner II, *et al* argued, "Whereas the organizers of these gatherings usually measured 'success' by the number of converts, the people were more pragmatic. 'However great may have been the need for salvation,' one plains woman recalled, 'the need for recreation was given preference.'"[21]

In 1855 Fort Worth, Indians still camped on the outskirts and cowboys frequented the saloons. Yet some of the women, such as Mrs. Carroll M. Peak, swept parlor floors, washed chintz curtains and dusted furniture in preparation for Sunday services in their homes. The traveling preacher brought the Word of God to worshipers who were attired in calico and buckskin—their Sunday best.

Circuit riders also held services in secular buildings prior to the time the hamlet had grown enough to erect even modest churches. Lewis J. Wright and William Bates conducted Methodist services in the Masonic Hall during the mid-1850s. Father Vincent Pairier, following the Civil War, held Mass in the homes of Catholics or in the Lake and Nash Hardware Store. Presbyterian W. M. Kilpatrick preached in the loft over Knight's Livery Stable at Calhoun and Third. Howard Peak recalled that a concrete building erected in 1857 stood ". . . about where Lamar Street joins West Belknap. This was used by all denominations who were fortunate enough to secure a preacher of their faith to fill the pulpit."[22]

James M. Moudy, retired chancellor of Texas Christian University and long-time member of University Christian, told the story of one "horseback preacher" who advertised his presence by going to the local school and telling the children to hold up their five, outstretched fingers. "Now I'm going to give you the five parts of my sermon," he designated each finger—faith, repentance, etc.—"now close your fingers and go home and tell your parents what the sermon is going to be about tonight."[23]

Some who ministered to the spiritual needs of the community held full time jobs and preached whenever settlers gathered at a camp meeting. Typical of these servants of God was the Rev. A. M. Dean. He harvested wheat on Col. Nathaniel Terry's farm north of town during the day, and preached at night. Dean's saddle bags contained a Bible, a hymn book, and a trusty revolver. The Bible and hymnal he used to protect the villagers from eternal damnation, and the pistol he used to protect himself from rattlesnakes or roaming Indians.

During the 1850s and 1860s when congregations met in log cabins or public buildings, at least one armed man stood guard in case of an Indian attack. The danger passed in 1869 when Company H of the Eleventh Infantry defeated a band of thirty warriors at the Battle of Marine Creek and ended unwelcome incursions.

Howard W. Peak remembered Sundays as days of rest from the week's labors. "Most everyone attended church, if there was a chance. . . . It was no uncommon occurrence for the family to hitch up the wagon, all pile in, and drive 10 or 12 miles to worship, taking commodious baskets well-filled with substantial foods, prepared the previous day. The whole congregation would seek a shady place after the preaching was over and there enjoy the feast, discussing the sermon and talking of crop conditions and affairs of local interest."[24]

Several churches were built in the county prior to those established in the city proper. "Isham Chapel, oldest church in the county, erected in 1849, remained abandoned for many years and Mount Gilead Baptist Church, (not the current one on Grove Street) also is being revived. . . ,"[25] John M. Burns wrote in 1922. He listed other county congregations such as Minter's Chapel, and Birdville, Benbrook, Smithfield and Pleasant Run Baptist Churches as originating before the Civil War. Lonesome Dove Baptist Church was the inspiration for the title of Larry McMurtry's Pulitzer Prize winning book. Alas, some of these historic congregations have been disbanded or merged with other flocks.

The editor of the *Fort Worth Democrat*, in February 1873 lamented, "The editor decries the lack of church edifices in Fort Worth 'which is improving so rapidly in all other respects.'"[26] At the time of Fort Worth's incorporation as a city March 1, 1873, congregations belonging to four denominations met in dedicated sanctuaries and served the population of 4,000. A hundred years later *Fort Worth Press* reporter Marvin Garrett wrote of the early churches. "By

1880 six denominations could count congregations in the outpost town: The Christian Church (Disciples of Christ), Baptist, Methodist, Catholic, Presbyterian and Episcopal." He concluded by saying, "Church people helped build Fort Worth. They built schools and hospitals and brought it from a rowdy cow town to a respectable city."[27]

The editor of the 1878-79 City Directory noted, "Our religious denominations have severally provided themselves with church buildings of ample character for their several wants. Their places of worship are regularly occupied and filled on the sabbath day with as devout and appreciative audiences as are anywhere congregated."[28]

These small congregations joined together from time to time. In June 1887 the Fort Worth Gazette reported, "Evangelists Claggett and Birch of St. Louis begin with fairest auspices a series of open air meetings. 2000 people gathered under the big tent to listen to fine preaching and most excellent music."[29] Perhaps the two enjoyed a perk offered by the Star Artesian Bath House, which notified via the Fort Worth Daily Gazette that after May 31, 1888 only ministers could take baths free of charge.

During the last quarter of the nineteenth century new churches sprang up to meet the needs of an expanding population, and a number of established congregations built larger buildings. Carol Roark stated that "Most were still located in the central business district and followed traditional styles for ecclesiastical architecture. . . . Saint Andrew Episcopal and Allen Chapel AME were of the Gothic Revival mode; Mount Gilead—Neoclassical; and First Christian—Renaissance Revival. The first suburban churches were also built during this period to provide a place of worship closer to home. Saint Demetrios Greek Orthodox Church chose the Byzantine style for its North Side church, an appropriate design given the national origin of its members, but unusual in Fort Worth."[30] On the city's South Side, the Missouri Avenue Methodist selected a more eclectic design—a vaguely Prairie-style form with Sullivanesque (form following function) and Gothic detailing.

At the turn of the new millennium, the Chamber of Commerce boasted of the growth of religious centers. "As did most western cities, Fort Worth welcomed different churches and denominations. Diverse houses of worship were proof of the pluralism and democracy that America embodied."[31]

By 1903, "There were 44 white churches and seven colored churches,"[32] according to Mack Williams. Associated with them were 66 church societies, including youth groups, altar guilds and societies, and ladies' aids and auxiliaries. B. B. Paddock, in 1922 noted, "(there were). . . in the city and its immediate suburbs 111 churches, embracing all the more prominent and well known sects and denominations, and several that are more obscure."[33]

In the mid-1950s, reporter Frances Edwards labeled Fort Worth as "One of the 'Church-Goingest' Cities in the Nation." Edwards cited statistics showing that of the 300,000 residents, 200,000 or more attended church. "The city," she wrote, "now has 427 churches representing 24 denominations."[34] According to survey responses, 66,000 identified themselves as Southern Baptists; 30,000 Methodists; 20,000 Roman Catholics; 12,000 Church of Christ; 10,000 Disciples of Christ; 6,000 Presbyterians; 6,000 Fundamental Baptists; 3,500 Episcopalians; 2,500 Jews; and 600 Church of the Nazarene. The survey did not include data from African-American congregations.

A more recent study, reported in September 2002 by Brett Hoffman and Jeff Claassen,[35] revealed a diverse picture of religious participation. The largest number (over 400,000) identified themselves as Evangelical Protestants, with Catholics and Mainline Protestants ranking second and third. Approximately 20,000 declared themselves "other." Many who participated in the survey worship at historic Fort Worth churches described in the following chapters.

Chapter Two

THE CHRISTIAN CHURCHES (DISCIPLES OF CHRIST) CONGREGATIONS

"Decline in moral and religious life at the close of the 18th and the beginning of the 19th century caused a number of men in America and abroad to locate the source of the trouble in the *divided condition of Christendom*."[1] (author's italics) Lars Pederson Qualben's statement led, early in the nineteenth century, a group of pastors from various denominations to begin a movement toward a unity of all Christians based on New Testament teaching. Among them were Barton W. Stone of Kentucky, and Thomas and Alexander Campbell, father and son, of western Pennsylvania. They considered themselves restorers, not reformers and sought to restore worship to its non-creedal simplicity as they understood the New Testament to require. The Campbells believed "Where the Scriptures speak, we speak; where they are silent, we are silent." This became the slogan of the Disciples Church.

H. C. Armstrong in 1924 quoted Thomas Campbell's plea. "O that ministers and people would but consider that there are no divisions in the grave, nor in the world that lies beyond it! There our divisions must come to an end! We must all unite there! Would to God we could find it in our hearts to put an end to our short-lived divisions here; that so we might leave a blessing behind us; even a happy and united Church."[2] Campbells' plea found favor on the Texas frontier.

■   ■   ■

The First Christian Church—1855

In 1855 Franklin Pierce resided in the White House, Abraham Lincoln argued law in Illinois, and Carroll M. Peak practiced medicine in Fort Worth. On June

10 of that year, a small group met in the parlor of Dr. and Mrs. Peak's double-log cabin. Those in attendance were Mr. and Mrs. Benjamin P. Ayers, Mr. and Mrs. James K. Allen, Mrs. Frances M. Durrett, Mrs. Alfred D. Johnson, Mr. and Mrs. William A. Sanderson, and Mr. Stephen Terry. They established a church. Thus the first Christian church was the First Christian Church.

"Mrs. Florence (Chalfant) Peak was an enthusiastic church woman. . . . From that early day (June 10, 1855) to her death, Mrs. Peak was untiring in her efforts for this church and in good works. She taught in the Sunday School continuously for 45 years and considered this one of the outstanding privileges of her life,"[3] according to a First Christian Church history. She also brought evergreens to Fort Worth, and these were used in weddings and funerals.

In the beginning these Disciples met in various homes. First Christian Church organized the first Sunday School. By this time, 1857, the congregation was meeting in the newly constructed two-story brick Masonic Lodge, located near Calhoun and Belknap Streets. J. C. Terrell explained, when he came, "The only pretentious structure in the embryo city was a lodge building of Fort Worth, No. 148. . . . In Texas, as a general rule, Masonic buildings were erected first, then came church edifices."[4] Laymen, or preachers if available, held religious services downstairs on Sundays, and John Peter Smith taught school there during weekdays. Lodge members met in the second-floor area.

Howard Peak, speaking to a reporter in 1922, reminisced about early spiritual life. "When I reflect on such men as Brother Allen (James), Stephen Terry, William Sanderson, the Clarks, Major and Dr. Van Zandt and others, and the loyal sisters who consecrated their time and means to the up-building of the early Christian Church . . . I can but exult thereat."[5] He wasn't the only one in spiritual awe. Local Indians, gawking at young Peak's red hair, believed such distinction gave him supernatural powers.

Ten years after Texas became a state, A. M. Dean worked on Terry's plantation which was located at the end of Samuels Street. Dean blazed the way for hundreds of ministers of the gospel who were to follow. *Fort Worth Press* reporter Allan Carney wrote, "He preached each night while the harvest season lasted, and then returned to his home in an adjoining county, to return each Sunday thereafter."[6]

Howard Peak described the lodge meeting room as having a ". . . rough board pulpit, seats fashioned from long cottonwood slabs supported on oak pegs, with a box stove in one corner and a water bucket and dipper in the center of the room."[7] Reverend Dean's services were simple, but earnest. They began with a deacon or elder offering a prayer, and a full-fledged discussion of the reading of Scripture. Dean owned the only hymnal, so he led the singing— sans instruments. To aid those who did not know the hymn, he sang one line at a time and the tiny congregation repeated them. Stephen Terry looked after the Sacraments and every Sunday morning neighbors saw him carrying bread and wine in a basket, covered with a white cloth. Following the singing and preaching, the worshipers partook of the Lord's Supper.

Under Dean's leadership the church grew steadily. Many from other denominations united with the Christians for two reasons. First, and the practical one, it was the only church in the village. Second, and the theological reason, Disciples did not require joiners to relinquish prior held Christian tenets nor swear to a new, multifaceted creed. Campbell's plea for unity was the main catechism.

After Dean, Dr. B. F. Hall became the next minister. Hall was also Fort Worth's first dentist. "It was under Dr. Hall's ministry that Col. John Peter Smith and his wife took membership in the Church,"[8] according to church history.

Physician and cattleman Dr. Mansil Mathews (also spelled Matthews) succeeded Dr. Hall. Like Abraham of the Old Testament, Mathews and forty members of his family traveled north and south with their flocks and herds, following the grass each year. In the early 1860s his preaching at the Masonic Lodge raised no hackles, but his outspoken political views did. The High Vigilance Committee, judge, jury and executer concerning allegiance to the Confederate States of America, declared Mathews a traitor for his opposition to slavery. The event was the subject of an oft repeated bit of lore. Oliver Knight told it best.

"During the purge the committee arrested and brought to trial . . . Rev. Mathews . . . who was very popular in Fort Worth. Mathews was informed that he stood accused of treason, a charge that invariably brought the death penalty." Hearing of the evangelist's plight, Captain E. M. Daggett appeared before the committee and dramatically pleaded that Mathews' mind might be with the North, but his heart was with the South. "'If that be treason,' he said, 'then, I, too, am guilty.' Reconsidering, the committee decided that Mathews should not die, but stipulated he remain behind bars for three days more without knowing his life had been spared."

Daggett, enraged by the stipulation, stomped off to Mathews's cell, determined to enlighten his friend. At the jail Daggett was admitted, but only with a guard present. "Burdened with sorrow and anxiety, Mathews was spending what he thought were his last hours with his Bible. Taking advantage of the circumstance, Daggett began a long biblical discussion. He talked on and on, drawing Mathews ever further into theology. Eventually Daggett noticed the bored guard was ignoring them. That was his chance. Into the conversation he shot the question, 'What is your favorite Bible quotation?'

"Mathews answered and then put the question to Daggett. Piously the visitor intoned, 'Fret not thy gizzard and frizzle not thy whirligig, thou soul art saved.'"[9] The preacher got the message and the guard didn't.

With many of the men off to battle, and shortages of all kinds plaguing the settlement, church activity was at a low ebb during the Civil War, but a few hardy souls kept the flame alive. Dr. Mathews was succeeded by Daniel Barcroft, as minister of the congregation. Mr. Barcroft was a lay preacher who engaged in farming throughout the week. Another lay-preacher, Rev. Terrell Jasper, fed the flock for a time. He was succeeded by Rev. J. A. Clark, father of Addison and Randolph Clark, founders of Texas Christian University. Kentucky native and Confederate General R. M. Gano came after Reverend Clark. Then H. F. Bantua led the congregation, only to be replaced by Elder Murphy according to church archives.

In the winter of 1865, during Jasper's pastorship, Major K. M. Van Zandt and his family came to Fort Worth and united with the church. He was followed by his mother and sister, Mrs. L. V. Clough, Major J. J. Jarvis and Dr. E. J. Beall and their families. They brought new vitality to the church. For nearly three quarters of a century these households gave outstanding leadership and support to the congregation.

Major Van Zandt, soldier, legislator, merchant, banker and community builder, at the age of ninety-two, met with biographer Sandra Myers.

Recalling the early days, he said, "Some of the members of the Masonic Lodge thought it did not look right to have "Campbellites" preaching in their hall, so we were forced to get a building of our own. We raised $200 and purchased the block bounded by Main and Houston and Fourth and Fifth Streets. . . . There was a small frame building on this lot, so we moved into this and named our congregation First Christian Church. Later we employed a man to make brick for us and built a small brick church. . . ."[10]

The one-room structure of which Van Zandt spoke ". . . had separate doors for men and women since the sexes were segregated during services. Children who might drop off to sleep were awakened by an usher using a rabbit's foot attached to the end of a long pole."[11]

He continued, "I have held practically every church office there is to hold—janitor when we could not afford to hire one, teacher, superintendent, and once I baptized a lady when we had no preacher. I think I have been Chairman of the Board of First Christian Church ever since we have had a board."[12] Van Zandt, a student of the Bible, took the New Testament, literally interpreted, as his guide for daily living. He customarily read the entire Bible every year from Genesis to Revelations. K. M. Van Zandt died in 1930 after a life that spanned almost a century. Myers in an epilogue wrote, "(He) was not the hard-shooting, hard-fighting, hard-drinking, hard-talking Texan of myth and legend. Rather he was one of the quiet men who built homes, plowed the land, engaged in business, promoted towns and cities, opened schools, and enforced law and order. These men were truly typical Texans and K. M. Van Zandt was one of their number."[13]

Van Zandt's sister, Ida Van Zandt Jarvis, contributed much to the First Christian Church. She was born in Washington, D.C. in 1844, while her father, Isaac, was Minister from the Republic of Texas. A poet and Sunday School teacher, Mrs. Jarvis was best known for her support of religious and educational opportunities for young people. One youth she helped, E. B. Bynum, graduated from AddRan College and later wrote of his mentor in *These Carried the Torch: Pioneers of Christian Education.*

Addison and Randolph Clark served as pastors to the congregation, but are better known as educators than preachers. They organized a private school, which met in the church building, later moved it to Thorp's Spring.

It became known as AddRan College, the forerunner of the present Texas Christian University. Rev. T. W. Caskey followed Randolph Clark. Reputed to be an outstanding pulpiteer and author, Caskey was succeeded by A. L. Johnson.

Because of the growing membership, the congregation found it necessary to erect a building larger than the one on Houston Street. Desiring to "get out of the congestion of the downtown," they sold their property for $5,000 and purchased another at the corner of Sixth and Throckmorton Streets for $1,500. In 1878 the "Rock Church," described as a very imposing structure, was erected at this location. Without a baptistery during its early days, if someone came forward for baptism, the minister and the congregation walked to the banks of the Clear Fork, sang a hymn or two, then the preacher led the candidate into the water and baptized him.

At first the Disciples of Christ sang unaccompanied. When the Gavin family moved to Fort Worth they became members of the church. Son George Gavin, a good singer, was asked to lead the singing. He produced from his pocket a tuning fork. Many were astonished and some displeased. A heated discussion arose as to the orthodoxy of a musical instrument in a New Testament Church, and the tuning fork was the only thing used for years to assist the singing. But times change. The James Harrisons gave the first organ to the church. Later the Burk Burnet family donated a grand pipe organ, replaced in 2001 by a $250,000 Allen electronic organ.

In 1912 the much lauded Dr. L. D. Anderson accepted the call from First Christian. This proved to be one of the most significant ministries in the entire denomination. Third generation member George Stephens, who said he "was born into First Christian," remembered Dr. Anderson as having an aura about him of great dignity and reserve. "I could anticipate the next word of his invitation to join—'Won't you come, just now, as we stand.'"[14]

When Anderson assumed the pastorate, the congregation experienced phenomenal growth. With its 3,000 members, it became the third largest congregation in the denomination. Due to this rapid increase, the membership saw the necessity of erecting a larger building, so in 1914 the little 'Rock Church' as it had been known throughout the years, was demolished to make way for the present imposing structure.

First Christian Church 612 Throckmorton. Courtesy UTA Special Collections Library

Influential members such as cattleman Samuel Burk Burnett and banker K. M. Van Zandt led the congregation in retaining the services of Van Slyke and Woodruff to design the new church. In 1915 the *Star-Telegram* boasted, "The new First Christian Church . . . will have the largest pipe organ in the Southwest, with the possible exception of that in the Scottish Rite Cathedral at Dallas."[15] It cost $12,000, a lot of money in 1915. This was the beginning of an outstanding music ministry, evident today under the leadership of Charles Duke.

Congregant George Stephens detailed the architecture. "Like St. Paul's in London, Fort Worth's First Christian Church has a dome. It's clad in copper, lighted with windows and illuminated at night. In Roman Empire Renaissance style, the building, veneered with manufactured limestone, is framed by ranks of soaring Corinthian columns on two (east and south) sides. At front (facing Throckmorton) three Roman arches lead to double copper-clad doors. They open on the ground floor. Iron gates guard the covered inner court. Ascending divided stairs lead to the second level. Three double doors open to the foyer. The white tile floor with contrasting black borders, said to have been laid by Italian artisans, leads to Doric columns, then doors into the sanctuary."[16]

Carol Roark, in *Fort Worth's Legendary Landmarks*, described the 1600 seat interior. "Most of the church's windows are art or stained glass casement windows depicting lilies and the cross. The windows, as well as the church's seating, organ case, and pulpit furniture were all designed by Van Slyke and Woodruff. . . . The sanctuary follows the Akron or auditorium plan which was developed to focus the attention of the audience on the preacher's pulpit."[17]

According to Stephens, "Entering the sanctuary the eye travels to the front where a great bas-relief frieze in wood of Michaelangelo's Last Supper covers the wall. On the right a mural showing Jesus being baptized by John highlights the baptistery. Above the baptistery the choir loft houses a $250,000 organ and space for a forty-five voice choir."[18]

A twenty-four foot diameter stained glass dome crowns the sanctuary ceiling. "With the exception of the urns on the front portico, which replaced four original light posts, the church exterior is unaltered, and the interior retains much of its historic fabric,"[19] Roark observed.

On March 28, 2002, seven years after this 1995 description by Roark was published, a Force 2 tornado tore through downtown Fort Worth. It totally destroyed the Bank One Building across the street from the church, but in the quirky nature of such storms, caused only minor damage to the sanctuary. Stained glass windows beneath the cupola were cracked, but the major problem for the church related to the destruction of the damaged bank building. At first it seemed implosion was the best solution. Structural engineers proposed wrapping the church to protect it from the vibrations when the bank fell. Pastor Tom Plumbley facetiously envisioned the whole building encased in some kind of bubble wrap. On further study, the engineers determined that an implosion would destroy the moldings of the historic edifice, and three years later what once was a landmark bank in the downtown area remained a boarded-up eyesore. The staff at First Christian referred to it as "the world's largest purple martin birdhouse," but in late 2003 tentative plans are afoot to turn it into a people house.

Dr. L. D. Anderson led the church through storms of a different nature. He was finishing his first five years when the United States became embroiled in the First World War. The young men of his congregation answered the call, and some never returned. In the years of the Great

Depression he saw contributions plummet and much of his ministry was to the poor. Still another World War, and then the Korean Conflict, prompted him to console parents and wives of men fighting in far flung parts of the globe. Through all the years his sermons inspired and comforted.

There were many milestones in his long tenure. Property north of the sanctuary was acquired in 1928 and a seven-story education building was erected. It housed classrooms, assembly areas, a gymnasium and a swimming pool. Nine years later, 1937, more than 2,000 couples married by Dr. Anderson were honored at a reception. The *Press* reported a membership of 5,000 and a property evaluation in excess of $1,000,000 just five years later.

In 1947, interviewed by reporter Robert Wear on the occasion of his thirty-fifth year at First Christian, Anderson spoke of the need to include new thoughts and insights into his sermons. "It isn't easy to keep out of a rut, speaking to the same group of people at morning and evening Sunday services for 35 years," he said. The memory of a preaching visit to a neighboring church many years ago kept him on his toes. "I learned my lesson . . . . the woman sitting beside me asked: 'Are you going to tell us about Florence Nightingale today?' I was surprised and asked: 'Why no, I hadn't thought of it—but why do you ask?' The woman looked relieved and replied: 'Our own minister has talked about her almost every Sunday for so long we were hoping you would tell us about someone else.'"[20]

The soft-spoken pastor recalled the topic of his first sermon, "His name shall be called wonderful," taken from Isaiah 9:6 preached in Athens, Texas. Over the years Anderson held fast to his policy of never preaching the same sermon more than once, and he believed "preachers should have something to say before they try to say it." He directed many of his topics to the young people of the church. Devotion to the youth motivated him to incorporate experiences from his own boyhood and the influences of teachers and ministers as they nurtured his religious growth. Anderson credited Sunday School teachers and circuit riders who came to his Ozark village as introducing him to the Bible. His parents were not members of any denomination, yet supported him in his desire to enter the ministry. At the age of twenty-seven he conducted a revival in his hometown and one of the people he had the privilege of baptizing was his mother.

The First Christian congregation in 1952 helped the Andersons celebrate their fiftieth wedding anniversary with a four-tiered cake and the gift of a television set. This was at a time when television was in its infancy and all sets were bulky pieces of furniture with only black and white programming. In 1955 Rev. Anderson noted with pride the longtime relationship between the church and its members. "Families have maintained the old ideas of their forebears in attending this church," he told a reporter. "This is a church of generations. We have had six generations of one family involved in our church membership,"[21] he said.

At a reception honoring him for forty-three years of ministry, it was revealed he had received 10,262 persons into church membership—4,106 by baptism and 6,156 by transfer. He had conducted 7,000 funerals and officiated at 3,500 weddings. During all this time, Dr. Anderson's only absence from his pulpit engagements was in 1915 when he was stricken with typhoid fever. A story in the *Fort Worth Star-Telegram* detailing his accomplishments noted the church budget rose from $5,000 in 1912 to $124,436.66 in 1954.

For most of Anderson's tenure, he was aided by financial secretary Nellie Straiton. In honoring her for twenty-nine years' work, Isaac Van Zandt, himself a member for seventy years, said, "Miss Straiton's services to the church have not been limited to the secretarial duties. Also for 29 years, she had taught the Jarvis-Love Bible Class, a group of young business and professional women."[22]

Besides caring for his local flock, Anderson found time to participate in regional, national and international church business. He served as president of the International Convention of Disciples of Christ, and as president of the Texas Christian Missionary Society. For a decade he co-edited the *Christian Courier,* and for years lectured once a week at the Brite College of the Bible.

In addition to the preparation of thousands of sermons, he used the early morning hours, working in his church study, to write four books: *The Business of Living, Perfected into One, Strangers and Pilgrims,* and *What We Believe.* Dr. Anderson served as pastor of the congregation more than forty-nine years. Only his death in 1961 removed him from the pulpit that he loved and served.

Dr. N. Quenton Grey came from a pastorate in Pennsylvania and served the church from 1961 through 1973. He led the church as it completed an extensive remodeling program and paid off all indebtedness on its property.

Known as an innovator, in 1965 he proposed an interfaith worship service for downtown workers. During Holy Week services, an average attendance of 550 persons ate a seventy- cent light lunch, and heard ministers from several churches present a fifteen minute message. Choirs from different high schools sang, and all enjoyed the spiritual nurturing. Also under his leadership Dial-a-Prayer was begun.

Following the death of Dr. Grey, the congregation called several ministers, but none stayed as long as Anderson or Grey. In 1995 Reverend James Cobb pastored the church during its 140th year. The gala celebration included parishioners attending worship services dressed in 1850-era costumes. Cobb and his family arrived in a horse drawn buggy. Parking lot festivities included music by the Light Crust Doughboys, a barbershop quartet, a clown to entertain the children and an old fashioned barbecue feast.

But the church had been in a period of decline. In 1978 Classified Parking System offered the congregation two million dollars for the property. A divided membership considered the options—stay in the revered building or move to a neighborhood location and erect a new sanctuary. Instead they sold the aging education building to Rattikin Title, yet kept the sanctuary. Reporter Jim Jones wrote of the period, "First Christian once . . . was one of the largest congregations in the Christian Church. But the church broke into several pieces during the flight to the suburbs and the exodus of downtown retail businesses."[23] Many members left to form new churches, but a loyal remnant remained. As civic leaders spearheaded the renewal of downtown, the church was vindicated in its decision to remain and at the turn of the twenty-first century was in a growth mode.

In July 2001 Reverend Tom Plumbley, a Texas Christian University Phi Beta Kappa graduate, preached his first sermon at the historic church. Leaving his post at Midway Hills Christian Church in Dallas he told reporter Jones, "I've always wanted to come back to Fort Worth. . . people seem to have an attitude that 'we can do things together.' I'm hoping I can play some kind of role in that."[24]

Plumbley didn't plan to be a minister. The son of a minister, he vowed his children would never face the slings and arrows of being a "preacher's kid." Instead, he wanted to be a different part of the church, such as an activist for

Christian ventures. With that goal in mind, he attended law school for a year before he realized his calling was in the pulpit. He holds a Master of Divinity from Vanderbilt University and was ordained in 1980.

Plumbley said he was drawn to First Christian because of the mix of leaders of different age groups, and the vitality and vision in the prospect of being the "neighborhood church for the downtown neighborhood." His goals include increasing the membership and leading the church as it strengthens its understanding of itself in the community of Disciples and the ecumenical community as well.

Capable assistants support the senior minister. Charles Duke joined the staff of First Christian in 1968 as Minister of Music. In addition to award winning choir presentations, he led the way in furnishing the "1855 Room," named for the year the congregation organized. This small parlor, furnished in Edwardian style, is open for noon time meditation.

Rev. Janet Fowler is Associate Minister of Evangelism-Singles. She sees First Christian as special "Because this is the oldest church, it has the frontier spirit of being creative and starting new things and doing things that are different."[25]

First Christian Church's history is significant to Fort Worth because it listed among its membership some of the outstanding leaders of the community in education, industry, government and religion. George Stephens's memories include an Easter Sunday morning looking out over what appeared to be "a sea of spring flowers on the women's hats; of witnessing one hundred white-robed people being baptized; of his mother's singing in the choir." As other congregations left the area, feeling there was little future for a centrally located church, First Christian Church envisioned the possibility of serving the downtown area and dedicated its ministry to this end.

Since the stone church was built in 1878 at Sixth and Throckmorton and the present structure built in 1913, it has spawned nine other congregations. What would become Magnolia Avenue Christian Church was the first one.

■   ■   ■

Magnolia Avenue Christian Church—1897

In 1897 as a result of a controversy at First Christian Church, some members formed a new church under the leadership of Rev. Homer T.

Wilson. He had been pastor of First Christian. Magnolia Christian Church historian Imogene McCue, as part of their seventieth anniversary wrote of the early days.

"On January 16, 1898, a resolution to form a new congregation was signed by 32 members and the next Sunday, January 23, 1898, the Third Christian Church, Inc. was formed with 64 members,"[26] according to a 1979 church history. (In 1892 a group broke away and later became the Southside Church of Christ. If they were called the Second Christian Church, research does not support it. See page 205) Third Christian Church first met in Hoffman's Hall, Greenwall Opera House. As the congregation strengthened, they purchased a lot at the corner of Fifth and Throckmorton Streets. The growing fellowship met in the basement of the courthouse while a sanctuary was built. The group chose the name Christian Tabernacle and by 1903 counted 1028 members.

After several years the church leadership realized that two churches of the same denomination within a block of each other was not in the best interests of all concerned. They further realized that the rapid growth of the city south-ward offered a better field for their services, so in 1908 they bought a lot on Magnolia Avenue, on which they built a house of worship and moved there.

W. D. Thomas wrote in 1909,"The pastors who served this flock are Homer T. Wilson, James S. Myers, Guy Inman, A. E. Dubber and E. M. Waits, the latter being called to the new organization."[27] In speaking of the reorganization of Third Christian Church, he noted, "The one who was cho-sen in 1898 to formulate and make vocal the first declaration of the new church life, by a strange coincidence is made the messenger of the expiring breath of the CHRISTIAN TABERNACLE (capital letters his). How we love that name! (sic) because of its memories and associations. May its mantle fall in resplendent glory and power on the Magnolia Avenue Christian Church."[28]

A small congregation, Bellevue Christian Church, already met in the 1300 block of Lipscomb, according to McCue. Minutes of the March 4, 1909 meeting detailed the merger of the two under the name Magnolia Avenue Christian Church.

The board hired Walter-Shaw and Field to design the sanctuary. Stained glass windows and pews, saved from the Throckmorton building, became part of the new one. McCue chronicled the careful detailing, such as three coats of Sherwin-Williams paint or stain, that went into the structure. "In large capital letters the specifications said: 'ALL STAINS RESULTING FROM TOBACCO JUICE WILL NOT BE TOLERATED AND MATERIALS HAVING THE SAME TO BE REMOVED.' Also: 'ANY INCOMPETENT OR DISORDERLY WORKMEN MUST BE PROMPTLY DISCHARGED. IT IS SO ORDERED BY THE ARCHITECTS AND WITHOUT ANY ARGUMENT WHATSOEVER.'"[29]

Apparently the tobacco chewers were careful and the worshipers dedicated the church on Easter Sunday, March 27, 1910. Over 600 people, carrying Bibles and hymnals and singing "Onward Christian Soldiers," marched the three blocks from the Tabernacle to the new sanctuary.

The style of the red brick building reflected a Moorish influence, with arches over windows and doors, and flowing parapets of brick and cast stone. The main entry featured a domed ceiling with clerestory lighting. According to McCue, "The new church was the finest church plant in Texas with an auditorium that would seat 1100, many, many Sunday School class-rooms, robing rooms for baptism, preacher's study, office spaces, and storage spaces."[30] For

Magnolia Avenue Christian Church. Courtesy Imogene McCue

seventy years the majestic structure topped with a red clay tile roof drew worshipers from the neighborhood.

When E. M. Waits took the presidency of Texas Christian University, Henry Clay Garrison filled the pulpit. John Underwood pastored there from 1919 to 1925. J. Graham McMurry's tenure was cut short by illness and after only two years the congregation called J. Leslie Finnell. During his time they dedicated a new three-story educational building. He served for seventeen years, the longest of any pastor.

"In 1945 while Bayne E. Driskill was pastor, lightning struck the sanctuary building, and gas which had accumulated in the ceiling causing great damage to the roof,"[31] McCue recalled. Extensive repair and remodeling resulted in an even more impressive sanctuary.

The church continued to grow under the leadership of Reverends Bradshaw and Driskill. From 1951 to 1957 Amos Myers served as pastor. It was a time when many teens and college students joined. For them, a popular event was a monthly Saturday night dance in the Fellowship Hall. Young married couples chaperoned the event and considered it a wholesome opportunity for youth to bond with each other and the church. Neighboring churches were "jealous or horrified, depending on their view of dancing," one former chaperone recalled.

Ever concerned with the needs of the young, Myers led the effort to establish a class for mentally retarded children, the first of its kind in the nation.

Roy Ford was the next minister. Although influential in the life of the church, he stayed only two years.

In the 1940s many community leaders attended Magnolia, including W. Lee "Pappy" O'Daniel and his family. Prior to his term as governor, he served as an elder. He campaigned "for the common man" and declared the Golden Rule and the Ten Commandments to be the primary planks in his platform. O'Daniel believed that honoring thy father and mother meant every senior Texan should receive an "old age pension."

By the 1960s the neighborhood began to decline. "As young people married and moved to the suburbs or out of town, Magnolia lost,"[32] McCue stated. Rev. Johnny Hughes, 1960-1967 diligently served the changing community.

Nimmo Goldston won the hearts of the parishioners, but could not stem the tide of urban change. His successor, Ralph Sells, brought great plans and ambitions. He urged the congregation to sell the property, but the older members were not receptive to the idea and he left after only one year. By 1975, when Mac L. Lee became minister, the church was in dire straits.

Dwindling attendance, an aging congregation and a huge plant requiring high insurance and utility bills forced the elders to take action. In 1983, after a year-long study of various options, Rev. Donald McClenny said, ". . . the members voted to 'plan its demise with order, dignity and grace. The church's ministry will continue,'" McClenny explained, "through the giving of the congregation's physical assets to other church bodies . . . . Its memorial fund amounting to approximately $50,000 has been given to Brite Divinity School of Texas Christian University as a named endowment fund for the granting of scholarships to members of the Christian Church (Disciples of Christ) preparing for Christian ministry.'"[33]

The board deeded the property to the Trinity-Brazos Area of the Christian Church in the Southwest with the expressed desire that it be used for religious purposes. TBA formed a special committee to study various possibilities for use or disposal. The property sold for $317,000 and with interest amounted to $412,507 when the proceeds were distributed among four Christian churches. St. Andrews Christian Church in Arlington received $200,000. A new church site in Keller was purchased in April 1992. The rest of the fund aided *Camino de Paz* Christian Church and West Wind Church in 1995 and 1996. Thus the sad demise of Magnolia Avenue brought new life to four deserving churches.

At Magnolia Christian Church, Pastor McClenny conducted the last worship service on June 26, 1983. Saddened parishioners sought communion elsewhere, but harbored fond memories of the once vibrant church.

■   ■   ■

University Christian Church—1873/1933

"Any church that can survive for sixty years without having a 'meeting house' of its own must have some genuine vitality. This is the case of University Christian Church, for although its first church house was erected in 1933, its beginnings root back to 1873,"[34] historian Colby D. Hall wrote.

University Christian Church has been a continuous body since that time, allowing for a few brief gaps and two definite changes in location.

A congregation of Disciples first met in the chapel of Add-Ran Christian College at Thorp Spring, Texas. The school's ample auditorium, the only one in the village, served both town and gown. For twenty-one years the college church was the only one in the community. Led by Addison and Randolph Clark, it welcomed the leading preachers of the day for regular services and revival meetings.

In 1895, following the move to Waco of the college, now called Texas Christian University, the story became more complicated. For the first six years no organized church existed adjacent to the school. The campus, on the edge of town, was not conducive to attracting worshipers, and students and faculty made the difficult, and expensive, trolley ride to attend Waco's Central Christian Church. In 1902 President E. V. Zollars helped establish a campus church and hired a part-time pastor. President Clinton Lockhart also supported the church, and in 1909 Colby D. Hall took the reins of ministry. A short eight months later fire destroyed the campus and the church. The college moved to Fort Worth and Hall moved to Central Christian in Waco as pastor.

From 1910 to 1912 Texas Christian University students and faculty worshiped at First Christian or Magnolia Avenue Christian. In the fall of 1912 President F. D. Kershner met with others and organized a congregation. They elected deacons and elders, and again tapped Colby Hall to be the minister/professor. For the next five years the congregation met in the chapel to hear Hall, visiting men of the cloth or professors preach the gospel.

Some say it would be impossible to overstate the importance of Hall to University Christian. Since 1912 he served as minister, board chairman or active member. In 1953 "Dean Colby Dixon Hall, whose life has been tied in with the ups and downs of TCU and University Christian Church since before the turn of the century, was honored by church members on the congregation's 80th anniversary celebration . . .,"[35] according to the *Star-Telegram*. At that event the education building was named for him. Granville Walker nicknamed Hall "Prime Minister of University Christian Church." Generations of students and parishioners agree. But Hall missed teaching and after five years resigned the ministry, and for more than thirty years he was Dean of TCU's Brite College of the Bible.

The Horned Frog, TCU's campus newspaper, told of the congregation's progress. "September 15, 1917, the University Christian Church was organized with sixty charter members and now has two hundred thirty-five. . . It is meeting now in the Brite College Chapel, but as soon as the awful unsettled conditions caused by the World War become normal again, a magnificent church building will be erected."[36]

Financial drives raised some money, and it appeared their prayers were answered in the person of oilman A. C. Parker. A preacher as well as wildcatter, Parker pledged to build the church, so money collected from the drives was spent on building a gymnasium. Parker gave his note for $80,000 and a down payment for five lots at Gibson (now Cantey) and Forest Park Boulevard (now University Drive) was made. "Then came heartbreak," Hall noted. "The oil boom simmered. The preacher-millionaire lost his fortune. . . . And the campaign money was already spent on the gymnasium."[37] It was back to the drawing board.

The members experienced a bleak year in 1922. They lacked a pastor and a building. For the next six years the old reliable plan of using visiting preachers and professors held the group together. Adding to their burdens, progress in the form of paving University Drive meant a city assessment and no money to pay it. The university covered the real estate lien and paid the assessment in exchange for the deed to the Gibson Street property. In 1925 the university donated the site of the present structure and again the worshipers joined in the search for ways to build.

"When T.C.U. held a state-wide drive for funds for the University, a first priority on all funds subscribed went to a building for a church. More than $20,000 was raised,"[38] so stated a church pictorial directory.

Church leaders explored other local and regional sources, but currency was scarce. In 1928 a committee, headed by Lockhart, hired A. Preston Gray as pastor and fund-raiser at an annual salary of $3,600. On April 3, 1929 the excited congregation held a ground breaking ceremony. Pouring the building's foundation took almost all their cash and the elation sagged as pledges were slow to dribble in.

Membership of the church in 1931 numbered about 151, largely TCU teachers, staff and students as well as neighbor-patrons, all concerned with the the national economy. Strapped for money, the building committee recommended a return to gratuitous preaching. After much debate, it was approved and professors again led the congregation.

The committee also revamped the design of the sanctuary from a $120,000 noble Gothic to a simpler Old Roman design at half the cost. A. F. Wickes, the advisory architect, greeted this move with overwhelming support. He wrote, "I like it all very much because the design has such a charming simplicity and directness." He explained his efforts to promote the type of architecture compatible with the Texas climate. "It takes a real artist to take a few common bricks, ordinary timbers, and a little wrought iron and achieve a noble architecture."[39]

"The laying of the cornerstone on March 5, 1933, was an occasion more gladsome than elaborate,"[40] Hall noted. The printed program, a paltry three mimeographed sheets, included the plea for $6,500 to pay pressing bills. Moreover, the event was pushed off the front pages of the newspapers by another action—President Franklin D. Roosevelt declared a moratorium on banks that same day.

The flock called young Perry E. Gresham as full-time minister. A recent graduate of TCU's Brite College of the Bible, he began his pastorate on September 1, 1933, in the shell of a building furnished with cane-bottom chairs. Gresham led in developing an orderly worship service, later adopted in whole or in part by other Disciples churches. He made a strong bid for neighborhood members and when he moved to a new pastorate in 1942 the membership was about 700. That membership contained many local business and civic leaders.

Prior to ending his pastorate, Gresham took sabbatical leave to pursue graduate study at Columbia University. Granville Walker served as interim pastor in 1940-41. When Gresham accepted the call from a Seattle church, Walker in 1943 began a ministry that lasted for thirty years.

He had joined University Christian Church in 1932 as a student, and earned degrees from TCU and Brite College of the Bible (later renamed Brite Divinity School). Now he found himself preaching to his former professors. They and the forty ordained ministers in the congregation might have given some preachers stage fright (pulpit fright?), but not the man with the gentle smile. Walker earned his Ph.D. at Yale University and subsequently received an honorary D.D. degree from TCU. Just as Gresham liked to be called "Perry," the new minister was already known to many as "Granville."

Walker soon introduced a service of worship at 9:30 am, identical to the 11:00 service. The two services drew additional members. The church enlarged the sanctuary and added an educational building. A gift from Mrs. H. B. Herd's family in 1950 provided funds to build and furnish the Chapel of the Good Shepherd. These facilities were first occupied in 1951. By 1954 it was necessary to add Church School classes at 11:00 o'clock. Special funds made it possible for a new organ to be installed in 1958, replacing the first electronic one in the city, donated in 1935 by the Cecil Morgan family. The church hired Q'Zella Oliver Jeffus as organist. In 1962 tower bells were given in memory of W. J. Laidlaw, Sr.

After a seven-year study, a second enlargement and remodeling of buildings began. It more than doubled the size of the church plant, and in just two years worshipers met in the new facilities for the first time on September 2, 1967.

"GRANVILLE T. WALKER DAY' ON FEBRUARY 11, 1968, CELE-BRATED THE 25TH ANNIVERSARY Of DR. WALKER'S MINISTRY HERE, the program announced. The use of all capital letters denoted the enthusiasm of the event. When University was featured in the *Star-Telegram*'s "This Week's Church," the reporter wrote of Walker, "Perhaps the greatest compliment that he can receive is that his colleagues in the ministry, both here and elsewhere, consider him probably the greatest pulpit and ministerial personality in our Brotherhood."[41]

TCU and UCC celebrated their Centennial in 1973. One feature of that celebration was a joint 'Picnic-Pilgrimage' on Sunday, September 23, to the original site of Add-Ran College at Thorp Spring. About 1200 persons attended. Many were dressed in a manner reminiscent of the 'olden days.' Performances by the Chancel and Handbell Choirs of the church and by the Drama Department and Band of TCU followed a catered 'picnic on the lawn.' The celebration concluded with a specially written litany, led by Dr. Walker and Dr. James M. Moody, Chancellor of TCU, which focused on the past, present and future of the church and the university.

Granville Walker achieved state and national recognition in his denomination. He held the office of president of Texas Disciples, and in 1957 presided over the International Convention of Christian Churches (Disciples of Christ). He requested retirement from University Christian as of December 31, 1973, and was named Minister Emeritus. At that time membership of the church was in excess of 3,500.

In the spring of 1974 the church called Dr. A. M. Pennybacker to the position of Senior Minister. He came to University Church from the Shaker Heights Christian Church in Ohio. Pennybacker's energetic leadership was felt throughout the whole congregation. Under his leadership the church continued to expand its program resources including an increased awareness of the church's life in the community. Also, the pastoral role of the church, the need of the church to have Biblical awareness and vision, and the church's concept of the Brotherhood of all Christians, were all undergirded by his dedication to sound financial planning.

One example of his community involvement was leadership in the creation of an informal group of ministers called the "Cattle Country Clerics." Senior pastors and rabbis of mainline denominations met once a month in someone's home, socialized, heard a presentation of current interest, and enjoyed a meal. The underlying purpose of this non-political gathering was to allow clergy to get to know each other so that when a crisis in the city arose, they could exert practical leadership based on the foundation of knowing each other's strengths. "When you pick up the phone and call someone for help with a problem, whether it be school busing or a natural disaster, it helps if you know the person on the other end of the line," said a retired minister who valued his association with the group over the years. The membership changed as ministers retired or accepted new pastorates, but the group still functions, ready to assist when needed.

Described as an interesting, friendly minister, Pennybacker's insightful preaching and grasp of Biblical theology was both a blessing and bane. One parishioner described his sermons as complex and "one dare not day dream" for fear of losing the thread of the message. A coed said it more succinctly, "I *love* to hear him preach. I just wish I knew what he was talking about." Indeed, many parishioners found his preaching profound and challenging.

Penny, as he preferred to be called, through his messages sought to move the congregation in ever increasing directions of spiritual life development.

Pennybacker helped develop the "Boar's Head and Yule Log Festival." Preparations for the first production of the ancient English festival required two years of work, including costume design and construction, set building, music and acting rehearsal. Several church members, specialists in theater, church music, design, art history, and religion in arts, traveled to Cleveland, Ohio to see the production at a large church there. They returned home and began preparations with teams of hundreds of people. Now a tradition, this portrayal of the ancient festival of pageantry and faith involves more than 300 participants and plays to thousands of local viewers and groups from distant cities on Epiphany weekend in January each year.

Near the end of Pennybacker's tenure financial resources weakened, and membership dropped over the direction of church policy. Citing irreparable differences, he resigned in August 1990. His resignation was met with both cheers and tears.

A search committee selected TCU and Yale educated Eugene W. Brice to calm the troubled waters. Leaving a church in Kansas City, he returned to Fort Worth. Reporter Jim Jones said, "While addressing social and economic issues, Brice does so in a more diplomatic fashion."[42] Pennybacker said of his successor, "He's a good choice. He has a fine mind and a keen wit; he is a good writer and a good preacher."[43]

Of his preaching, Brice told of an experience early in his ministry. "My elocution teacher was sitting near the front, and I noticed she frequently took out a pencil and made a note on the small pad in her lap. I, thinking she was writing some of my words of wisdom, beamed. After the service, she commented, 'Eugene, you mispronounced. . . ' and corrected me as if I were still her student. That has kept me humble as I try to preach today."[44] In his five year ministry, Brice kept the congregation together and led it to financial stability. Interviewed at the time of his retirement from University Christian, he spoke of his love of preaching. He maintained that people often come to church hurting and needy. They want an encouraging sermon to help them get through another week. After retirement, the Sulphur Springs native looked forward to writing and traveling.

In 1996 the church called Indiana-born R. Scott Colglazier as senior minister. He majored in Greek and Hebrew at David Lipscomb College in Nashville, then earned a Doctor of Ministry degree from Christian Theological Seminary in Indianapolis. In 2001 that institution awarded him an honorary Doctorate of Divinity. His preaching style combines deep theology, utilizing themes from Buddhism, Christianity, Judaism, psychology and spirituality with common experiences, all delivered in a contemporary style. As one congregant noted of the personable preacher, "The future belongs to the storytellers, and Colglazier is a great storyteller."[45]

Colglazier has published four critically acclaimed books, including the best-seller *Finding a Faith that Makes Sense*. His articles on contemporary spirituality have appeared in numerous national journals, and he writes a monthly column in the *Fort Worth Star-Telegram*, an activity he began as pastor of the Bear Grass Christian Church in Louisville, Kentucky where he wrote a column for the *Louisville Carrier-Journal*.

As a community leader, Colglazier helped negotiate volatile racial situations within the school district, and shared in creating positive Jewish-Christian rapport throughout the area. He served with Mayor Kenneth Barr and Congresswoman Kay Granger to address issues of race and culture in the city. He serves on local and national church and community boards.

When asked why he came to University Christian, he replied, "I was interested for a variety of reasons—this is a church that for many years has been considered a flagship church of our denomination, known nationally and appreciated by people around the country, so I thought coming here would allow me to be a part of that history."[46] Colglazier extols the make-up of the congregation as the reason the church is special. "There are a lot of people who care passionately about this church, a lot of people who have a history and investment in it."[47] The 5,000 plus members constitute Disciples from all walks of life. Because of its proximity to TCU, and its close ties, many parishioners are faculty or students. However, other members, representing all ages and backgrounds, come from throughout the city.

University Christian is the second largest Disciples church in the nation. And it's still growing. In September 2002 the congregation, under Dr. Colglazier's leadership, dedicated a $6.7 million, 20,835 square foot addition.

The expansion created more educational space both for adults and young children, a four room youth center, a multi-purpose fellowship hall, an art gallery, a bookstore, and a multi-media learning center. The first major project in three decades, the total area for the complex now is 140,185 square feet. The *Star-Telegram* noted, "The church also has a new front entrance, improved accessibility for the disabled, new audiovisual equipment and a new sanctuary organ."[48]

In addition to the completion of the plant expansion, Rev. Colglazier sees "opening doors" as a major emphasis in the coming years. "I believe that far too many walls divide people from churches. We want to create open doors so people can access God and their spiritual lives in a significant way."[49] He also

University
Christian Church
2720 S. University Dr.
Courtesy University
Christian Church

cited a need to be more innovative as the church reaches out to a new generation, a new century and a new era in University Christian's dynamic history.

■   ■   ■

Community Christian Church—1909

About the time Texas Christian University was moving from Waco to west Fort Worth, the Southside Christian Church (Colored), forerunner of East Annie Christian Church, and Community Christian Church, became a reality. The church grew out of the relationship between Negro and White Disciples dating back to the time of Alexander Campbell, according to church historian Mrs. H. V. Shanks. Campbell, Barton Stone and other leaders in the Disciples Movement were slave owners. Thomas Campbell, Alexander's father, in 1819 invited a number of Negroes to his school to hear the Bible read. "They obeyed with alacrity and remained to sing hymns and hear Christian instructions,"[50] historians Winifred E. Garrison and Alfred T. DeGroot noted.

Mrs. H. V. Shanks, a student at Brite Divinity School, wrote the history of East Annie Christian for her thesis. She found the South Side Christian Church, alternately called East Annie Christian, had its origin in the thought of two persons, Brother W. H. Littles, its only living charter member (in 1949), and Major K. M. Van Zandt, Fort Worth citizen and philanthropist. Brother Littles gave the following oral history.

"One night in the summer of 1909 a group of us met on the second floor of the Masonic Hall (White) at 9th and Jones streets."[51] "Our History," the Community Christian Church 2001 Homecoming account, placed the number of original members at forty.

Again from Littles' narrative,

"We continued to meet there for quite a while. I think that the Christian Woman's Board of Missions paid our rent. . . . There was a little White people's church at Eleventh and Steadman streets (sic) no longer in use and that building was given to us. . . .This was a good spot for a church where many Negroes lived but the Church caught fire and burned up. We held a meeting at Virginia and Tucker Streets and decided to

buy a lot for $400.00, $20.00 apiece we were to give. We let
the lot slip and took on the lot I bought on Annie Street for my
house. My house was on the back of the lot."[52]

The site was near the homes of many African-Americans. Bounded by the
Frisco Railroad on the east and the on the west by a white neighborhood, in
the immediate area of the church modest houses were graced with flowers and
well-kept lawns. Major Van Zandt, President of the Fort Worth National Bank,
and Dr. Bacon Saunders, a pioneer physician, each gave $500 toward the con-
struction of the church. Architects Van Slyk and Woodruff gave their services.
It was a smaller version of First Christian, designed by the same firm, and in
keeping with the style of the period.

Elder Littles described the work. "We laid bricks and poured concrete at
night. . . . Everyday we went as far as we could on the church and when our
materials played out, we stopped."[53] To raise money they held fish fries at
night, then purchased materials for the next day.

Littles continued his oral history.

"We had trouble paying for the lot too. They gave me notes
on the lot, and when it looked like the members just couldn't
pay (the notes), they were sold to the Stock Yards National
Bank. The bank was going to foreclose, George Webb and I
went out to try to buy them. We were on the street car coming
back from the North Side and were very down hearted and
Brother Webb said for us to pray. He said he thought he knew
a man he could get to take the notes. He got off in town, and
I came on home. Later, I learned they were taken by the Fort
Worth National Bank. The lot cost about $500.00 in all. It is
50 by 100 feet. When we began to build the church, my house
on the back of the lot was moved off."[54]

At the dedication Rev. L. D. Anderson, Mrs. Ida V. Jarvis of First Christian,
and Waco evangelist J. E. Dinger joined W. H. Littles, G. W. Webb, Munro
Tucker and other members in celebrating the milestone. First Christian donated the pulpit and sanctuary furniture.

East Annie's red brick church had a sizable auditorium. The baptistery,
large and ornate, ran across most of the south wall. A center aisle divided the

pews, which accommodated sixty parishioners on each side. The eight member choir, noted for its beautiful and appropriate singing, sat to the left of the elevated pulpit and lectern. Deacons and elders were seated to the right. The outdoor playground space was a vacant back lot owned by the church.

Shanks reproduced portions of the 1909 to 1912 congregation's board activities recorded in *Day Book, First Minutes of East Annie Christian Church, 1904-1914.* "April 10, 1912. Treasurer report $14.00 for the lot fund: $3.36 on the general fund and $2.00 in the sinking fund. . . . . Feb. 13 records: The minutes read- Then the books were balanced up to Feb. 1, 1913 which left a balance in the treasury of $7.42   . . . ."[55] At that same meeting the board agreed to hold communion at 11:00 o'clock and ". . .we agreed to have our board meetings the first Monday night in each month, rain or shine. . . . We paid Sister L. B. Webb, janitor $1.50 and $1.00 for wood." Other minutes showed expenses including money spent for grape juice and weed cutting. The April 7, 1913 account records the hiring of a preacher.[56]

William M. Alphin, a state evangelist, served as the first pastor. His salary was $12.50 a month, paid by the First Christian Church. Next was Rev. Arby Jacobs, a contractor and electrician who helped build the church. The third pastor, Rev. R. Love, although he had no formal education, "did a good work with the church," Littles recalled. Reverend Samson, the next to pastor the church, had been a professor at Jarvis Christian College. He, his wife and their five children, lived in the basement of the church until heavy rain flooded their living quarters.

By the 1930s enrollment rose to 200-300. Shank wrote, "The Bible school, eleven o'clock Preaching Service, the Sunday night service, Christian Endeavor (now the Christian Youth Fellowship), the mid-week prayer meeting, choir practice, and meeting of the Missionary Society constituted the official church program until the Summer of 1948."[57]

In 1924, when J. E. Quarles was minister, the congregation voted to officially change the name to East Annie Christian Church. He and other leaders kept the church afloat during the difficult days of the Great Depression.

Reverend L. F. Sledge, pastor from 1946 to 1951, and graduate of Fisk University, had been trained in sociology as well as theology. His background, plus the opportunity he saw, led him to solicit funds for a center to serve the children of the community. Using the large basement, he and volunteers from East Annie and other churches, opened an activity center. Sixty-five children showed up the first day. Shank reported, "A month after the opening the Center still did not have any chairs. . . . The Center's friend, Howard Edwards, again come to the rescue with an 'idea.' . . . . make chairs out of orange crates. Leonard's Department Store furnished the orange crates and the Center boys the power for the hand-saws that the Recreation Department lent."[58] Soon the children had chairs, but until another church donated regular sized chairs, adults stood. But, said one volunteer, "We were really all too busy to sit anyway!"

As community programs sponsored by Camp Fire and other organizations began to meet the needs of the children, East Annie Church members found another way to aide its neighbors. They established a Child Day Care Center, the first of its kind under an all-Negro leadership. Elder Johnny Smith explained that the day care center moved to another location when the congregation vacated the East Annie building.

That structure, long a beacon in the south side neighborhood, was in need of extensive repair. In 1971 the congregation disbanded the East Annie Street Christian Church, and reorganized itself. This new congregation was established ". . . as a joint program of all the Christian Churches (Disciples of Christ) of the Fort Worth area, and with both a traditional main line church and a center program serving not only members, but the whole community,"[59] the 1988 historical profile noted.

Later, according to a 2001 homecoming document, "In a called congregational meeting . . . under the leadership of the Reverend Paul A. Sims, with Chairman W. G. Wiley presiding, it was voted that the present East Annie property (Lot 10, block 31, Union Depot Addition . . .) be sold by the trustees and the proceeds of the sale be applied on the purchase and remodeling of the new site. . . ,."[60] On June 15, 1971, veteran treasurer Elder Gilbert Raleigh announced to the Board of Directors of the Fort Worth Area of Christian Churches that the name of the new church in the black community would be Community Christian Church. The fellowship hall now bears the name of the esteemed treasurer.

At 1800 E. Vickery, perched high on a bluff, Community Christian is a beige stucco building of modified mission design. The wide auditorium features three sets of white, oak-topped pews and polished pine flooring. Geometric designed stained glass windows in marbleized pink, brown and aqua, give worshipers a feeling of enveloping serenity.

During the period leading up to and during the move, Dr. Paul A. Sims led the church. Elder Johnny Smith described him as "a people person. He could bring black and white people together."[61] Sims is also remembered as a steadfast champion of justice and equality. The late Bert Cartwright, area minister of the Trinity-Brazos Area, said, "In a time of racial turmoil, when Christians were unsure how best to respond, Dr. Sims affirmed the rightful aspirations of an oppressed people. He called everyone to rise beyond passion and rhetoric to build a better community in which all have their rightful place."[62]

Sims resigned from Community in 1977 when he was named Director of Development at Jarvis Christian College, and later he served as Associate Regional Minister of the Christian Church in the Southwest.

Both at East Annie and Community Christian, the congregation has led in programs to help those in need. Historian Lucy Fountain fondly recalled the Emergency Food Program, Economic Development Program, Nursing Home Visitation Program, and Operation Diploma. Sewing classes, pastoral care classes, a religious library, and a tutoring and latchkey program were just some of the ways in which they reached out to the community. Other efforts involved support of Sojourner Truth Players, the Jubilee Theater, and the Tarrant County Black Historical and Genealogical Society, founded by long-time member Mrs. Lenora Rolla.

Columnist Bill Fairley wrote of that indefatigable woman, "'Been there. Done that,' Lenora Rolla could say quite confidently."[63] In her ninety-seven years she followed many vocations—taught school, proof reader for the *Fort Worth News*, a reporter for the now defunct *Dallas Express*, Jarvis College newspaper managing editor and later Dean of Women, Baker Funeral Home director, community activist, and the first female elder at Community Christian. Lucy Fountain, herself a member for fifty years, said "Everybody loved Mrs. Rolla, and anyone who needed help knew to go to her."[64]

Yet she is best remembered for her love of African-American history. In the 1970s Rolla was researching local black history and found a dearth of printed data. She interviewed elderly people and started a formal collection of

Bibles, diaries, newspaper articles and photographs. She died June 29, 2001 and the community lost a giant.

Jarvis College graduate Clarence Hodrick, Jr. served as pastor from 1978 to 1982. He first had been youth minister.

On January 1, 1983, the congregation called the Reverend Clarence H. Howard from the Durham Christian Church in Cleveland, Ohio. Active in ecumenical circles, he was a member of the Fort Worth Interdenominational Ministerial Alliance, the Southside Area Ministers, and was Vice-President of the District 2 of the Disciples of Christ Church. As a civic leader, he served on boards of the Sickle Cell Anemia Association, the Community Action Agency, and Bethlehem Community Center. Described as a "Christian gentleman," his ministry was cut short by his untimely death three days before his fifty-eighth birthday in 1988.

After Rev. Howard's death, the congregation called Paul Sims out of retirement. He returned as interim pastor in July 1988, only to die in August of that year. Dr. Wayne Stewart led the flock from 1989 to 1993. Alfred Dotson pastored in 1993, then an interim minister served until 2001.

In the fall of 2001, Dallas native Max Morgan left his staff position at the Oklahoma Disciples Regional Office to lead Community Christian. Full-time Christian service is a second career for him. For twenty years he worked in critical care nursing before acting on the call to ministry. A graduate of Phillips Theological Seminary, Morgan pastored two churches in Oklahoma and was campus minister at Jarvis Christian College. His preaching style is low key accented by points of drama. Vibrant phrases such as "God makes a way out of no way," pepper his sermons.

Morgan sees Community as special because it has spawned two other churches and continues to be active in community ventures. He speaks with pride of the history of the church and the many in the congregation who lend their talents to the betterment of the city. More than a neighborhood church, Community's members live throughout the area. Morgan expressed their cohesion by saying, "We know who we are, we know who we represent, and we want to share that love with others."[65] Elder Littles and Major Van Zandt would be proud of the results of their long ago efforts.

Chapter Three

THE CATHOLIC
CONGREGATIONS

The history of the Roman Catholic Church in Texas began with the Spanish exploration and conquest. Under first the Spanish flag, then the Mexican, a few priests ministered to Texas Catholics in settlements near San Antonio and Goliad. The early Irish settlements at Refugio and San Patricio came later. Mexican law required Stephen F. Austin's colony to be Catholic, but few Anglos practiced that religion. In 1841 an estimated 10,000 Catholics lived in the Republic of Texas. By the time of statehood, 1845, immigration from the United States and Europe caused that number to double. German Catholics settled in the central part of the state and still constitute a significant population there. Like their Baptist and Methodist brethren, other Catholics came to Fort Worth following the Civil War.

St. Patrick Parish—1870

Before the Civil War, a priest came from time to time, carrying the altar stone in his saddlebag, but 1870 marks the first organization of Ft. Worth Catholics. Father Vincent Pairier came twice a year from San Angelo to say Mass. The early facts are sketchy, but according to a *Star-Telegram* article, "The history is specific enough to note that in those days Father Pairier became too heavy to ride one of the Texas mustang ponies then widely used for transportation and that, as a consequence, the good father utilized a buckboard driven by a Mexican boy."[1]

In 1876 Father Thomas Loughrey became the first resident priest. The Diocese paid $300 for lots in the E. M. Daggett Addition at Eleventh and Throckmorton Streets. Despite the good price, some objected to the location, not because the church faced "Hell's Half Acre," the notorious gambling and red light district, but because it was so for from the center of town.

They named it for Stanislaus Kostka, a Polish Jesuit Saint, and held opening services in October. Fr. Loughrey welcomed the Irish Catholic immigrants who worked on the new railroad. Many stayed and formed the nucleus of the congregation. In Jean Andrus' paper on the history of St. Patrick's she wrote, "Kay Fialho, parish archivist and historian, said that Vincent Duross, a long-time member of the church recalled his father explaining that the membership had more Irish than Polish members."[2] When they voted on a new name, the Irish won and renamed it for St. Patrick, their patron saint. Fr. Loughery left for another parish in 1884.

Father Jean Marie Guyot answered the Bishop's appeal for a replacement. Born in 1845 in a village near Paris, the youth's wealthy parents supported his desire for a religious life. Guyot landed in Galveston in 1879, and arrived in Fort Worth in 1885. At St. Patrick, "In the early days," according to a 1907 *Star-Telegram* article, "Father Guyot contented himself with keeping his little flock together and instilling in them the teachings of the Catholic faith."[3]

As time went by Guyot conceived the idea that to complete his work and crown his efforts, a church of which the city could be proud, took root. Church historians credit the French priest with being the force behind the grand church in what is now the center of downtown. He hired local architect James J. Kane to design the Gothic building. It was to be constructed of ". . . rusticated or roughly-finished limestone blocks with twin towers flanking the triple-portal central entry,"[4] according to Carol Roark in *Fort Worth's Legendary Landmarks*.

Eight hundred people watched on October 14, 1888 as Galveston's Bishop Nicholas Gallagher blessed the cornerstone and sprinkled it with holy water. But then as now, plans sometimes hit a snag. Fr. Guyot wanted tall twin towers flanking the front entrance, but he conceded an engineering flaw after the towers reached the level of the church roof. "The foundation would not hold the added burden. The work had to stop,"[5] the *Press's* Jean Wysatta reported.

Fr. Guyot insisted that no major debt be incurred and thus it took four years to finish. The priest not only guided the construction, he did part of the work himself.

The *Fort Worth Gazette* wrote of the July 10, 1892 dedication witnessed by the ". . . Rt. Rev. Bishop Brennan of Dallas and the Mt. Reverend

St. Patrick Cathedral
1206 Throckmorton St.

Archbishop Janssens of New Orleans. . ." and numerous other visiting church dignitaries. The article continued:

> "The richly decorated altars, the magnificent vestments of the attendant priests and of the Rt. Reverend Bishop and Archbishop, the former with mitre and crozier and the latter in the gorgeous vestments of a prince of the Church, coupled with the solemnity of the occasion and the sweet strains of music all conspired to make the dedication of this church to the service of the living God and the Faith of our Fathers a most successful one, and one to be looked back to by all Catholics of this city as an occasion long to be remembered."[6]

Worshipers filled the sanctuary and Father Guyot celebrated the solemn High Mass. The newspaper article printed the entire sermon, preached by "Rev. Dr. Coffey of Dallas," and listed the names of choir members.

When the French priest first arrived here, twenty families made up the Catholic population of Fort Worth. Thirty years later, he witnessed to over 2,000 members of his parish. In his twenty-two years here Fr. Guyot earned the devotion and respect of parishioners and the city as well.

Described as a man of 'simplicity and humility,' he made such an impact that his ideas became a vital part of the city and continued their affect long after his death.

The beloved priest's health deteriorated following surgery in 1905. He died August 4, 1907. The *Fort Worth Record* summed up his major accomplishment. "Father Guyot's life has been one of unselfishness, and with him passed away the great sacrifices of his life, the sacrifices which he had made in order to establish the Catholic church in this City."[7]

The *Star-Telegram* editorial lauded him as a builder. "There are many people. . . who will sincerely mourn the death of Father Guyot, who never were inside his church and who would not know a litany from an ave."[8]

Kansas native Father Robert M. Nolan came to Fort Worth after the death of Guyot. A graduate of St. Benedict's College in Atchison, KS, Nolan taught English, Greek and Latin at his alma mater for five years. He was ordained to the priesthood in St. Louis Cathedral June 4, 1898. In Texas Fr. Nolan served parishes in Gainesville and Weatherford before he came to St. Partick's. For thirty-two years he ministered to thousands of newcomers seeking work in the packing houses or on the railroads. Demographers estimated the Catholic population in 1931 to be about 12,000.

Fr. Nolan died in December 1939. Pallbearers, active and honorary, represented a cross section of parishioners and of distinguished Fort Worth citizens. Among the clergy paying their respects were Rabbi Philip Graubert from Ahavath Sholom, and J. Frank Norris from the First Baptist Church. In tribute to his successful career, the diocese named the new Catholic high school in Nolan's honor.

As the city grew, sparkling new churches flourished in the neighborhoods, but centrally located St. Patrick's took on a tired look. Father Joseph

O'Donohoe, Nolan's successor, led in the restoration. Fr. O'Donohoe, a convert to Catholicism, was born in Fort Worth November 18, 1893 and attended the old First Ward Elementary School. While traveling in Europe, the Holy Land, and Mexico he came to appreciate art and church history. "He had a mind full of ideas of what the church could be and a heart full of impressions of devotion and beauty seen or heard of in distant places and times gone by,"[9] Father William R. Hoover wrote in *St. Patrick's: The First 100 Years.*

Under Fr. O'Donohoe's watchful eye, the exterior of the sanctuary received a new coat of plaster and paint. On the inside, window frames were walnut grained, the side altars replaced, the main altar reworked and new statues added. A new communion rail matched the altars. Declaring that God prefers baroque with its curvaceous lines, he replaced the straight Gothic Revival lines. "His plans, his art, and his love of the grand pageantry of the church became a reality at St. Patrick's,"[10] according to Andrus. By 1953 the church had become so influential that Bishop Thomas K. Gorman received permission from Pope Pius XII to designate it a co-cathedral.

Fr. O'Donohoe set about remodeling the basement, which had been used for storage and maintenance operations. He converted it into a crypt to hold the remains of priests, including himself when the time came. He encountered problems in the reinterment of the body of Fr. Guyot. City officials objected on the grounds it illegally established a cemetery. Funeral director and parish member Guy Thompson solved the dilemma. He said, ". . . there is a relic under the altar, and the relic is . . . a part of a body of a saint. . . . (Therefore) We have had a cemetery in St. Patrick's since 1888. We are simply enlarging it."[11] The City Attorney agreed. The remains of Fr. Guyot even now lie below the high altar.

In 1949 Fr. O'Donohoe buried his mother in the crypt and four years later they placed the body of Fr. Joseph Vann, victim of an automobile accident, there. Following the innovative priest's death in 1956, now Monsignor O'Donohoe, he too was buried in the crypt. Three spaces are empty and the crypt is kept locked. At one time a sign above the narrow stone stairway leading to Fort Worth's only crypt within a church warned, "Watch thy step."

O'Donohoe's successor, Monsignor Vincent J. Wolf, graduated with highest honors from Texarkana's Sacred Heart Academy and attended

St. Mary's College in Kansas. He studied for the priesthood at two St. John Seminaries—one in Little Rock and the other in San Antonio. Ordained by Bishop Patrick J. Lynch in 1938, Wolf served parishes in Tyler and Dallas before coming to St. Patrick's. Msgr. Wolf celebrated eight Masses April 6, 1956, at his new station.

It had been years since the church had undergone repairs and adaptations. Msgr. Wolf persuaded the congregation to undertake the needed work. In his six years at St. Patrick's he led in the complete restoration of the sanctuary. "He erected a new shrine of Our Lady in the Co-Cathedral,"[12] according to the *North Texas Catholic*. An icon of the Blessed Virgin with the Infant Jesus, brought from Russia in 1917, is the central object of devotion at the shrine. In May 1968 Holy Family, his parish after leaving St. Patrick's, honored Msgr. Wolf on the thirtieth anniversary of his ordination.

Following Wolf's tenure, Pennsylvanian Lawrence M. DeFalco came to St. Partick's. DeFalco entered St. Vincent's College in Latrobe, Pennsylvania in the fall of 1933. A year later, due to budget cuts, the Catholic Diocese of Pittsburgh dropped half of the class, including DeFalco. He found a place at St. John's Home Mission Seminary in Little Rock, Arkansas in 1935. After ordination at St. Andrew's Cathedral there, he was immediately assigned to St. Patrick's.

The *Star-Telegram* introduced Father DeFalco by noting, "On June 26, 1942, a newly ordained priest unpacked his few belongings at the rectory. . . and prepared to take up his assignment as second assistant."[13] Almost twenty years later, in January 1962, Msgr. DeFalco again unpacked his few belongings at the rectory when he returned as senior minister of Fort Worth's oldest Catholic parish. In the interim the Pennsylvania native spent two years in Rome, studying at Gregorian University. He received a master's degree in canon law. Back in the United States, he served as head of the matrimonial tribunal, and pastored Our Lady of Perpetual Help in Dallas. *The Handbook of Texas Online* noted, "He was named papal chamberlain with the title of monsignor in February 1961."[14] In 1963 Pope John XXIII promoted DeFalco to bishop of the Amarillo Diocese. Exploratory surgery in July 1979 revealed advanced pancreatic cancer. Bishop DeFalco resigned the following month. Declaring to his family "I am ready," he died September 22, 1979 and was buried in Llano Cemetery, Amarillo.

Monsignor Joseph Erbrick pastored during the turbulent 1960s. On April 8, 1968, he ordered the bell tolled thirty-nine times to coincide with the funeral of thirty-nine-year-old slain civil rights leader and Baptist preacher, Martin Luther King.

Erbrick was a popular priest and builder of churches. Thousands of parishioners enjoyed his sense of humor during his fifty-four year ministry. After his death friends established a seminary endowment in his memory.

October 21, 1969 was a momentous day for St. Patrick's—the Diocese of Fort Worth became a reality when pastor John J. Cassata was named the first bishop. In a ceremony attended by visiting dignitaries, he occupied the *cathedra*, the episcopal chair, and received the crozier. Representatives of clergy and laity paid homage. "Archbishop (Luigi) Raimindi was then chief celebrant at a Mass at which all the bishops of Texas were celebrants,"[15] Hoover wrote.

One year later St. Patrick's turned 100 years old. To recognize the centennial, Bishop Lawrence DeFalco joined former pastors Monsignors Erbrick and Wolf in the festivities. Msgr. William J. McCoey, new to the parish, welcomed them. Bishop DeFalco recounted the parish history, noting that three pastorates, Guyot's, Nolan's and O'Donohoe's spanned seventy-two years. He also praised the Irish pioneers who played such an important part in the early days of the church.

Philadelphian Msgr. McCoey, ordained in Dallas in 1945, served parishes there and in Abilene. He developed and led St. John the Apostle Parish in Richland Hills before his assignment to St. Patrick's. Illness cut short his ministry. He died February 4, 1973. "He, by force of will, had remained as active as possible until the very end,"[16] Hoover noted.

Monsignor John M. Wiewell took up his charge on Mother's Day, May 13, 1973. The Oklahoman had served as secretary to Bishop Joseph P. Lynch, and pastored St. Bernard's Parish in Dallas before coming to Fort Worth. Throughout his tenure, he included a sermonette in the bulletin as a personal message to his parishioners. He felt privileged to preside at the marriage of Dennis Crumley and Malinda Rhoades—special because Dennis was a fourth generation member of his family to be married at St. Patrick's.

Msgr. Wiewell is remembered for his restoration and enlargement of the facility. He also observed a dual celebration in June 1987: his Golden Jubilee as a priest and his retirement from active ministry.

"St. Patrick's attained the rank of co-cathedral on December 8, 1953, when the name of the Diocese of Dallas was changed to the Diocese of Dallas-Fort Worth,"[17] according to Hoover. Sixteen years would elapse before John J. Cassata became Fort Worth's first bishop.

Following Bishop Cassata's 1980 retirement Father Joseph P. Delaney was named to the post. Delaney began his seminary training at Cardinal O'Connell College in Boston. He later earned a master's degree in philosophy at Catholic University, and was ordained to the priesthood December 16, 1960 in Rome. Known as an able administrator, prior to his elevation to bishopric, he modernized the Brownsville diocese by making it the first to use computers. Archbishop Patrick Flores praised Delaney's work by saying the South Texas diocese was thought to be the best-organized one in the United States.

On Sunday afternoon, September 13, 1981, his parents, Joseph and Jane Delaney, and an estimated 7,000 other people crowded into the Tarrant County Convention Center to observe the reverent ceremony. Jim Jones of the *Star-Telegram* wrote, "The height of the ordination came as Archbishop Patrick Flores of San Antonio, the ordaining bishop, silently laid his hands on the head of the kneeling Delaney."[18] Community leaders, including Mayor Woodie Woods, and representatives of Jewish, Protestant, and Orthodox congregations witnessed the event.

Fr. William Hoover, 1987-1995, is best remembered for compiling the centennial history, *St. Patrick's" The First 100 Years*. He resigned in 1995 and died a year later.

Msgr. Hubert J. Neu came to St. Patrick's in the fall of 1995. A native Texan, he received his religious education at St. John's Seminary in San Antonio. He inherited a restoration program and it has been his goal to complete the project. Indeed all who enter the century old building feel the blend of the old and the new. The communion rail is old, the carpeting is new. The stained glass windows are old, some of the lighting is new.

What makes St. Patrick's Catholic Cathedral special? Longtime member and historian Kay Fialho said the traditional classical Masses, its downtown location, and most of all, its congregation have contributed to the legendary church's appeal.

■   ■   ■

All Saints Catholic—1902

All Saints is the second oldest Catholic parish in Fort Worth, and the first north of the Trinity River. It originated with twelve families meeting in the home of Mrs. Annie Mulholland at 1305 N. Commerce in the spring of 1902. Fr. J. A. Campbell of the mother church met with them, but gave up on the group's hope for a new parish after three weeks. Yet resolute organizers saw the need for a ministry to Catholic European immigrants who poured into North Fort Worth to work in the packing houses.

Mrs. Mulholland donated property on Berry Street, which was raffled off for $2,000. With the proceeds the group built a small frame church on the corner of Lake (later N. Houston) and N. W. 20th Streets. "The church was dedicated in 1903 and served the needs of its English-speaking parishioners until December 1952, when a modern and much larger brick-veneer facility replaced it,"[19] historian Carlos Cuellar wrote. Father Martin A. McKeogh served as the first priest. In 1905 Fr. James Molloy came, the second to serve. He is remembered as an outstanding orator as well as overseer for the building of the rectory. Until that time he lived in the south sacristy and took his meals with the John Kelley family. "Father Malloy used a fireplace for heat, and when the wind would be from a certain direction the sacristy would fill with smoke, which prompted him to remark that he had heard of all kinds of priests, but that was the first time he had heard of a smoked priest,"[20] according to a church history.

The Sisters of Charity of the Incarnate Word came from San Antonio in 1906 to establish a boarding school for girls —All Saints Academy. Later, boys were admitted to the elementary grades.

Fr. Daniel R. Harrington, who followed Malloy, often drove a horse and buggy, accompanied by his two Bernard dogs, (Saints, of course) to take care of parish business.

Other priests during these early years were J. M. Byrne, Y. Pohlen, F. Marti, R. Atanes, and James E. Malone. The latter, known as the "mayor of the North

Side," was a close friend of New York Giants manager J. J. McGraw. The New Yorker brought his baseball team to Ft. Worth for spring training and the priest delighted in watching them play. The leadership was busy during his pastorate. The members completed the rectory and the Sisters of Charity opened the Mt. Carmel Grade School. Fr. Malone died in office November 19, 1921.

The Rev. J. Krukkerts ministered to the growing flock for two years. In 1923 Fr. John Maher, the seventh pastor, began a twenty-four year tenure at All Saints, the longest of any priest of the parish. A devout man who never took vacations, he is remembered for always trying to keep the old church warm in winter and cool in summer. Seeing the futility of these efforts, he originated the fund for a new sanctuary.

Following Fr. Maher's death in 1948, Frs. Joseph Erback and Thomas Zachry ministered to the children and neighbors of the original members in the old church until the new one was ready for occupancy in 1952. Rev. Charles Redfern succeeded Monsignor Zachry and ministered until early 1955 when All Saints and San Jose were combined into one church under the name All Saints.

In the first decade of the twentieth century, The *Star-Telegram* noted that more and more, "Mexican workers were part of north Fort Worth's influx, and Catholic Church authorities recognized the neglect of Mexican parishioners as their numbers grew."[21] The diocese chartered Mission San Jose, in a cottage at Ross and 21st. streets, as a church within the boundaries of All Saints for these communicants. In 1919 the diocese moved the San Jose Chapel to the corner of Rusk (Commerce) and N. E. 14th Streets.

The Claretian order was founded in 1849 by the Spaniard, Antonio M. Claret. This order branched out into Africa and Latin America before coming to the United States in 1902. In 1926 the bishop entrusted the parish to the Claretian Fathers. For the next thirty-six years San Jose was under their supervision and guidance. They cared for the physical, educational and spiritual needs of the Mexicanos. Rev. Eugenio Herran, the first of his order to serve the community, later became one of the General Counselors of the Congregation residing in Rome.

The mission thrived as a center for Catholic families. In addition to the San Jose School, during the 1930s the Claretians operated a free health and dental clinic, staffed by Spanish-speaking professionals. "The mission grew rapidly as priest and parishioners blended Mexican rituals and traditions with other Catholic practices, nearly a century before Pope John Paul II called for Mexicans to honor their native cultures. . . ,"[22] reporter Taneya Gethers noted.

Frs. Sebastian Ripero, 1930-1932; and Bonifacio Mayer, 1932-1937, served during the first ten years of the Mexican church. In 1930, during Ripero's pastorate, the old church was torn down and a new sanctuary built. On October 26 an overflow crowd witnessed the blessing and dedication of the new church, a Gothic design constructed of brick and tile.

Cuellar wrote of the congregation's pride. They worked hard to sustain San Jose by raising money, supporting activities, or maintaining the building. "Those who had no money to give in *la colecta* helped the church by doing volunteer work; some cleaned the church every week."[23] The parish men's club, Holy Name Society, poured sidewalks, painted, and made repairs when needed. "Longtime member Michael Ayala recalled that 'the Claretian priests had the knack of making it seem as if it were your idea, and ultimately it was, for the entire North Side community benefited from the improvements.'"[24] The women did their part by cooking for the *jamaicas* (summer festivals) and organizing religious pilgrimages.

San Jose School grew as the parish numbers increased. During the 1930s Sister Lawrencia, SSMN, used her persuasive skills to obtain supplies for the children. The nun organized annual Christmas programs in which girls received dolls, boys toy cars, and all collected bags of candy, Michael O. Ayala told historian Cuellar. When Sister Lawrencia took the children on field trips to Forest Park, she cajoled Swift and Company into donating hot dogs to be put on Mrs. Baird's Bakery donated buns. "Taking the streetcar downtown . . . the determined nun went from store to store, especially Leonard Brothers, asking for shoes and clothing for her poor students."[25]

The city condemned the San Jose school in 1943 and the Sisters of Notre Dame de Namaur opened a new one nearby for grades one through six. Five years later they added grades seven and eight. Father Celestino de la Iglesia, during his pastorate, raised enough money to field a football team. They won a championship in 1949.

From 1937 to 1945 Frs. Ignacio Azumendi, James Tori, and Antonio Nebrada led the congregants, with Fr. Mayer returning for a year in 1941. Father Celestino served in the mid-1940s.

Father Aloysius Dot, 1948-1954, devoted a great deal of his time to visiting parishioners. In *A Celebration of 68 Years of Service of the Claretian Order to San Jose and All Saints Parishes*, the editors tell this anecdote:

"He'd go to peoples (sic) houses without invitation, sit down at the kitchen table and chat. One day he arrived at the home of a man who was cutting his three boys' hair. After the boys were finished, Father Dot asked to have his hair cut, since it was sort of long. Thereafter, Father Dot came to visit whenever he needed a hair cut."[26] Once he accidentally left his celluloid collar stay. Three years later he died and the stay is a treasured souvenir of a loving friend and priest.

Richard Trevino, 1954-1955, nurtured the congregation in the last decade prior to San Jose's merger with All Saints. According to the church history, "By a decree of His Excellency, Bishop Thomas K. Gorman, D.D., the Parishes were merged or integrated into one unit on February 11th, 1955."[27] Clearetian Father Richard J. Trevino, C.M.F. (*Cordis Mariae Filius*) became the first Claretian pastor of All Saints.

It fell to Father Louis Vasquez, 1957 to 1962, to cement the merger of the two congregations. Of the years of dual churches, Daniel Anguiano, unofficial historian of All Saints, said, "There was definitely a racial divide that didn't break until the '50s."[28] Anglo Catholics worshiped west of North Main and Mexican Catholics worshiped east of the street. Of the merger, parishioner Michael Ayala noted, "The transition went alarmingly well. . . . We [San Jose and All Saints] came together with the same goal."[29] The building which housed San Jose is now used by the Catholic Mens' Club.

Rev. Leo Delgado, the last Claretian priest, served until 1994. In his thirty-nine year ministry the Kansas native recalled counseling with everyone from migrant workers to inner-city troubled youth. Mostly he devoted himself to building neighborhoods. Speaking of the lack of young people going into ministry, he told reporter Elizabeth Campbell, "For me, I think the church is going into a phase where lay people will have a prominent role."[30] Before coming to Fort Worth, Delgado served parishes throughout Arizona and California. He left All Saints for a church in San Marcos.

Third generation congregant Hope P. Ayala, wife of Michael O. Ayala, served as All Saint's secretary from 1961 until her retirement in 1994. In an interview she fondly recalled some of the clergy with whom she worked. There were many because the Claretian order routinely reassigned priests every four years.

Light-hearted Father Al Lopez, 1978-1981, centered his efforts on getting people more involved in the activities of the parish. Ignacio Blanco, 1981-1984, was born in Spain. He left All Saints to pastor *Corazon de Maria* in San Antonio. Father Manuel Marrufo, who followed Blanco, and led the church until 1987, had a military bearing, perhaps related to his years as a major in the chaplaincy. Father Ron Alves, 1987 to 1990, Mrs. Ayala remembered as a jolly person and easy to get along with.

Franciscan Esteban Jasso felt his appointment to All Saints was a homecoming of sorts. The Waco native spent seven years in Europe, where he earned a Masters Degree in Theology from the University of St. Thomas Aquinas in Rome, and later earned a masters in business leadership in Mexico. Fr. Jasso served four years in Central and South America and twenty-four years in Mexico before his 1994 assignment to the historic North Side parish.

Described as having a gentleness of manner, combined with a determination of spirit, he sees education of his parishioners, and Mexican-Americans in general, as a key to the future. "Education in every sense of the word—religious, civic and training for leadership," he said in an interview.

The growth in the Mexican-American community makes it imperative that the church join with society as a whole to train leaders from this population, ". . .otherwise that growth would not be as fruitful as it should,"[31] he declared.

While proud of the achievements of All Saints, such as sponsorship of *Cinco de Mayo* and *Dies y seis de septiembre* festivals, Father Jasso looks forward to the time when the parish can finish raising money to enlarge its facilities. In his office he points to a model of a new community center—complete with classrooms, meeting rooms, kitchen, and recreation room. He calls it a "place to accommodate the needs of the parish," and sees a bright future for All Saints. Of Father Jasso, Mrs. Ayala said, "He's very understanding and calm in his dealings with people. He listens and says 'Things have a

All Saints Catholic Church 2020 N. Houston St. Courtesy All Saints Catholic Church

way of working out. God never forgets us, but you have to keep faith and not give up."[32]

From twelve families a hundred years ago, the congregation, numbering between 12,000 and 15,000, fills the sanctuary for its one Saturday service and six Sunday masses. It seems Father Campbell gave up too soon.

■   ■   ■

Our Mother of Mercy—1929

"In June 1928, Bishop Joseph P. Lynch of Dallas wrote to Father Pastorelli: 'Things are now at the state that we should proceed with the work in Ft. Worth,'"[33] according to the brief history in *Our Mother of Mercy Parish*.

Father Narcissus Denis, of the Josephite order, which is dedicated to work exclusively with black congregations, was named the first priest. The Diocese bought property on Evans Avenue and Verbena Streets for $11,500. The house facing Evans became the rectory after Father Denis cleaned and repaired it. On January 3, 1929, he celebrated the first Mass. About fifty people made up the congregation. In the spring he tore down the building and used the lumber to build a new 150 seat church. On June 9, 1929, Bishop Lynch dedicated the first Catholic church in Fort Worth for African-Americans. Within a year the parish listed seventy members.

"The Klu Klux Klan was very active and violent in Ft. Worth, and Father Denis was an object of their hostility."[34]   More than once the hate group burned crosses as a warning to the congregation and its white priest. "The red neon light which Father had installed on the steeple of the church was shot out several times but he kept replacing it,"[35] the church historian noted.

The growing congregation purchased three houses across Verbena. They converted them into a convent and a two-room school—housing and work area—for the three Holy Ghost nuns who came in 1930. Father Denis switched from clerical robes to "work clothes" when he began construction of a modern brick and tile school building in 1931, and back to "Sunday clothes" for Masses. On September 16, Bishop Lynch again traveled from Dallas for a dedication, this time for the $5,600 Our Mother of Mercy School. The student population grew from fifty to more than 150, taught by five sisters. Many years later, retired educator Frank Staton credited the school with providing him the foundation he needed for his long and successful career helping Fort Worth students.

Father Denis served as pastor until 1938. He left with the love of the congregation of 200, and with the gratitude of the black community. Churches in the then segregated city were more than places for Sunday worship, and Fr. Denis led parishioners beyond sharing the liturgy. "Efforts to fill the need for social life, especially for the young, was a part of Our Mother of Mercy from the beginning,"[35] Jerry Thomas wrote in *La Vida News*.

Fathers Thomas Brophy, T. Collins, E. Bowes, J. Rawlins, J. Geeslin, C. Crowley, H. Gregory, and M. Kenney, led the parishioners during the forty year interval between the first priest and their first black priest, Father Kenneth

Howard. During all these pastorates Our Mother of Mercy experienced continued growth and influence in the community.

Because of racial segregation they could not join the Knights of Columbus, so men of the parish established the Knights of Peter Claver, Inc. as their fraternal organization. Their mission reads in part, ". . . for giving edification by good example . . . in word and deed, especially to the youth who emulate these virtuous deeds; of rendering mutual aid and assistance to its sick and disabled members; of promoting such social and intellectual association. . . . . May every Knight aspire to true manhood in all its glory!"[36] African-Americans may now hold membership in the Knights of Columbus and some men of Our Mother of Mercy have joined the larger association.

In 1952 the congregation moved to the former site of Holy Name Church at New York and Terrell Avenues when that congregation relocated to the Polytechnic neighborhood. Built of true stucco with buttresses lending an aesthetic touch, the church and rectory were larger than their previous quarters. The nuns lived in the new rectory until the church built another convent.

"Parishioners performed the needed repairs and in September 1953 the school moved to the new location,"[37] the church historian noted. But two years later building engineers found a structural flaw in the school and the city condemned it. In the summer of 1957 the congregation signed a contract for an $87,500 building containing eight classrooms and a cafeteria. The Holy Ghost Sisters moved into their new school on E. Terrell in 1958. Former Principal Sister Roberta Fulton in 2002 affirmed their mission. "Our Mother of Mercy Catholic School was established in 1929 to serve the African-American Community. We strive for holistic formation of the human person based on Christian values. Our foundation is fundamental in leading students to reach their full potential and to prepare them for tomorrow's world."[38]

Sixty-two years after the founding congregation met with the first Josephite priest, a turn of events brought Father Vincent Inametti, of the Missionary of St. Paul order, from his home in Africa to Fort Worth. Okon, as he was known prior to his baptism, was a member of the Efik Tribe, living in a village near Calabar, Nigeria. He attended a school taught by Kiltigen

Fathers from Ireland. One day, curious about the Mass ritual, instead of going directly to the community water well, he sneaked inside the church next to the school. "Only the Mass lasted an hour and a half," the priest told Pat Poundstone of the *North Texas Catholic*. "To explain why it took me so long that Sunday to get water, I told my grandmother that there was a big crowd at the well, and that I had to stand in a long, long line,"[39] When Okon's grandmother found out the truth she spanked him, not for going to the church, but for not telling the truth—a lesson he carried with him the rest of his life.

The youth persisted in his efforts to learn more about the Catholic faith and was accepted into a catechumenate class. After three years of evening and Saturday sessions, he received a certificate indicating his readiness for baptism. "But I had to have a Christian name," he recalled. He looked around the church and spied a St. Vincent de Paul Poor Box. "I will be called Vincent."[40]

In 1978 he enrolled in the pioneer class at Missionaries of St. Paul Seminary in Nigeria's capital city. Ordained by Cardinal Etedem in the Cathedral in Abuja, Father Vincent learned he would be assigned to the

Our Mother of Mercy Catholic Church 1009 E. Terrell

United States. He served parishes in several Southern states as a "swing priest" before coming to Fort Worth in 1991. Only the second black priest to minister to Our Mother of Mercy, he was the first African. Although his path to ministry was atypical, his message to the congregation was not. "We are family." In a Nigerian accent, he said, "Because of our baptism, we speak the same language that challenges us to love one another, nurture each other and be witnesses of the Gospel to all,"[41] he exhorted his flock.

Frank Staton remembered Father Vincent as one who liked to sing, who sometimes preached from the center aisle, and interacted with the parishioners. After leaving Our Mother of Mercy, Father Vincent served the Diocese in several capacities. Beginning in 2003 he served as chaplain at the federal corrections facility at the Joint Reserve Base in west Fort Worth.

As part of Our Mother of Mercy's seventieth anniversary Father Dan Bastianelli led communicants on the original walking trail from Verbena to the Terrell Street sanctuary. Each recited the rosary on the pilgrimage.

Father Michael Farrell came to the near south side parish in 1997. As a youth growing up in New York City, Michael pondered what vocation he should choose. In his senior year a representative of the Josephite Order visited Michael's high school. Intrigued by the order's commitment to ministering to black congregations, he applied and was accepted for membership.

Following his graduation from St. Joseph Seminary in Washington, D. C. more than forty years ago, Father Farrell served in that city and several cities in the Deep South. In the 1960s he experienced, along with his parishioners, the last vestiges of Jim Crow practices. Recalling that time, he spoke of a bygone incident. After saying Mass in a Virginia mission the priest suggested that he and a member of the flock have dinner at a local restaurant. "I can't go in, I'll have to go to the back door," the man said. It made Jim Crow very real to the New Yorker. Father Farrell recalled another time when he and a fellow priest ate at a national chain restaurant. They asked "Do you serve Afro-Americans?" The manager replied they never had, but would. Father Farrell then dined without incident with one of his parishioners. The only problem the manager had was keeping his black cooks in the kitchen rather than gawking in disbelief.

Father Farrell led a parish in Houston before he came to Fort Worth. Speaking of Our Mother of Mercy he said, "This congregation comes from all over the city and the suburbs. We're the only Afro-American Catholic Church in the entire Diocese."[42] His goal is to continue that historic ministry and to bring more people into the church. Frank Staton says of his priest, "His is a teaching ministry. He explains the readings."[43]

Reporter Jerry Thomas recently stated, "Our Mother of Mercy has been a 'Yeast' for social justice for Afro-Americans in the Catholic community for Fort Worth and beyond."[44] Confirmation is the fact that the church has contributed leaders of Diocesan organizations, and one member became president of the Texas Catholic Conference. A retired judge, a former Tuskegee airman, a city council member, and community business and educational pacesetters consider Our Mother of Mercy their spiritual home.

Chapter Four

THE PRESBYTERIAN CONGREGATIONS

"Presbyterian churches represent those features of the Reformation emphasized by Calvin,"[1] Allen Carney wrote in his series on historic Fort Worth
denominations. Their doctrine, developed in Switzerland, was modified some-
what in Holland and France. The Scots, under the influence of John Knox,
readily adopted the tenets of worship and transported Presbyterianism to
America. In *Why I Am A Presbyterian*, Park H. Miller wrote, "Although there
were previously many scattered Presbyterian ministers and congregations with
Presbyterian beliefs, Presbyterians in America first formed an organization
in 1706."[2]

The Presbyterian churches, prior to the Civil War, included three major
denominations: the Presbyterian Church in the United States of America
(1706), the Cumberland Presbyterian Church, a split-off, (1810), and the
United Presbyterian Church of North American, a union of the Associate
Presbyterian Church and the Associate Reformed Presbyterian Church
(1858). Another division occurred in 1861 when a group meeting in Augusta,
Georgia, broke with the Presbyterian Church in the U.S.A. and formed the
Presbyterian Church of the Confederate States of America. Following the
Civil War this group took the name Presbyterian Church in the United
States. "After 1861 churches of this former denomination were affiliated
with the U.S.A. (Northern), the U.S. (Southern), or one of the other two
Presbyterian denominations,"[3] according to First Presbyterian Church histo-
rians Dorothy Iba, Rose Marie Jennings, Gail Barham, and Dan Goldsmith.
More than 160 years after Presbyterians organized in the United States, the
formal beginning of the Presbyterian movement in Fort Worth became a
reality.

■   ■   ■

First Presbyterian Church—May 1873

The history of the pioneer church in Fort Worth is woven into the fabric of the five denominations mentioned above, as Iba *et al* wrote in *First Presbyterian Church; Our History.*

". . .and each division, union or reunion, directly affected the life, ministry and broader relationships of this local congregation."[4]

On Sunday, May 25, 1873, a new congregation of ten charter members formed the Fort Worth Presbyterian Church, of the "Southern" denomination. Among the ten were Mrs. W. P. Burts, wife of the newly elected mayor; Captain and Mrs. B. B. Paddock, publisher of the local newspaper; S. P. Greene, an organizer of the volunteer fire department; E. M. Field, Mrs. J. F. Cooper, and Mrs. Henrietta Knight. Services first were held in a room over Knight's Livery Stable, then moved to near-by Evans Hall.

Dan E. Goldsmith said in an interview, "Jesus was born in a manger—our church was born in a livery stable."[5] Goldsmith, Pastor Emeritus and gold mine of information (pun intended) chronicled the complicated story of the church in such a way that is easily understood.

W. M. Kilpatrick, the first supply minister, (approved by the Presbytery rather than called by the congregation) had been traveling through the country in a covered wagon and stopped in Fort Worth for provisions. He served from 1874 to 1876. W. W. Brim, the first called minister, began his work in March of 1877. He supervised the construction of a frame church on Jones Street between First and Second. The *Fort Worth Daily Democrat* wrote, "The new building is only 30 x 52, in size, but is finished throughout; plastered, painted, seated, lighted, carpeted, heated, blinds to the windows, and everything neat and tasty!"[6]

The growing congregation called Reverend William George, D.D., as their next minister. Installed May 1, 1881, he served until the fall of 1884. Under the leadership of their next pastor, Robert H. Nall, the members requested a name change. The Dallas Presbytery approved and Fort Worth Presbyterian became First Presbyterian of Fort Worth. Within a few years they needed larger quarters. In 1890 the flock erected a white brick and stone building at Fourth and Calhoun. It had red quoins as corner trim, and cost $65,000. In *Press* reporter Allen Carney's 1934 history of the church, he described it as "large and commodious," with twice the seating capacity of the old wood church. Within twenty-five years the membership grew to 636.

Meanwhile, at the coming of the railroad in 1876, the town experienced rapid growth. With this boom came all-night saloons, dance halls, gambling houses—and hotels.

Cumberland Presbyterian had its beginning in 1878 when C. A. Daniel, a local hotel owner, invited A. H. Stephens to preach a Sunday service at the hotel. Stephens, a graduate of Trinity University, who was traveling through Texas selling subscriptions to the *St. Louis Presbyterian Observer*, met with twelve people. Encouraged, Rev. D. R. Bell and thirty-three charter members organized the Fort Worth Congregation of the Cumberland Presbyterian Church on June 9, 1878. The first pastor received a two-month contract of $25.00 a month and board. At the end of the two months the contract was extended for ten months and his pay increased to $40.00 a month. Services were held at Evans Hall until the next year, when the congregation bought a lot at the corner of Fifth and Taylor Streets.

"The Rev. Stephens visited ranches in the countryside in a borrowed horse and wagon, soliciting donations for a new church building,"[7] Iba noted. With cash in short supply, he accepted cattle and hogs which he sold for $1,500. They built "a grey frame structure," Carney wrote.

Stephens resigned in 1879 to finish his Biblical studies and for the next five years a succession of ministers preached until the Rev. R. M. Tinnon arrived in October 1884. "The church grew under Dr. Tinnon to be one of the largest in the city,"[8] according to a church feature story in a 1913 *Star-Telegram*. He stayed until 1892 and saw the congregation incorporate and adopt a new name—Taylor Street Cumberland Presbyterian Church of Fort Worth.

In 1888 the stone church of Gothic architecture was dedicated. The copper box in the cornerstone contained a confession of faith of the Cumberland Church, copies of the *Fort Worth Evening Call, Fort Worth Evening Mail, Sunday Mirror, Fort Worth Daily Gazette, Texas Commercial Reporter* and a church paper. This same cornerstone can be seen in the narthex of the present church at 1000 Penn Street.

Another relic of the old church, the Harrison Memorial Bells, were also installed in the new church. In 1911 Mrs. John C. Harrison donated the fourteen bell carillon in memory of her husband and his grandparents. Anne Goerte, known as the "bells lady" played them for fifty-seven years. For a period of twelve years, she never missed a Sunday. *Star-Telegram* critic E. Clyde Whitlock noted, "To watch her in activity one is impressed by the earnestness and devotion she lavishes upon her assignment."[9] John W. Floore, architect of the Penn Street edifice, observed the hoisting of the fourteen bell, ten ton carillon as workmen prepared to remove the historic bells for restoration and then to their new steeple home built especially for them.

Rev. A. B. Buchanan served as pastor from 1893 until 1902. He helped establish other congregations, including what would become Hemphill and Westminster Presbyterian Churches. In 1897 the women of the Taylor Street church began a social ministry for needy women. First known as the Cumberland Rest Home, today it is the sixteen-story Trinity Terrace, a retirement home open to the community.

In 1906 the church affiliated with the Presbyterian Church, United States of America (Northern) and dropped "Cumberland" from its name. Meanwhile Rev. William Caldwell, minister of First Presbyterian from 1904 to 1915, approached the minister of the neighboring Taylor Street Presbyterian, Rev. J. W. Caldwell, regarding a cooperative effort to eliminate duplication of services. After several years of cooperation, both groups met to consider a merger. "On January 30, 1916, the two congregations, meeting simultaneously a few blocks apart, approved the Articles of Federation,"[10] according to historian Jennings. Under terms of the federation, which was different from a union, separate membership and officers rolls were kept, but assets and expenses were shared, and there would be only one minister and program. J. W. Caldwell died and Reverend French McAfee served from 1913 until the federation. Old records noted he "attended seven funerals, preached seventy-three times and made six hundred and thirty pastoral visits."[11]

Dr. Arthur E. Holt pastored the newly formed church from 1916 to 1919. While at the helm, apartments next to the church were bought, faced with stone to match the church, and remodeled to provide office space, a kitchen, dining room, library and gymnasium. This addition greatly increased the monetary value of the property.

Pastor Emeritus Goldsmith pointed out the 1916 date was strictly local. "After 1916, members and their children of the Northern (or Southern) branch were kept on that church roll for the Federation. New members could choose, and those who didn't were put on the roll with the smaller number." This caused concern for a woman in Goldsmith's Church History class. She discovered she was Southern and her husband was Northern. "Fabulous!" Goldsmith responded. "You are an example of what our church is about—a coming together."[12]

Rev. James K. Thompson began his twenty-five-year ministry in 1919. In addition to guiding his flock through the agony of the Great Depression, he is remembered for his collaboration with William J. Marsh, organist and choir director from 1905 until 1942 at First Presbyterian. During that time the church became famous throughout Texas and neighboring states for its annual Christmas presentation of "The Innkeeper of Bethlehem," written by Thompson and Marsh. Marsh is best known for composing the state song, "Texas, Our Texas."

"Following World War II and under the ministry of Dr. Robert F. Jones. . . the congregation decided to meet its space needs by building a new church building,"[13] Jennings wrote. The deteriorating sanctuary, and lack of parking space prompted a committee, headed by Dr. C. A. Hickman, to choose a site just west of downtown on Penn Street. They paid $140,000 for the entire block bounded by Fournier, Texas and Thirteenth Street. A modern styled brick sanctuary, with steeple drawing the eye heavenward, became their new home. The grand opening service, December 23, 1956 was so large the crowd spilled out into the street.

After the retirement of Jones, the congregation called Dr. Robert W. Bohl. The Oklahoma native encouraged members to provide expanded opportunities for social outreach. Habitat for Humanity, Meals on Wheels and the Stephen Ministry benefited from his leadership.

The idea for a haven for homeless people came from Bohl's reading in the newspaper that three homeless men froze to death one winter night. He and St. Stephen Presbyterian minister, Dr. R. W. Jablownowski, gained the support of community and church leaders and the Presbyterian Night Shelter became a reality. In 1996, when the National Jewish Center honored Bohl with its Humanitarian Award, the *Star-Telegram's* Valerie Fields noted, "Since its opening, the Night Shelter has grown from serving about six homeless people per night to 790 men, women and children on Saturday, the coldest night this winter."[14]

During Bohl's tenure the James L. West Presbyterian Special Care Center for Alzheimer patients opened. The visionary pastor also participated in national activities and led the almost 3,000,000 member Presbyterian Church (USA) in the 1990s. After sixteen years, Bohl resigned in 1996.

Cumberland Presbyterian Church, circa 1888. Courtesy First Presbyterian Church

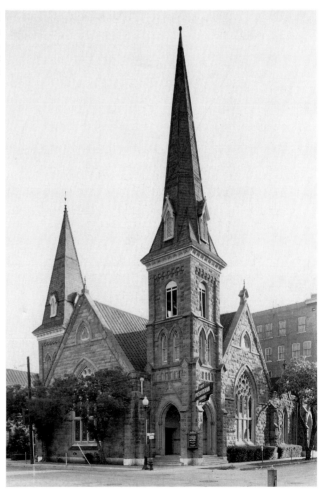

The new minister was trained as a lawyer. Perhaps this explains why Rev. Dana C. Jones' sermons are described as articulate and organized, delivered with a bit of New England accent. He came to First Presbyterian in July 1998. A fellow Presbyterian minister credits Jones with the ability to choose associates that enhance the ministry of First Presbyterian. Another noted Jones' ministry is one that incorporates pastoral leadership, compassionate caring and faithful proclamation of the Word.

Historian Goldsmith in the 1985 church directory summed up the influence of his church. "Tied very much to the city where the west begins, but reaching out in influence much beyond our locale, First Presbyterian Church

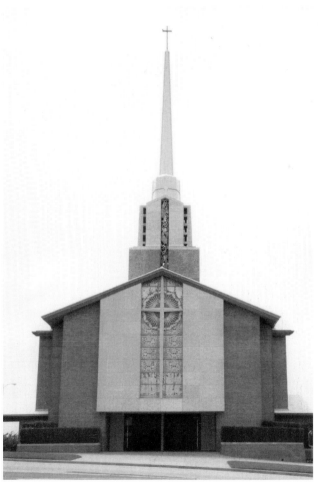

First Presbyterian Church 1000 Penn St. Courtesy First Presbyterian Church

is a congregation with a past, but one which holds a vision of what the future must be. With early worship being invaded by the sounds of horses being saddled and hitched, to modern worship being penetrated by the sound of supersonic planes flying overhead, (it) absorbs the varying sounds . . .and sends out the pealing of steeple bells to the community.[15]

■   ■   ■

St. Stephen Presbyterian—1883

What is today one of the most impressive Presbyterian sanctuaries in the city started out as a mission of the First Presbyterian Church. In the 1880s neighborhoods along Samuels Avenue to the east, Summit Avenue to the west, and stretching from the Trinity River to Railroad Street, (now Vickery) became crowded. People looked to south of the Texas and Pacific railroad for places to build. There was no church in the area and it was too far to walk "to town" for services. "This prompted four elders from the First Presbyterian to go before the Session (the ruling body of a congregation consisting of the elders in active service) on December 12, 1883, and petition the Session to sponsor a church on the south side of the tracks,"[16] St. Stephen historian Juanita Cowan wrote. Given permission, the elders purchased a lot on the corner of St. Louis and Broadway for the sum of $1,250. They paid $400 down, and elders C. H. Fry and H. H. Kerr signed a note for the balance. The Dallas Presbytery donated $300 toward the cost of a building.

Evangelist R. W. Cooper helped in the initial stages and within two months the church took form. On March 3, 1884 the congregation resolved that ". . . the first service to be held in the Mission Church south of the T & P Railroad be at 3 P.M. next Sabbath, at which time a Sunday School be organized provided the building can be gotten ready."[17] It was ready, and Elder James Roe became the first Superintendent.

On May 11, 1884 twenty-two members, the original four and eighteen from First Presbyterian, signed the charter for the Broadway Presbyterian Church. Cowan's 1997 history, kept in the St. Stephen archives, lists these founding members.

The congregation called W. L. Lawrence as their first pastor. The elderly minister died after only eighteen months in the pulpit, the record saying he "was called to a larger field." S. M. Luckett served one year. The third preacher, Canadian William Mitchell, oversaw the building of two wings, giving the sanctuary the shape of a Greek Cross, and a manse on St. Louis, added to the church's value. Membership soared to 110 and in 1887 a charter for fifty years was granted.

Some parishioners objected to Mitchell's programs and the $5,000 indebtedness caused by the building program. Membership dropped to forty-five. In August 1890 elders dissolved his contract with the church.

The Presbytery proposed the name of Dr. Junius B. French and the congregation called him in November 1890. "It was the year of the great depression of the '90's, and people were depressed in spirit and purse, a gloomy time to take over a dispirited church. . . ."[18] The thirty-two-year-old preacher, described as a man of commanding appearance and untiring energy, vowed to reverse the fortunes of the small congregation. Cowan told of one of his efforts to increase membership. ". . . word got out that a wealthy cattleman was coming to town. First Presbyterian had a delegation at the station to meet him. When the train stopped, off stepped Dr. French with Mr. and Mrs. D. C. Campbell. He had gone to Bowie to meet them and ride in with them."[19] They became the first of three generations of Campbells to be members.

French's compassionate care for an ill man, Frank Ball, paid unexpected dividends. The man's family donated enough money in 1901 to build a new sanctuary. "The beautiful church was of Gothic architecture, seating 950."[20] Mr. Ball's mother donated a handsome pipe organ and silver communion service.

In May 1905, for the first time ever in Texas, the General Assembly met at Broadway Presbyterian. This was one of many civic and religious activities during the first decade of the growing congregation. But tragedy in the form of a devastating fire halted the church's progress.

It was front page news for days. Cowan put a personal touch to the catastrophe. "On Saturday morning April 3, 1909, two little boys playing with matches in a barn on the corner of Jennings and Peter Smith started a conflagration that, fanned by a brisk wind, took everything in its wake from Peter Smith to Railroad Ave. and from Jennings to Jones. Three churches:

Presbyterian valued at $55,000; (Broadway) Baptist at $47,000; and Swedish Lutheran at $30,000."[21] Many members lost their homes. The heroics of two neighbor women, even though their own house was ablaze, saved the silver communion set donated by Mrs. Ball.

A front page story in the *Fort Worth Star-Telegram* pegged the financial loss at $2,000,000, an enormous sum in 1909 dollars. "All of the houses on the south side of Peter Smith between Jennings Avenue and St. Louis Avenue were burned to the ground. Scarcely a post standing."[22]

Broadway parishioners worshiped the following day at First Presbyterian, but by the next Sunday a tabernacle had been erected on the corner of Jennings and Peter Smith, across the street from where the fire started. For the remainder of 1909 and all of 1910 they conducted services in the makeshift quarters. "On January 1, 1911," Cowan wrote, "the congregation gathered at the tabernacle and marched to the new building singing 'Onward Christian Soldiers.'"[23] The new building's exterior was of red brick. The main floor held the sanctuary, parlor, kitchen, rest rooms, choir room, closet, Session Room and secretary's office. The second floor contained rooms for various Sunday School classes.

"One of the attractions in the new building," Mrs. R. B. Rawls told a *Star-Telegram* reporter, "was a huge chandelier that served as the principal lighting fixture in the sanctuary. . . ." Reverend French had purchased it in New York. "We were so thrilled over it we could hardly keep our eyes off the ceiling."[24] A unique feature of the huge light fixture was a cable and geared crank installed above the sanctuary ceiling to lower it when it needed to be cleaned or relamped. When wreckers razed the building almost fifty years later, the lowering device still worked.

Historically, Presbyterians consider Bible study an important element in their spiritual lives. John I. Winter taught a Bible class that was so popular men from other churches attended Sunday School at Broadway and rushed back to their home congregations for preaching services. B. B. Cobb, Secretary of Texas State Teacher's Association, taught a class that as part of their social ministry "adopted" a five-year-old when her parents were killed in a car crash.

Juanita Cowan, a Sunday School member since she was one week old, recalled her days in the Primary Department. "We sang 'Jesus Wants Me for a

Sunbeam' and 'Broadway Is the Sunday School We Love." The brown-toned sanctuary inspired reverence, especially in a small child. "I felt I should whisper,"[25] she said. "Another feature of the sanctuary was a huge clock on the north wall near a back entrance. It kept perfect time due to the diligence of Mr. Fred Fry who worked in the clock repair department of Haltom Jeweler's. As the service went on, . . . the small child would whisper 'How much longer, Daddy?' 'When both hands are straight up.'"[26]

In 1912, after twenty-two years the revered Dr. French left to pastor a church in Florida. Dr. Archibald Carr took the helm of the rapidly growing flock. After six years at Broadway, he accepted a call from a congregation in Savannah, Georgia. "On his last Sunday the church was so crowded, chairs were set up and people were standing in the balcony—so highly was he esteemed in the city,"[27] Cowan noted. It was during Carr's tenure that Sam Losh brought widespread recognition to the music ministry.

Preachers from the Baptist Seminary filled the pulpit in the interim before they hired Dr. David McConnell. The new pastor, his wife and their son moved into the manse on Fairmount Avenue in 1921. Like a good diplomat, historian Cowan recalled the man "had a good speaking voice and there was never a complaint that he could not be heard."

In addition to the death of Mrs. McConnell, several important events took place in the 1920s. Losh moved to another location and noted musician E. Clyde Whitlock became choir director. Broadway's foreign mission field, always important, expanded.

McConnell relinquished the pulpit to James F. Hardie in 1935. "It was under Dr. Hardie's leadership that the church purchased the present location and elected a building committee to plan a new church overlooking Park Hill," Cowan penned. She recalled, "We held a barbecue on the grounds, and decided to hold an evangelistic tent meeting on the site . . . . The tent blew down twice, but early Sunday morning 30 or more members took it upon themselves to bring a glorious victory out of a seeming defeat. Before the morning hour of worship, they had the tent up stronger than before and had sawdust on the tent floor."[28] Hardie accepted a call from a church in San Saba in 1949. It would be up to another pastor to guide the congregation in their new location.

Dr. R. W. Jablownnowski brought an array of skills when he accepted the 1949 call to Fort Worth. A graduate of Baylor University School of Law, he also held a divinity degree from Austin Presbyterian Theological Seminary. Before and after serving in the Pacific as a Navy chaplain for two years, Jablownowski was pastor of the Seguin Presbyterian Church.

"Bill Jab" preached the last sermon in the church on Broadway, then preached in the auditorium of McLean Junior High (now Paschal High School) until the structure on Merida Street was ready for occupancy.

After much debate concerning architecture, cost, size, and tradition, the communicants resolved to construct a sanctuary worthy of God and consistent with their resources. Albert S. Komatsu designed the building to enhance its commanding position atop a rocky escarpment. They hired James H. Conlee and Frank H. Sherwood as contractors. *To The Glory of God: A Building for Worship* chronicles the progress of the Park Hill cathedral-like edifice and much of the following description came from that document.

The modified Tudor Gothic design, cruciform in shape, was constructed principally of native variegated limestone and accented with white cast stone. It measures 260' in length and 130' at its widest area. "The central Tower

St. Stephen Presbyterian Church 2600 Merida

measured from the Robert Street level rises one hundred fifty feet,"[29] according to the document. A peal of five bells, that weighs 12,000 pounds, rests on the tower.

The church is built on three levels, with the basement, twenty-six feet beneath the Sanctuary, housing electrical controls and heating and air-conditioning equipment. The undercroft contains restrooms, storage and unfinished areas. The Sanctuary occupies the topmost level, its principal entrance being from the south into a spacious narthex. A giant tile mosaic, dominating the south facade, contains symbols of the Christian faith. Worshipers enter the nave through three sets of double doors from which point the entrance to the chancel lies 147 feet to the north, almost half the length of a football field. A five foot wide center aisle divides the pews. The nave is composed of six bays, each of which is eighteen feet, delineated on both sides by stone arches. Outside clerestory aisles, ten feet in width, parallel the center aisle.

At the rear of the nave, constructed above the area of the narthex, is the choir gallery, which houses the Gallery Organ and provides space for eighty choristers. A leaflet, available at St. Stephen sets out the exact properties and specifications of the organ. The sanctuary is acoustically designed for music and groups such as Schola Cantorum of Texas perform there.

"As one moves forward in the nave the soaring open tower becomes steadily more apparent. Upon entrance into the crossing, a large open space of 1,521 square feet, a contemplative glance up the tower, with its interior elevation of 100 feet, will disclose the vertical dimension of awe it is designed to convey, silently promulgating our dependence upon God."[30]

Beyond the transept, "The entrance to the chancel from the crossing is by three wide steps interrupting the Chancel Balustrade into which the Gospel side . . . is built the Lectern and through which on the Epistle side . . . is the staircase up to the Pulpit. Balancing the base of the pulpit in the crossing, immediately in front of the lectern, is the Baptismal Font. In the center of the chancel on an elevated dais is the Holy Table on which . . . is the Chalice. . . . Behind the Holy Table is the Retable on which are displayed the two candlesticks, floral arrangements (and) offering basins."[31]

To The Glory of God, notes "The beautiful appointments in needlepoint in St. Stephen express the Christian Faith of its communicants in an ethos of beauty and in unique medium."[32] Located throughout the sanctuary, the work was done by the Needlepoint Guild, known state-wide for their excellent stitching.

Stained glass windows, created by the Gabriel Loire Studio in Chartres, France, depict biblical events such as the Lord's Supper and the martyrdom of St. Stephen. Other windows depict the prophets and the apostles.

Minister of music since 1975, Mark Scott expressed the view of many concerning the grandness of worshiping in such a sanctuary. "The building itself states our feeling about worship. The whole reason was to build in material goods an expression, albeit tiny, of our faith. The grandness of God is evident when you walk into the building and your eyes are immediately drawn upwards."[33]

In his thirty-eight-year ministry Jablownowski not only presided over the physical construction, he moderated the debate over the name change. Historian Cowan recalled the long process of balloting—some felt that *Saint* was too Roman Catholic, some even left the church. But in June 1950, with a new name and a new location, the flock began a new phase and growth in church life.

Jablownowski, trained in the law, attracted a large number of lawyers to the congregation. St. Stephen also is home to doctors, teachers and other professional people who appreciate a formal, high-church style of worship. Mark Scott credits Jablownowski and former music minister Elza Cook with educating the membership to expect a worshipful experience in both music and sermon.

Reverend Jablownowski also is remembered for his support of the Presbyterian Night Shelter. According to historian Cowan, it came about because of his outrage over the death of a homeless man. "This is a scandal. . . .In a nation such as this, in a city full of Christian people, there is no reason that a human being should freeze to death for lack of shelter."[34] Within days he and other pastors met, and within weeks they arranged meetings with business and civic leaders. Before another winter held the city in its icy grip, in an old school building, the shelter's volunteers provided sandwiches, medical services and a detoxification program.

Following "Bill Jab's" retirement, St. Stephen welcomed Patrick J. Willson as minister. Only the eighth man to lead the congregation, he was viewed as a scholar and wonderful teacher. Willson left in 1995 to become pastor of the First Presbyterian Church of Williamsburg, Virginia.

Next they called Dr. William F. Galbraith, III. Young, and "young thinking," he shared his interest in mission causes. "He has taken us to a higher level of understanding our responsibility as a church in the world at large,"[35] Mark Scott said. In late 2002 Galbraith left to pastor a church in Fort Smith, Arkansas.

The new minister will find a warm congregation made up of people with diverse political views, but who share an expectation of a thought-provoking message steeped in awe, mystery and a feeling of "otherness," Scott commented.

■   ■   ■

Hemphill Presbyterian Church—1889

Inside the landmark red-bricked Georgian-style building located at 1701 Hemphill, a History Wall tells the story of Hemphill Presbyterian Church, decade by decade. In 1889, in Washington, D. C. Grover Cleveland prepared to vacate the White House; and in Fort Worth on Chambers Hill a dozen people met to organize a Sunday School.

Mr. and Mrs. Andy J. Chambers invited friends and neighbors to hear J. H. Hodges teach the Bible. The school grew so rapidly the group erected a brush arbor for the meetings. Within a year it became evident a mission could be established there. On June 6, 1892 Chambers deeded Lot #1, Block 14, Chambers Hill Addition, just east of downtown, for the site of the new church. Known as Tabernacle Cumberland Presbyterian Church, the charter members were: Mrs. and Mrs. Chambers, Mr. and Mrs. W. A. Sexton, Mrs. Etta Sexton, Erving Sexton, J. D. Brown, Mrs. W. H. Dixon, Mrs. E. L. Calnon, Madison Phenix, Mrs. Mary Phenix and Thomas Bratten. Bratten served as first Session Clerk until the union between the Cumberland and Presbyterian Church, U.S.A.

"The Rev. J. C. Calnon was chosen to serve as the first pastor of this church from its organization, February 8, 1891 to November 3, 1891,"[36] according to church historian Lois White Deaton. A Rev. Tinnon, as interim, watched over and preached to this little flock for a month. The Rev. J. M. Martin became the second pastor and gave the church his full attention until July, 1897. The membership at this time had reached 181. Rev. W. B. Fitzhugh pastored the congregation from 1897 to 1899.

As members migrated southward, the leadership voted to follow. They purchased a lot at Hemphill and Cannon and moved the original building there. At the first meeting, in November 1898, the congregation changed the name to Cannon Ave. Cumberland Presbyterian Church. Rev. M. W. Robinson, minister from 1899 to 1902, oversaw the repayment of the $1200 indebtedness and burning of the mortgage.

The flock continued to grow under the leadership of its fifth pastor, Rev. R. E. Chandler. By 1907, 143 Presbyterians called Cannon Ave. Cumberland their home church. Two major changes occurred during Chandler's ministry. "In the year 1906," Deaton wrote, "when the U.S.A. Presbyterians and part of the Cumberland Presbyterians united, the Hemphill Cumberland Presbyterian Church, with almost all of its members, united with the U.S.A. Presbyterian Church,"[37] and changed their name to the Hemphill Presbyterian Church, U.S.A.

Rev. J. P. Hicks, 1907-1912, served during a period of extraordinary progress. In his five-year tenure, he received more than 300 new members. Again the church was on the move, literally and figuratively. In July 1909 the congregation bought a lot on the corner of Hemphill and Laurel Streets for $7,500 and built a tabernacle there. But the people longed for a brick church.

Miss Cora Bridges' Infant Class donated the first monies to the Building Fund—$20.00. Others donated larger sums and the brick structure was assured. The cornerstone, laid July 9, 1911, contained the congregation's constitution, a photograph of the first wooden tabernacle, a copy of the *Fort Worth Record* dated July 3, 1911, and a pamphlet, "Five Reasons Why Church Members Should Attend the Sunday School," written by pastor Hicks. On the History Wall hangs a faded photograph of the Sunday School. It shows little girls in white dresses, and boys in stiff-collared shirts and ties, looking as uncomfortable as Tom Sawyer. Women held onto their large flower-trimmed summer hats to keep the wind from snatching them, and men, some bearded and some clean-shaven, in dark suits and polished shoes, stared at the box camera.

Dr. M. E. Chappell led the congregation for fifteen years of expansion of both membership and plant. In a summary of his ministry he noted 1385 new members, and wrote at length about the progress of construction. "The Sunday School building of two stories above the ground and a basement was not finished on the inside."[38] A receipt on the History Wall describes a 1913 purchase of furniture at a cost of $443.48. The building required $1,500 and free labor valued at $500 to finish the structure. He listed debt at $10,500. In September of that year they raised $11,000 in pledges, grants, and loans. The building, which could hold a thousand worshipers, was finished and in 1922 the congregation voted to construct a gymnasium on the rear of the lot. The members used it for revival services as well as for athletics. They were now ready to build a proper sanctuary.

The leadership designated November 4, 1923 as "Pledge Day." At the close of the morning service, 175 members responded. Their pledges, ranging from $2.50 to $1,250 amounted to more than $30,000—$5,000 above the goal of $25,000. A loan of $15,000 augmented the pledged cash.

Deaton quoted Elder J. P. Wear concerning the early days. "(Hemphill Presbyterian Church). . .received the fostering care of Taylor Street Church. Its pastors and membership encouraged, counseled and gave financial support."

Hemphill Presbyterian Church 1701 Hemphill St. Courtesy Hemphill Presbyterian Church

He singled out Noah Harding's family "who not only gave cash monthly payments to its current expenses, but perhaps saved its existence at two crisis. A business institution that held the lien on the property for approximately $1,000.00 became impatient on account of its not being promptly paid and in 1898 tacked up a notice of sale on the door of the church."[39] Harding advised the pastor to raise what money he could and he (Harding) would pay off the rest.

Noah's son, Ellison Harding, later gave $600 in memory of his father. "This aid from the outside," Wear noted, "encouraged (others) . . . and resulted finally in this strong and prosperous organization, well housed, such as is the Hemphill Presbyterian Church today."[40]

The sanctuary's white walls and ceiling exude an air of light and spaciousness. Polished hardwood floors lend a feeling of continuity with yesteryear's congregation. Like generations past, modern day worshipers, savor the magnificence of the stained glass windows. *Star-Telegram* religion writer Jim Jones noted, "In the peaceful confines of a historic church here are . . . windows recalling a deadly shootout in Cowtown's old 'Hell's Half Acre.'"[41] He referred to the March 22, 1907 death of crusading prosecutor, Jefferson D. McLean. (For details see *History of the Fort Worth Legal Community*.)

The stained-glass windows of which he spoke, above the front doors, feature two small crosses and pay tribute to those who enforced the law in the city's early days. The most resplendent window, of many, installed and dedicated in 1935, portrays larger-than-life figures of Jesus, Moses and Solomon. It was given in honor of McLean's father, Judge William P. McLean, Sr., a U.S. congressman and Civil War veteran who signed the Texas Constitution.

Despite hard economic times during the ministry of Dr. Everett B. King, 1928-1939, the congregation accomplished a great deal. He recalled, "God gave us the increase enabling us to complete and furnish the basement; to install the stained glass windows. . . place cushions in the pews; to re-carpet the sanctuary; and to landscape our church lawn."[42]

A mural style photograph on the History Wall tells the story of growth. In 1941 there were 1,100 enrolled in Sunday School, making Hemphill the largest Presbyterian church in Tarrant County at that time.

In 1966 Dr. J. Hoytt Boles looked back on his years at the church. They were turbulent years, 1939-1944. Only one day after he and his family moved into their Fort Worth home, "We were awakened before daylight. . . with news-paper boys on the streets selling extra editions of the paper, announcing what we were to know as World War II had begun."[43] Young men of the congregation went to war, some not to return. Yet Boles saw the loyalty and willingness to make the best of bad times as the real inner strength of the congregation.

The church observed its fiftieth anniversary during Boles' ministry. He noted, "One of the highlights of that celebration would have to be the fact that the people, wanting to express their appreciation to those who had gone before, raised the money and paid all debts of Hemphill."[44]

Two important milestones occurred in the decade of the 40s: according to the *100th Anniversary Time Line* on "August 14, 1945: VJ Day found Hemphill meeting for a prayer of rejoicing, then piling into Hazel Rounds (sic) car to join the happy throng in the streets of Fort Worth."[45] And in early 1946 Mary Huey became the first Director of Christian Education, organist and director of the children's choir and bell choir. It was the first bell choir in the state.

Membership grew to 900 and a new education building was finished. Dr. Robert Boshen served as pastor during these events. He helped establish the Fort Worth Council of Churches, was an officer in the Boy Scout Council, chaplain of the Guild of Organists and active in the Fort Worth Ministers Association. "After 12 of the best years of their lives, the Boshens left Hemphill in 1956 to accept the pastorate of the First Presbyterian Church of Santa Fe, New Mexico,"[46] he wrote in 1966.

Dr. Jack Prichard's ministry is remembered as one of compassionate vis-itations and prayers at the bedside of the sick and dying. Pastor from 1957 to 1964, he and his family were the first to reside in the new manse at Jessamine and Ryan Place Drive. One of those he visited was Mrs. Charles C. Miller, church secretary for forty years. She died in 1960 and the flock lost a stalwart.

Hemphill Presbyterian, in the 1960s, faced the same problem other long established churches faced: remain in a central location or move to a newer neighborhood. The congregation voted to remain. Years later, Reverend William R. Kimbrough, minister from 1968 to 1991, spoke of this decision. "My most important memory of the church is how loyal and dedicated the members were to presenting the Gospel on the southside of Fort Worth." As other churches were closing or leaving the area, "Hemphill Presbyterian Church stayed and continued to be an effective witness for Jesus Christ,"[47] he said.

Rev. Raymond E. Judd, Jr. led the members as they rededicated themselves to serving a changing community. Of his introduction to the church, he wrote, "Our ministry here began with a 'bang,' for during the first month of the pastorate in January, 1965 we experienced all of the adjustments of a new church, a new home, a new city, and a new baby!"[48]

When Judd took a position at Trinity University in 1967, the membership called William R. Kimbrough as pastor. "Pastor Bill" opened the church to community groups such as the Girls Club of Fort Worth. In the summer and after school 500-700 girls used the facility. Tutoring for dropouts working to obtain a GED diploma aided another segment of the community. "We had youth night every Friday night," the retired minister said. A fully equipped game room with ping pong, table games and pool tables provided recreation in a wholesome environment for both teen age members and young people from the neighborhood. They played volley ball on the parking lot.

During Kimbrough's tenure, the Southside Area Ministries, a coalition of churches in the neighborhood, organized a program to help needy families in the area. It was housed at Hemphill Presbyterian. As the service grew, it became the South Central Alliance and served an even larger part of the community.

Recognizing another need, he organized an employment counseling and job information clearinghouse for Hispanics. "While I was pastor we opened our door to *Centro Evangelico*, a Spanish speaking community church which began in our chapel in 1980. They are still conducting worship services and hold church school classes,"[49] he recalled. Kimbrough also represented his church in community endeavors such as Bread Basket Ministries and the Presbyterian Night Shelter. For ten years this energetic man of the cloth sponsored a gathering for senior citizens at MoRanch, the denomination's retreat.

In addition to wearing his ministerial robe, from time to time Kimbrough donned Navy blues. For thirty years he served as a naval reserve chaplain. He retired in 1985 with the rank of Commander in the U. S. Naval Reserves. Six years later Kimbrough retired from active ministry, but remained a staunch supporter of Hemphill Presbyterian.

For the next four years the congregation was ministered to by interims Kenneth L. Mauldin and John W. Thompson. Ben H. Stewart III was pastor for a short time as well.

Soft-spoken Reverend Robert J. Thomson came to the church in 1995. The Princeton Theological Seminary graduate led churches in Pennsylvania and New Jersey, spent eighteen years as a National Presbyterian Church administrator in New York, then pastored North Woods Presbyterian Church in San Antonio, from which he retired. But he missed being in the pulpit. He looked for a church where he could be useful and found one on Fort Worth's South Side.

His first year at Hemphill Presbyterian he conducted more funerals than infant baptisms. Thomson sees a turn around in those statistics. "I don't know how long it will take, but this part of town will be revived." He cited the renewal of the Fairmount neighborhood as an example. He thinks the dedication of members hanging on in tough times makes the church worthy of commendation. "We have a mission here,"[50] he offered as the purpose that invigorates the congregation.

Thomson's goals are, theologically to help people meet Christ through worship services and preaching, and to build up the congregation, ". . . not only among ourselves, but to reach out to the community where we live. We have a ministry to Sudanese (immigrants), and helped build a Habitat for Humanity house for them." He rejoices in a more diverse flock of young and older families. Speaking of *Centro Evangelico*, he explained "This is an independent group, but we share special occasions, such as Christmas Eve services."[51]

Summing up his calling to Hemphill, he said, "This is an old historic church with a bright future. I couldn't have asked for a better place, a better challenge, than what we have here."[52]

■   ■   ■

Westminster Presbyterian Church—1897

Funeral services are often held in church houses, but Westminster Presbyterian is the only congregation to have held church services in a funeral home. The church, now sitting on five acres at 7001 Trail Lake Drive, in the late 1920s met on the second floor of Harveson Cole Funeral Home while awaiting the building of a new sanctuary.

Westminster began as a small mission of First Presbyterian Church in 1897. The actual history dates back to March 25, 1888 when R. R. Keith, G. W. Hornbeck and F. L. Crosby met in the home of E. A. Bowman. They wanted children living just outside the southern perimeter of the city to have an opportunity for Bible study. "At that time there was no Sunday school or Church (sic) south of the Mulkey Memorial Church on St. Louis and Leuda Streets, and the boys of the neighborhood spent Sunday afternoons playing baseball and other games,"[53] according to *Our Church History: 1888-1938.*

Although Presbyterians, the men formed a non-denominational Sunday school. Fifty adults and children met in the 1500 block of Alston in an old rented dwelling used as a schoolhouse. When the building was razed, members cut down trees from near-by woods—later known as Forest Park—and constructed a brush arbor at the corner of Lipscomb and Myrtle. There they met until the new school was built.

The Bible study class continued to grow, and in 1890 offered itself to any Protestant church that would maintain it. First Presbyterian, getting ready to move into its new building at Fourth and Jones, offered its old one to the Sunday school group. The class bought a lot at 1515 College Avenue for $1 and a note for $1,000. "Men of the Sunday school dismantled and rebuilt the structure board by board at (the new site),"[54] a *Star-Telegram* reporter noted.

Taking the name College Avenue Presbyterian Church, they officially organized on December 15, 1897, under the leadership of Rev. J. H. Davies. With twenty-three charter members, the new church, located in one of Fort Worth's fastest growing neighborhoods, was near the prestigious Fort Worth University. Mrs. John A. Mitchell, who came to Fort Worth in 1858 to be the hamlet's first music teacher, donated one of her Pilcher organs to the church.

In 1898 the church issued a call to thirty-one-year-old Rev. C. L. Altfather. This began a long and mutually affectionate relationship. Clifford Williams, E. A. Bowman's grandson, recalled being baptized in 1918 by the revered minister. "I was about seven. He talked to my mother and dad and said I'd answered all the questions that he knew to ask and couldn't see any reason why I couldn't go ahead and join the church. So I did."[55] A Rev. Mr.

McCady baptized Clifford's sister, Kathryn, about 1909, Their mother held the office of president of women of the Texas Synodical—quite an honor. The Williams family has had a warm relationship with Westminster over many years now.

Altfather, ordained in 1896, received his bachelor's degree in 1899. He stayed until 1903 when he resigned to further his religious education. In the interim between Altfather's two periods of leadership, Rev. Frank T. Charlton pastored the growing church for two years. Rev. S. L. Rieves led the congregation from 1901 to February 1912. Interims filled the pulpit until the return of Rev. Altfather.

Reunited in late 1912, this time Altfather ministered to the congregation for ten years. During this pastorate both the congregation and the building grew. Historian Wilbur Klint wrote, ". . . in 1913, the 23-year-old church proper was enlarged to nearly three times its original size to provide more Sunday School space and seating for 400 in the Sanctuary. This project cost nearly $4,000."[56] Altfather initiated the "Women's Missionary and Aid Society," as well as the "Westminster League," the church's first youth group.

In 1920 his devoted flock scraped together $395 and bought a 1920 Model T touring car for Altfather. There was just one problem—he didn't know how to drive.

"Dr. Altfather served as secretary and treasurer of the Fort Worth Presbytery from 1918 until 1922 when he left College Avenue Presbyterian to accept a call to a church in Bowie, Texas,"[57] the centennial history noted.

Novice Rev. Frank R. Young, a youthful twenty-nine-years-old, began his first ministry in 1922. "Soon after he arrived the church was again remodeled: a gymnasium was built and a pipe organ, a gift from Mr. and Mrs. G. A. Bounds, was installed to replace the aging reed organ,"[58] according to the church history.

In 1926 the flock called Rev. John Leighton Green. During his tenure the school district bought the church property for DeZavala Elementary. Wanting to stay close to its neighborhood roots, the church relocated at 1425 Eighth Avenue, and with a new name—Westminster Presbyterian. "While construction proceeded, the congregation met in the Harveson and Cole Funeral Home which was then located in the (former) Southside Masonic Temple. . . ."[59]

Initially they excavated and finished a basement. On Christmas Day, 1928, the first service was held in the new location.

Green left in 1931 and missionary Rev. Archer Anderson served for two years. Before he left again for the foreign mission field he oversaw the doubling of membership, but not much was done in construction owing to hard financial times.

Next the congregation called Rev. Paul F. Bobb, who like his predecessor, had been a foreign missionary. Sometime during the 1930s, two small frame Sunday school buildings were constructed, but economics of the Great Depression caused the group to postpone the planned sanctuary. Twelve years and World War II would pass before they celebrated in their finished church. During this time Rev. James H. Patterson, a native of Scotland, and Dr. Livius P. McClenny also pastored the growing flock. McClenny led the first worship service "above ground" on Sunday, September 5, 1948.

However, friction between some of the 400 members over church policy and McClenny's leadership dampened their joy. He left to pastor an independent Presbyterian church in North Carolina. "Early in 1949 Rev. John Rodman Williams. . . came to try to smooth the troubled waters."[60] Unable to restore harmony in the congregation, he left in 1950. "At this time, 61 families (including nine elders) withdrew from Westminster to form Calvary Independent Presbyterian Church."[61] Wilbur Klint and Clifford Williams remembered this as the nadir of the church's history, but one which eventually strengthened them. Dr. Lyndon L. McCutchen's leveling influence was short-lived due to his accepting a call to the Wynnewood Church in Dallas after only three years.

Following a lengthy search, the congregation found a stabilizing force in Dr. Herbert E. Kann. He began his ministry in 1954. It was a homecoming of sorts. Twenty years earlier he met and married Fort Worth school teacher Margaret Tadlock. The Harrisburg, Pennsylvania native also had served for two years at Polytechnic Presbyterian while completing his divinity studies at Dallas Theological Seminary.

"During the next seventeen years the church made great strides in expanding its ministry under Dr. Kann's leadership,"[62] Klint wrote. On August 8, 1956, on a stormy night, both inside and outside, Kann led the congregation, literally, out of darkness in its move to the newly developed Wedgewood neighborhood. As a sometimes heated discussion ended, and ballots distributed, the lights went out. "Determined to carry on, candles were brought into the room, voting continued and the ballots were tallied by candlelight."[63] The ayes won by seven votes, electricity was restored, and the die was cast. After more than thirty years on the near southside, the congregation opted for another move.

Yet like earlier hard financial times, a new problem loomed. "The bomber plant," variously named Convair, General Dynamics and Martin Lockheed, downsized from 28,000 workers to 9,000. This hit Westminster, and other West Side churches, with a loss of membership and revenues. On occasion deacons dug into their own pockets to pay the bills. Kann remained optimistic and in 1959 the congregation proceeded with plans for the new structure on the four acre site fronting the newly proposed Loop 820.

This location afforded ample parking space and room for growth. The contemporary styled sanctuary, designed by architect Walter Koeppe, seats 300. The May 22, 1960 dedication, according to a *Press* reporter, indicated ". . . that one of the city's earliest Presbyterian congregations is keeping abreast of the shift in population."[63] Poor health forced Kann to resign in 1972, but not before the church saw an improvement in its finances and growth in its membership.

Dr. Billy P. Smith, described by long-time member Merle Scoggins as, "everything a man of the cloth should be,"[64] accepted the call to Westminster in August. Ordained by a Southern Baptist church in 1948, Smith held a doctorate of theology from the New Orleans Baptist Theological Seminary, and taught for fourteen years at Hardin-Simmons University. However, the Presbyterian system of church organization and government appealed to him, and he spent the last years of his illustrious career as a Presbyterian.

The congregation saw many changes in the decade of the seventies. "In 1973 Mrs. Donna Poe was ordained and installed as the first woman elder of Westminster Presbyterian Church,"[65] according to the church history. A year later the leaders held talks with Hemphill Presbyterian concerning a merger, but came up eleven votes short to make the change. The congregation called Dr. Jimmie Johnson in May 1976 to serve as associate pastor.

Under Dr. Smith's leadership the church continued to grow and soon needed more space. The Presbytery owned five acres at the corner of Trail

Westminster Presbyterian Church 7001 Trail Lake. Courtesy Westminster Presbyterian Church

Lake Drive and Alta Mesa Boulevard in the developing area of Candleridge. This time, by an overwhelming vote, the congregation was on the move. As the flock sold the old site and with the new one unfinished, ". . .once more, the congregation became a pilgrim people."[66]

Dan Danciger Jewish Community Center opened their doors to the Christian group. With the help of a substantial donation from John and Neva Wilson, and gifts from inspired members, the building progressed. Of modern design, the brick structure features a barrel vault roof line topped by a Celtic style cross. The flock worshipped for the first time in their new quarters in December 1983 and burned the mortgage ten years later.

Children were always special to Dr. Smith and the early learning program that now exists was started by him. He viewed Westminster as a caring congregation with a strong faith through the years and a strong understanding of the place theology has occupied at various periods of their history.

On the occasion of their centennial celebration, Mayor Bob Bolen, an elder at Westminster, brought greetings from the city. Wilbur Klint echoed Rev. Smith's observation. "Through the years we have been blessed with people who cared—cared about their God, His church and each other.

That's been our hallmark for the first 100 years. Let's keep it so for the next 100 years."[67]

Dr. Donald R. Hogg began his ministry in 1997. A graduate of Austin Presbyterian Seminary, he received a Doctorate in Ministry from Dubuque University in Iowa. He saw Westminster as a church where members were pro-active in service to the community and each other and he wanted to be a part of it. One of the strengths, as he sees it, is the spirit of family among the parishioners. "Not just husband, wife, children; but family in the larger sense. We consider all our members to be part of our family and we treat each other that way."[68] Despite a history of four major relocations, financial downturns, and loss of members, he sees a bright future for the church because of its location and message. "One of the things this church has learned over the years is that we weather the storms because of God's connection to us,"[69] Rev. Hogg affirms.

■   ■   ■

Iglesia Presbiteriana Getsemani (Gethsemane Presbyterian)—1927

"On January 1, 1927, Under the authority of Texas Mexican Presbytery, Synod of Texas, Presbyterian Church in the United States, the Mexican Presbyterian Church of Fort Worth, Texas was organized,"[70] as stated in an unpublished history of what would become Gethsemane Presbyterian. It answered a need for Spanish-speaking people.

As early as 1920 a study by Rev. W. S. Scott pointed to the large number of Mexican people receptive to a non-Catholic church. With help from First Presbyterian, Reverend A. B. Carrero opened a mission in 1921. It attracted children, but even with the help of the women of Broadway (now St. Stephen) Presbyterian, he struggled to maintain the ministry. He left in January 1925 and the women kept the mission open for the youngsters during the spring and summer.

Guillermo A. Walls, the son of a Scottish missionary to Mexico, was a graduate of Austin Presbyterian Seminary. Prior to entering the ministry he fought in the Mexican Revolution and served as an interpreter in the United States Army during World War I. He and twenty-three charter members signed the constitution of the officially organized Mexican Presbyterian Mission. Josias Balderas and Juan Frias were the first elders to be elected. Every Sunday, Balderas and his family traveled the thirty-two miles from Cleburne to attend services. Frias' son, Sam, is still an active member of the church on Bluff Street. Francisco Vega was the first deacon.

Walls' leadership began in September 1925, but he also pastored churches in Cleburne and Ladonia. Friendly, outgoing and resourceful, for two years he divided his time between the three before becoming the first full-time pastor of the mission. Walls made a survey of Mexican neighborhoods and determined a location near the court house, known as "Batter Cake Flats," would be the best site. Historian Carlos E. Cuellar in *Stories from the Barrio* designated this area located southwest of the courthouse between Belknap and Thirds Streets and Cherry and Burnet Streets as the barrio known as *La Corte*. Walls "managed to get a small group together for services in an old dilapidated house rented by the Men's Bible Class of the Broadway Presbyterian Church,"[71] the church's unpublished history read. Later the church purchased property on North Florence Street from the First Presbyterian's Hawes family, at below market value.

Members of College Avenue (Westminster) and North Forth Worth Presbyterian joined the aforementioned churches in getting the mission established. Mr. and Mrs. T. P. Wilkes spearheaded the renovation of the corner building and converted it into a sanctuary. The adjoining five room house became the manse.

As soon as the remodeling permitted, Walls began holding services. Not all the neighbors supported his efforts. According to the church's history, "There was an element. . . that resented the opening of the mission. These were the bootleggers, dope peddlers and others of that gentry."[72] Walls refused to let threats against his life from *Los Horobados* (The Hunchbacks) deter his work. With the help of county officers, he succeeded in getting most of the undesirables out of the area.

Reverend Walls identified about seventy children who were not in school, or were having difficulties because of the language barrier. Working with the Fort Worth school district that supplied a first grade teacher, Walls established a bilingual class in the sanctuary. The twice a week class was so successful in preparing the children for entry into the public schools that the board of education erected a two-room building on Henderson Street and hired two teachers. This arrangement lasted until 1930 when the classes were moved to a nearby school. The 1932 records listed 300 Mexicans studying English or vocational arts.

Along with helping the children, Walls turned his attention to their families. One historical account told of a Day Care Center "long before anyone thought about it." Homeless men could find food and rest at the church, then do odd jobs to offset the cost.

"Disease was prevalent in the neighborhood, especially smallpox and other communicable diseases,"[73] according to the history. Walls converted the front part of his house into a medical clinic. Mrs. Walls, a trained nurse, lent a professional hand to the endeavor. Westminster Presbyterian member, Dr. L. M. Whitsett, donated his time giving vaccinations and treating minor illnesses. Dr. Harold Williams, another member of Westminster Presbyterian and on the staff of the City Health Department, also donated his services. The Community Chest, forerunner of United Way, recognized the value of the work done at the Mexican Mission and allotted $300.00 a month for educational, social and health services.

The congregation grew as neighbors flocked to be a part of the church. During the summer months Reverend Walls held services outdoors, but he realized larger quarters must be built. From a membership of fifty, they raised $300.00 toward a building fund. Again local Presbyterian churches made liberal donations and the congregation worshiped in a new sanctuary in the fall of 1928. Sunday School membership reached 170. Young People's Society, Boy Scouts and Vacation Bible School offered Spanish-speaking young people opportunities to participate in wholesome activities.

By the late 1930s the Mexican Presbyterian Center operated a curio shop in which they sold Mexican art and crafts. "In 1938 Eleanor Roosevelt, accompanied by Secret Service agents, visited the center and inspected the curio shop,"[74] Cuellar noted. The First Lady bought several items, including handmade Mexican pottery and vases.

In 1939 the Federal Housing Authority bought all of the Mission property and the Walls home in order to build low-income housing on the site. The

Mission moved the sanctuary and school building to its present location at West Bluff and Lexington Streets. A basement under the school housed class and meeting rooms and a play area. Men of the congregation built a patio between the school and sanctuary and covered them both with asbestos shingles. New roofs and a beautiful stone front completed the renovation. The flock held a Dedication Service, complete with debt-free deed to the property on March 31, 1941. By this time 410 members were enrolled in Sunday School.

Cuellar wrote, "During World War II Guillermo Walls became directly involved in the *bracero* (hired hand) program, designed by the Roosevelt administration to alleviate domestic manpower shortages by actively recruiting and arranging transportation for Mexicanos, especially from San Luis Potosi."[75]

Reverend Walls retired from the ministry in 1949. Fifty years later he has not been forgotten. Sam Frias speaks for other members of the congregation in praising Walls for the many social as well as educational innovations he brought to the community. "The First Mexican Presbyterian Church was the center of religious and social life in *La Corte* as a result of his efforts."[76]

Reverend C. S. Guerrero, a former student of Walls, ministered to the flock from 1949 to 1955. The need for the church to provide the social services of years past lessened as Community Chest and other organizations met these obligations. Guerrero and later ministers still helped Mexicans with language and other services, but their main task was in the area of spiritual leadership.

Reverend Benjamin Gutierrez led the congregation from 1958 to 1963. He left to do missionary work in Ecuador, but returned and again pastored Gethsemane from 1997 to 2000.

Reverend David Cervantes led the church in the last half of the 1960s. It was a time of working with the Interreligious Task Force to help register undocumented workers. Dr. Daniel Garza continued the work of his predecessors from 1974 until 1979. Reverend Vincent Castro participated in the Presbyterian Church's Task Force on Mexican Migration. U. S. Congressman Jim Wright assisted in getting the church declared a "Qualified Designated

Interior of *Iglesia Getsemane* 960 W. Bluff. Courtesy *Iglesia Getsemane*

Entity." Jose D. Fajardo, 1987-1994, also helped Mexicans and those fleeing war in Central America to get green cards.

During this period Gethsemane, Fort Worth Independent School District, and Amherst College collaborated to operate a "College without Walls," the first and only one in the Metroplex. Partially funded by the Immigration and Naturalization Service, "We had a lot of resistance to accepting money for working with what some called 'Wetbacks.' We had some 700 or more students attending our School,"[77] according to a 1977 historical document. It told of a mother of five who worked as a cook. She pasted notes above her cooking station and studied history and English while she worked. After passing the 100-question INS exam and becoming a citizen, she won a scholarship to Tarrant County Junior College and planned to finish her education at Texas Christian University. Another success story from that document revealed that of thirty-five new citizens, half voted in the first election for which they were eligible.

From 2001 to 2003 Reverend Lewis Holmes led the church. English as a second language classes are still a large part of the church's outreach ministry, but providing a worshipful experience for its members remains the primary focus.

Chapter Five

THE BAPTIST CONGREGATIONS

▪ ▪

Early day Baptists were expected to adhere to certain "rules of order and decorum." Historian James L. Garrett, Jr., in *Living Stones* noted "(these rules) forbade absenteeism from public worship. . . failure to contribute to the 'treasury of the Lord,' attendance at or participation in 'balls' or attendance of 'the race-course' or 'other . . .worldly amusements,' and 'presence' in a drinking saloon or the use of alcoholic 'and fermented' beverages 'except for medicinal purposes.'"[1]

Lonesome Dove, in the vicinity of present-day Grapevine, became the first permanent settlement in Tarrant County. Lonesome Dove Baptist, the first church building in the county, began as an idea discussed by twelve settlers around a fireside in 1845. Legally formed February 21, 1846, the same day officials lowered the Republic of Texas flag over the capitol in Austin and replaced it with the State of Texas flag, the name seemed to symbolize its solitary location on the West Fork of the Trinity River. It stood as the only Baptist church for hundreds of miles, and the forerunner of later churches in the area, such as Mount Gilead (not the church on Grove Street), Bear Creek, and Fort Worth's First Baptist.

Much of the history of Fort Worth Baptists is connected with the life and influence of J. Frank Norris. With no middle ground concerning him, some reviled him, others revered him. All agreed Fort Worth has never produced another like him.

▪ ▪ ▪

First Baptist Church—September 1873

In 1867 Rev. W. W. Mitchell and Rev. A. Fitzgerald established the Fort Worth Baptist Church. Fitzgerald, not an easy man to get along with, weakened the already struggling flock with his sour disposition. He left and in the next six years three ministers tried to hold the group together. During this time, the Baptists, like other congregations, worshiped in the courthouse or the Masonic Building. They also attended worship services at the First Christian Church on Houston Street. On September 12, 1873 Rev. William Gough and J. R. Masters revived and reinvigorated a handful of the congregation. The renamed First Baptist Church survived. Pioneer attorney Hyde Jennings donated a lot at Ninth and Throckmorton and the group erected a building. Located near the cattle trail on what is now Jennings Avenue, in the summer a cloud of dust arising from the feet of bawling cattle swept through the open windows of the little red-brick church. Inside, worshipers strained to hear the sermon above the din of the passing herd.

"Rev. R. H. H. Burnett was the first regular pastor the Baptists had. . . .He was followed by Rev. Walter E. Tynes, Rev. J. D. Murphy and Rev. J. S. Gillespie, but it is not known the order in which they came,"[2] according to a draft document of early church history housed in the Special Collections Library of the University of Texas at Arlington. Other sources list Rev. Gough as pastor until 1877.

"Fearless, dynamic" Rev. J. Morgan Wells is remembered as the pastor who energized the young church. In a long tail coat, stove pipe hat, white gloves and cane, he cut quite a figure as he visited downtown bars to invite men to the church. At night he made the rounds of rooming houses to let drummers and travelers know the schedule of services.

Believing the original site to be too far south, he led in the building of a church on the southeast corner of Third and Taylor Streets. He solicited money from store keepers to saloon keepers for the new sanctuary. Completed in 1888 at a cost of $65,000, the large white limestone Gothic-style edifice could seat 500. Free of debt thanks to Rev. Wells' efforts, by the time of his death in 1896 the First Baptist Church was among the leading congregations in the city and the pride of the newly formed Tarrant Baptist Association.

Several pastors, including A. W. McGaha, Luther Little and Charles W. Daniel, ministered to the flock prior to the momentous 1909 call to John Franklyn Norris.

J. Frank was born in Dadeville, Alabama, September 18, 1877 to an alcoholic father and a devoutly religious mother. In 1888 the family moved to Texas and settled in Hubbard, near Waco. "When Frank was thirteen years old, an enemy of his father opened fire on the elder Norris, then turned the weapon on the boy, shooting him three times."[3] The father suffered minor injuries, but the shooting critically wounded Frank. Gangrene and inflammatory rheumatism developed. It took him three years to regain his health.

"As a lad growing up in the Hubbard City Baptist Church, Norris was influenced by the emotional excesses of Pastor Catlett Smith,"[4] doctoral student Lee Roy McGlone postulated. At age twenty Norris felt the call to ministry and graduated from Baylor University in 1903, and Southern Seminary two years later. He perfected the lessons he learned from Smith and preached powerful sermons based on his literal interpretation of the Bible's admonition to root out sin. Rev. Homer Ritchie wrote of his mentor, "From the first day he entered the ministry until he drew his last breath . . . Norris was consistently dedicated to one cause: he would fight social evils in high places or low." Ritchie continued, "Usually he attacked the major vices of the age but the minor ones were not too small to attract his attention."[5] Some of the "smaller ones" included urging the legislature to pass a law forbidding a woman to dance with anyone other than her husband, and forbidding women to smoke or wear short skirts and bob their hair. Norris left his mark as a leading proponent of fundamentalism.

He pastored a church in Mt. Calm from 1899 to 1903, and McKinney Avenue Baptist in Dallas from 1905 to 1907. However, he is most remembered for his turbulent leadership of Fort Worth's First Baptist. Biographer Barry Hankins noted, "While Norris' enemies often charged that he had no character, few have doubted that he was one."[6] He left no middle ground concerning his fiery preaching—critics claimed God cringed when J. Frank prayed, and his congregation believed him to be a prophet on the order of Elijah.

"Norris accepted the call to the pulpit of the First Baptist Church. . . in September, 1909. . . .From that time, until his death in 1952, his life and the life of the First Baptist Church were deeply intertwined. Neither was ever the same,"[7] Gwin Morris wrote in *Frank Norris: Rascal or Reformer?* When Norris accepted the helm of First Baptist, its membership included many of the most prominent and wealthy men in the city. The influential church, with its members seated in pews accented by gold-plated name tags, witnessed a change of cyclonic proportions. For two years, according to Norris' own words,

"I was drawing a big salary, wearing tailor made suits, preaching in the midst of a city of over a hundred thousand people, none paying any attention to me."[8] That did not suit his mission.

Earlier, as owner/editor of the *Baptist Standard*, he wrote stinging editorials crusading against alcohol and racetrack gambling—what he saw as major vices. Both were ultimately outlawed for a time and Norris joyfully took partial credit.

In a 1911 argument over three First Baptist deacons' serving on the entertainment committee for a function that served liquor at the Northside Coliseum, he demanded their expulsion. Instead they and their supporters left the church. "Six hundred members left the congregation within the next few weeks, taking most of the church income with them,"[9] according to Leonard Sanders.

Rather than accepting defeat, Norris saw it as an opportunity to put his stamp on the church. Prior to his resignation as *Baptist Standard* editor, Norris had learned that vividness achieved results and he put it to use at First Baptist. He filled the lull of activity in the summer months with as many as three rousing tent revivals. By advertising sermon titles, such as "Death and After Death," he drew huge crowds. He said, "The Lord came around and paid us a visit. And folks came. And salvation came."[10]

In addition to his expressive preaching, he formed well-organized evangelical teams that surveyed the city. From the survey data he sent out weekly visitors to prospects. His staff trained members to recruit any and all who showed an interest in membership. In an era of limited opportunity for communication and socialization, this encompassing approach appealed to the masses.

Next he turned his attention to closing "Hell's Half Acre" and his dramatic sermons attracted even larger congregations. He compared Fort Worth to Sodom and Gomorrah, and like prophets of old, named names of city leaders whom he denounced as profiting from the dens of sin.

His accusations split the city into two camps, just as the church membership earlier had been divided. One Saturday evening an assailant fired two shots into Norris' study, narrowly missing him. The resulting publicity brought even more people to hear the crusading preacher.

Having drawn a line in the sand, Norris now focused his sermons on city officials and a reported $400,000 in missing tax revenues. Mayor W. D. Davis denied the charges and in 1911 called for a mass meeting of every male in the city, but "no boys under twenty-one and no women." Davis harangued for two hours and observed, ". . . if there are fifty red-blooded men in this town, a preacher will be hanging from the lamp post before daylight."[11] The preacher countered by calling Davis and his followers liars.

At a calmer level, Norris supported the establishment of the Southwestern Seminary in Fort Worth and declared, "'the hope of all our work, every other denominational enterprise, is wrapped up in the Seminary' and advocated the raising of a million dollars for endowment,"[12] according to Baptist historian James Garrett. In one day the First Baptist Church raised $45,000 of the $100,000 inducement to bring the seminary to the city. Norris' support did not extend to the Tarrant Baptist Association, the Baptist General Convention of Texas and the Southern Baptist Convention. The rift came to a head in 1924 when the county association and First Baptist dissolved their relationship.

This action came two years after Dr. Norris led his congregation to embrace the tenets of fundamentalism. "First Baptist Church then became the mother church of Fundamentalism to hundreds of churches and thousands of laymen throughout the United States and the rest of the world,"[13] according to a *Star-Telegram* article.

The first of two criminal charges against Norris occurred in 1912 when fire destroyed First Baptist. Authorities indicted the zealous minister for arson. After a month-long trial a jury acquitted him and he built a bigger church. E. Ray Tatum described the main auditorium as having three balconies and a total seating capacity of 6,000. "In addition to the regular seating in the auditorium there was a circular choir loft which encased the front of the auditorium and contained several hundred seats. . . . The whole of the structure was designed to give the first place of prominence to the dark pulpit which was raised eight feet above the auditorium floor."[14] The interior was painted a dove gray and the pews stained a dark oak. A single cut glass chandelier hung from the oval ceiling. A two-page photo spread in the *Fort Worth Press* showed wall-to-wall people listening to one of Norris' sermons.

Another fire, in 1929, was of suspicious origin, but no charges were filed, and he rebuilt an even bigger church.

In 1926, after a heated argument with Mayor H. C. Meacham, a Catholic, the gravelly voiced preacher accused him of trying to enrich a Catholic church and school at the city's expense. Dexter E. Chipps, a friend of Meacham, confronted the minister in his office. Shots rang out. Norris admitted killing the unarmed man, claiming self-defense. Unable to seat a jury, the spectacular trial took place in Austin. Daily the *Fort Worth Star-Telegram* carried the entire proceedings and testimony. Norris' acquittal brought rejoicing at First Baptist. For a detailed account of the trial see *History of the Fort Worth Legal Community* or any of the several Norris biographies.

According to biographer Hankins, "By the end of the 1920s, Norris was a well-known fundamentalist figure across the South and in the North as he continued in the roles of populist preacher and dispensational prophet."[15]

In 1933 he founded a Bible school, the Premillennial Baptist Missionary Fellowship. (Premillennialism is the doctrine that the prophesied millennium of Christ's reign on earth will begin with the imminent Second Coming of Christ.) This fellowship led to the establishment in 1938 of the World Fundamental Baptist Mission Fellowship. Norris and long time associate, Louis Entzminger, with the support of the WFBMF, founded the Fundamental Baptist Bible Institute in 1939. The seminary, housed at First Baptist Church, emphasized support of foreign missionaries, stressed evangelism, trained preachers, and opposed "modernism." Dr. Louis Entzminger, "an able school administrator, was given wide latitude in laying the groundwork for what later became the Bible Baptist Seminary,"[16] biographer Roy Falls wrote.

In 1956 the seminary moved and in 1972 changed its name to Arlington Baptist College. On a rolling tree-studded campus, where a notorious gambling establishment once stood, students now walk past an eight foot tall bronze statue of Dr. Norris. Public guided tours are conducted for those interested in the history of both the college and the site's scandalous past. Standing near the Administration Building entrance is the original cornerstone from the downtown First Baptist Church, which Homer Ritchie secured for them. Also, a museum houses a pew from the little church where young Frank listened in awe to Catlett Smith.

In addition to establishing the seminary Rev. Norris made a momentous decision to further spread his message. In 1934 he preached a revival at Temple

Baptist Church in Detroit. "He found a religious and cultural environment immediately acceptable to the dramatic, energetic, simple, and sensational message which he preached,"[17] according to biographer Tatum. Appealing to the many Southerners who had migrated to work in the automobile factories, he drew crowds as large as 3,000 on any given night. Rev. Homer Ritchie recalled on one occasion Dr. Norris preached to over 40,000 in Detroit's Cadillac Square.

Always polemical, he attacked the Northern Baptist Convention, the Federal Council of Churches, and the Detroit ministerial association. "He accused all three religious organizations of being modernistic, ecclesiastical, and tinged with Communism,"[18] Ritchie noted. Following the close of the revival, the deacons invited Norris to lead the 800 member church. At first he considered refusing the offer, then word came to him that the "modernistic machine" was trying to silence him. He accepted the challenge and by a vote of 257 to 157 Temple Baptist called him. "'If they had gone on and behaved themselves,' he declared,. . ."[19] he would have declined. Instead Norris became the senior pastor of two churches, 1200 miles apart.

With the help of associate pastors filling in when he preached in the alternate city, and with a large staff handling day-to-day business, Norris expanded his ministry via radio and the two congregations to an estimated 25,000 followers nationwide. Biographer Falls noted, "From 1936 to 1939, Norris expended the greater part of his energies in the Detroit church, but the First Baptist of Fort Worth always remained his 'first love.'"[20]

During the Great Depression the members of the downtown church helped the needy by providing hot meals and medicine. "The war years from 1941 to 1945 afforded the First Baptist Church an opportunity to render service to the hundreds of servicemen stationed in the Fort Worth area.,"[21] according to Falls. Buses brought them in from their military bases and lavish hospitality kept them coming back. Dr. Norris estimated several thousand responded to his invitation for salvation.

In 1948 Norris asked his colleague, Beauchamp Vick, to assume the presidency of the seminary and relieve him of some of the day-to-day administration. After only two years Vick chafed at what he considered interference. Especially did he object to the seminary being a subsidiary of First Baptist.

He and his followers left and formed the Baptist Bible Fellowship with head-quarters in Springfield, Missouri. Among its alumnae is Rev. Jerry Falwell.

In the early 1950s, Norris realized he needed to relinquish some of his duties. He asked longtime disciple Luther Peak to pastor First Baptist. Peak accepted the call, but felt he did not have free rein to lead the church. Peak resigned after only six months.

J. Frank Norris died of a heart attack in August 1952. More than 5,000 attended his memorial service. The *Star-Telegram* editorial eulogy noted, "The newer generation may not fully recognize in the death of Rev. J. Frank Norris the passing of an unusual personality and the close of a life in which strife and storm and the exercise of dynamic leadership played dominant chords." The writer continued, "He possessed ambition, and brilliance, and the ability to gather others to his will. The force of his personality was tremendous. He built in beliefs, in numbers, and in stone. These monuments remain."[22] Almost thirty years later, biographer Mark G. Toulouse summed up the charismatic preacher's life, "J. Frank Norris was many things to many people; loyal friend, caring pastor, loving relative, troublemaker, confirmed enemy. Few people who encountered him could remain indifferent to him."[23] Certainly Fort Worth had never seen another like him.

He pastored the First Baptist Church for forty-three years before failing health prompted him to curtail some of his activities. "The irony may be that, what he failed to do in the 1920s—take control of the denomination—others were able to accomplish in the 1980s,"[24] Gwin Morris noted.

Dr. Homer Ritchie succeeded the icon of fundamentalism. In 1952, at the age of twenty-five, Reverend Ritchie left his post at Central Baptist Church in Athens and agreed to co-pastor the historic First Baptist Church.

Homer Ritchie and his twin Omer, were born in Mobile, Alabama in 1926. At age sixteen Homer became interested in entering the ministry. A year later he and his brother came to Fort Worth to study with Rev. Norris at the Bible Baptist Seminary. Young Ritchie viewed the First Baptist Church, the mega church of the 1920s, as the seat of the Fundamentalist movement and Dr. Norris as the driving force behind the movement. He found it galvanizing to be associated with both. At one time, for three years Ritchie had been a member of the staff, and Dr. Norris felt a young man who knew the church should lead the congregation. "I often wondered why he called me," Ritchie said in an interview. "I told Dr. Norris I would not become the pastor, but would co-pastor with him. I would do preaching, funerals, weddings, and he would only have to advise me and support me."[25] J. Frank Norris died five months later and Ritchie became senior pastor.

Homer G. Ritchie became the church's sixteenth leader. Under his leadership the church averaged 2200 worshipers in Sunday morning services. The *Star-Telegram* noted in 1955 that the "church has had 1,800 additions each year since Rev. Mr. Ritchie became pastor, and the annual income has been more that $200,000."[26]

In 1965 the congregation built a new $2,000,000 church at Fifth and Penn Streets. Situated on thirteen acres, the cream-colored brick in modern Gothic architectural style, featured a distinctive steeple and prayer tower. An auditorium-in-the-round seated as many as 4000. The arched domed ceiling, with its eighty-six lights of more than 55,000 watts, seemed to glitter like stars at night. Five stained glass windows, thirty feet high and five feet wide, plus an elegant rose window, gave diffused light to the sanctuary. Ritchie touted it as "the most complete and modern church plant in the Southwest."[27]

In 1979 the congregation again saw the need to move. They sold the Penn Street property to Calvary Cathedral. On Tuesday evening, March 28, 2000, a deadly tornado ripped through western and central downtown. Margie Young and Sue Billue of Calvary Cathedral were in the prayer tower when three sides of the structure blew away. Six blocks to the west, powerful winds tossed eighteen-wheeler-truck trailers about like soup cans. The women in the prayer tower were unhurt.

First Baptist leaders made a study to determine where they would build a new church. Many of their members, they found, lived north of the Trinity River and in the suburbs of northeast Tarrant County. They determined that the area had growth potential. The matter was put to a vote and the congregation chose the site on Loop 820. They erected a modern building with clean lines and room for expansion. In the beginning it served as both education and worship areas.

Having settled into their new facility at 5001 NE Loop 820, Rev. Ritchie sought ways to make worship services available to more people.

First Baptist Church 5001 NE Loop 820

Rolling Hills Baptist Church was once a mission of First Baptist. By 1980 the flock, made up of many young families, had relocated from their southeast Fort Worth location to 5617 Diamond Oaks Drive in Haltom City. Rev. Ritchie, whose congregation was graying, approached Rev. Johnnie Ramsey concerning the benefits of merging their two churches. Put to a vote, "One hundred percent of the Rolling Hills congregation and 98 percent of the First Baptist members voted for the merger,"[28] Evelyn Hernandez reported.

In 1981 Rev. Ritchie, and his twin, Rev. Omer Ritchie resigned their positions as co-pastors of First Baptist. It ended a thirty year association with the historic church. The brothers remained in ministry, conducting Prophecy Bible conferences throughout the nation.

Rev. Johnnie Ramsey, pastor of Rolling Hills for twenty-six years, became senior minister of First Baptist. Ramsey, born in Vernon, Texas, received his bachelor of divinity degree from Bible Baptist Seminary. Under Ramsey's leadership the church built a new balcony, and made other improvements. He is remembered for the extensive bus ministry to the community. Each Sunday thirty school-type buses rolled over the city, collecting children and parishioners who needed transportation. After thirty years in the ministry, in 1983 Dr. Johnnie Ramsey relinquished the reins of the church to his son.

Rev. Billy L. Ramsey had served with his father for ten years, but the younger Ramsey wanted a clear signal that the parishioners wanted him to be senior minister. "So in December, 1983 a unanimous call was extended to another young preacher, 26 years old, to become their Pastor,"[29] according to a church history. Like others before him, he is remembered for leading the church in another leap of faith. Through his efforts First Church rejoined in full fellowship with the Southern Baptist Convention.

Rev. Bill Ramsey preached his last sermon at First Baptist on February 9, 1997. He left to begin a new ministry, "Metroport Cities Fellowship" in Keller.

Don Wills' family joined Rolling Hills Baptist Church in 1967. He grew up in that congregation and when it merged with First Baptist the Wills family considered the church on the Loop their new home. Citing his experience as junior high, then college, then music director, then interim pastor, "I've had on-the-job training for everything except deacon,"[30] he said with a chuckle.

In 1997 Rev. Donald J. Wills became senior minister. The combined congregations, numbering about 1,500, worship in a red brick and tan stucco structure facing north. Of modern style, it is accented by a tall steeple—readily visible from Loop 820. Rev. Wills directed the work on the sanctuary and first preached in the new facility in late 2001. Additional parking lots and refurbishing the dramatic eighty foot high sign, which included a computerized message center erected during Rev. Ramsey's ministry, completed the expansion. The original building on the site now houses classrooms and offices.

First Baptist has a long and important history—but what of the future? Rev. Wills wants the church to continue to reach out and impact the city with the Gospel, and to become a hub for family activities. "We hope to minister to all, from young to old, at every life stage,"[31] he said.

■   ■   ■

St. John Missionary Baptist Church—1874

The faithful are familiar with the assurance that "the Lord will provide," but rocks and fill dirt? Rev. L. G. Austin testifies to it.

The Mosier Valley community is south of Euless on the north bank of the Trinity River and occupies a finger of far east Fort Worth. "It was founded by

Robert and Dilsie Johnson and ten other emancipated slave families, most of whom had been taken from Tennessee through Missouri to the J. K. or T. W. Mosier plantation,"[32] according to *The Handbook of Texas Online*. They farmed, worked as handymen, sharecroppers and nannies for neighboring white families. John Calhoun Parker built a widely patronized syrup mill around 1900. The community reached its heyday in the early 1930s, after which the population of about 300 began to slowly move away to find work and better opportunities.

In 1960 the anticipated construction of Dallas-Fort Worth International Airport caused the city to extend its boundaries eastward. Mosier Valley was part of the package. Over the years, commercial interests, especially the excavation of gravel and top soil, edged closer and closer to the few remaining homes. Yet old timers like Jimmy Parker held on. "'I feel free here, that's why I love it, . . . I can sleep at night without bars on the windows, without the noise and the crime they have in the city'"[33] he told reporter Whit Canning. He also stays because of religious ancestral ties. The historical marker near the St. John Missionary Baptist Church front door reads:

> "In 1874 a small group of former slaves met in the home of Frank Young and organized this congregation which originally was named Oak Grove Baptist Church. During the late 19th century pastorate of Rev. Jim Carroll the name was changed to St. John and a two-story church and Masonic Lodge building was constructed by Tennessee Blackburn. The congregation built its own sanctuary here in 1911. Throughout its history St. John's Missionary Baptist Church has been a source of service and leadership for the Mosier Valley community."[34]

The Oak Grove Baptist Church also served as the village school starting in 1883.

Rev. L. G. Austin knows the history well, since he has been minister since 1957. In an interview, he pointed at the parking lot viewed from his office window. "See that parking lot out there? They dug top soil and sand down to clay." He referred to the forty or so years in which the area became pock marked with gaping holes left by the indiscriminate selling of soil.

At one time, sand and gravel excavations left a 50-foot dropoff into a crater there. "When it rained our soil eroded so much it threatened the foundation of the church," he said. Rev. Austin tried to buy an acre adjoining St. John's boundary, but the owner wouldn't sell. After his death, his heirs let the property go for taxes in a sheriff's sale. Rev. Austin was the high bidder.

One skeptic chided that the reverend never would get that hole filled, but the preacher said he had heavenly help. "The Spirit told me to go out into the street and tell the truck drivers they could dump fill dirt and rock here at no charge."[35] (It cost $50.00 at the landfill.) This was about the time construction workers excavated a lot of dirt and rock in building the Dallas-Fort Worth International Airport. Word spread and soon drivers were making their way to House Anderson Street. A man with a bulldozer volunteered to compact the material. Today's visitor would never guess his parking space was once a hole deep enough to set St. John's sanctuary in it.

The hardwood floors, rare in churches today, speak to the age of the sanctuary. Wainscoting below beige walls and ceiling convey a feeling of warmth.

St. John's Missionary Baptist Church 3324 House Anderson Rd.
Courtesy St. John's Missionary Baptist Church

Maple pews, fitted with deep red cushions, provide seating for a congregation made up of families with young children and older members who no doubt recall years of interaction with St. John Baptist.

Despite the loss of homes and population in Mosier Valley itself, Rev. Austin, in a conversational tone and with a sense of humor, preaches to a full house. One particular Sunday the offertory prayer included blessings for "those who didn't have money to give; those who gave; and those who had money and didn't give." Concerning the congregation, Rev. Austin said, "People come from all over. Some who used to live here, but many who heard of us and want to worship with us,"[36] he said. In fact, the church has recently undergone a $300,000 expansion. Over twenty years ago, when the church celebrated its 117th anniversary, deacon Ollie Parker said of Mosier Valley, "This church has been the main spoke in the wheel."[37] With Rev. Austin at the helm, chances are good it will keep rolling along.

■   ■   ■

Mt. Pisgah Baptist Church—1875

Mount Pisgah's history dates back to 1875 and the Old Baptist Church at Fifteenth and Crump Streets. Rev. Steve Smith led the flock from 1875 to 1878. When he moved two blocks down Crump Street to another church not everyone went with him. The "old reliables" stayed at the Old Baptist Church, according to a church history.

In late 1878, the "old reliables" called Rev. T. W. Wilburn as pastor. They tore down the original building and started construction of a new one. Rev. Wilburn laid the first cornerstone and named the church "Mount Pisgah." He served about ten years before an evangelist, Rev. J. L. Griffin became the minister. His powerful preaching led many to the Lord and "The services were so glorious that the Old Baptist Church became the talk of the town,"[38] according to the 125th anniversary history. Alas, he was truly a man of God, but not a skillful pastor, and moved on after one year.

Rev. P. W. Upshaw served the flock from 1888 to 1892. With his white goatee and piercing eyes, he looked more like a prophet of old than the carpenter he was. Putting his skills to work, he enlarged the sanctuary during his pastorate.

In 1892 the congregation called Rev. H. W. Jackson, but asked him to wait six months to give them time to pay off some outstanding debts. He complied and when he came he stayed for sixteen years. The flock experienced a time of growth with his astute guidance.

The home of Mrs. Mattie McConnell became the parsonage, and the congregation provided a horse and buggy for Rev. Jackson's use. They installed a seventy-two foot tall bell tower and its peals became a tradition in the community. The original history recorded other actions.

> "About this time Sis. McConnell took a band of women and built a choir stand and carpeted the pulpit, bought a tread organ and played for the Sunday School until Mother Edwards' daughter, Miss Laura Edwards, came from college. Sis. McConnell had her to play and she gathered a band of children to sing for the Sunday School. . . ."

> Only later would the church accept a choir. "It was still a spiritual church with men and women who could sing hymns and spiritual songs as saith Eph. 15 (sic):18-20."[39]

The scripture citation refers to Ephesians 5 wherein the Apostle Paul encourages Christians to sing and give thanks for one's blessings.

When Rev. Jackson accepted a call to a church in Galveston, Mt. Pisgah hired Rev. Samuel R. Prince. The former professor preached much as he had taught—stressing intelligence over emotion. The congregation wanted a more spirited service. "He would preach when his time came," the historian noted, "letting us have our way of getting the Spirit running high for the service for a time, but we could see he was not satisfied with our old-fashioned way of singing, mourning, crying, praying and shouting in Jesus in the service, and no one took us out when we were shouting."[40] Evidently they reconciled their styles, for Rev. Prince stayed forty-three years.

In addition to his duties at Mt. Pisgah Rev. Prince held several denominational offices. He served as Superintendent of Missions, President of the General Baptist Convention, President of the State Sunday School Congress and Secretary of the National Baptist B.Y.P.U. Board.

As the congregation of Mt. Pisgah grew, the need for larger facilities became urgent. Rev. Prince oversaw the building of a three-story, forty room structure that housed both offices and classrooms. He is also remembered as a diligent steward of church finances. In 1952 the ailing Dr. Prince resigned his pastorate. He had been ill for months. In summarizing his ministry he said, "I was not slack in leading the Church to comprehend its worldwide mission, as well as its mission to the local community and its individual members."[41]

Rev. H. R. Bradley began an eleven year tenure in 1952 with some misgivings at first. Initially, in a letter to Mt. Pisgah's search committee, he declined the call. Historian Rosa Clay wrote, "Rev. Bradley said that as he dropped that letter in the mail-box; he felt that he wanted to reach in and pull it out."[42] After a restless night, he sent a telegram saying God had led him to accept their call. He preached the following Sunday.

"Those early years were difficult for Rev. Bradley,"[43] Clay noted. Associate pastor James Warren diligently took on added responsibilities during Rev. Prince's extended illness, but the members had been without the influence of a senior pastor for almost four years. With skill and tact Rev. Bradley brought stability to the congregation again.

In 1957 the church faced a major decision—where to relocate. Interstate 35 was slated to go right through the Old Baptist Church at Fifteenth and Crump. The first site chosen, on Tennessee Street, proved unworkable. For a while the congregation worshiped with the Antioch Baptist Church flock on

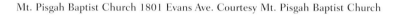

Mt. Pisgah Baptist Church 1801 Evans Ave. Courtesy Mt. Pisgah Baptist Church

East Rosedale. After much deliberation and soul-searching Rev. Bradley and church leaders opted to buy the Evans Avenue Baptist Church. Located at 1801 Evans Avenue, the building's magnificent entry steps and pillars form a pleasing visual flow from street to sanctuary.

"In the relocating process, some two hundred or more members went out from the church family and organized the Prince Memorial Baptist Church,"[44] according to historical records. That church at 1412 E. Cantey was named for their beloved Rev. Samuel R. Prince.

It became Bradley's task to get the congregation settled into their new home. He led in the physical remodeling and refurbishing of the building. He trained new leaders to replace those who left to form Prince Memorial. Mt. Pisgah was on the road to bigger and better things when his ministry ended with his sudden death in August 1963.

Visionary Dr. Nehemiah Davis became senior pastor in December 1963. He served churches in Robstown, Corpus Christi, and Cuero before coming to Fort Worth. Davis, reared in Dallas, knew something of the history of the church. He appreciated Mt. Pisgah's emphasis on the total person, education, mission, and community involvement. Those were his values as well. Also, when he attended Mary Allen College, the president's brother pastored at Mt. Pisgah, and the future minister learned more about its history through that connection.

A native of Centerville, Texas, Davis earned a B.A. in 1955. He believed church leaders should have a strong Christian education and set the example by enrolling in Southwestern Baptist Theological Seminary while pastoring his flock. After obtaining a Master of Divinity and a Master of Religious Education there, he received a Doctor of Divinity degree from Guadalupe Baptist Theological Seminary in 1992.

Dr. Davis' preaching style is gentle with touches of the dramatic to make a point. "He preaches with his hands," someone said. At times he turns to the choir to let them know he's preaching to them, too.

On the last page of the 1975 centennial history, Rev. Davis listed three goals for the future of Mt. Pisgah. "First, we faced a remodeling project." In the 1980s the church undertook a $1,000,000 make-over in three stages. They finished a new choir room and pastor's study in 1983. Next, workers installed air conditioning in the educational areas and added thermal windows to the Education Annex. The remodeling created a new chapel and atrium, and an elevator gave easy access to all three floors and the sanctuary. New carpets were laid throughout the building. This work was finished in 1985. The next year the sanctuary received a new central unit for heating and cooling. New lighting fixtures decorated Fellowship Hall. In the last phase, they expanded and paved the parking lot and improved the landscaping. That goal was accomplished.

Davis' second goal, still in progress, involved getting a historical designation for the "Prince Home" on E. Terrell. It is used to house seminary students and their families.

The minister's last goal champions his basic Christian philosophy—"Our goal is not what we do with things—but with people." When asked in a 2003 interview, he said, "In church work, goals are never totally accomplished, but you keep working at them as if you think they are. Helping people learn to make Christianity a vital part of everyday living is where we get the joy out of the committed life."[45]

Rev. Davis believes in ministering to the whole person. To better meet that goal he is a member of the National Association of Christians in Social Work, the Fort Worth Chamber of Commerce, the Fort Worth Metropolitan Black Chamber, and is president of the local branch of the NAACP. "This church has always been a strong supporter of organizations like the NAACP. We believe it is another arm of Christian help. Self-esteem and equal rights go together,"[46] he said.

In the area of community involvement, Rev. Davis was one of ". . .the civil rights leaders who have led or had a hand in engineering efforts from desegregation of the public schools in the early 1970s to a push for affordable housing and power sharing,"[47] according to the *Star-Telegram*. He served on the Fort Worth Independent School District Board of Education in 1980-1981.

His activities in denominational affairs range from lecturing at the National Baptist Congress to service as president of the Pastor's Conference, National Baptist Convention of America, and president of the Minister's Conference of that body. Rev. Davis writes Sunday School literature for the National Baptist Publishing Board, specifically the *Young Adult Sunday School*

Quarterly, and for R. H. Boyd Publishing Corporation. He is a member of the Committee on Uniform Lessons Series-National Council of Churches.

"Dr. Davis presently serves as Chairman of S. A. Pleasant, Jr. Institute of the Missionary Baptist Convention of Texas and Assistant Dean of the Congress. He is Dean of the Congress of the North Texas District Association; and a teacher in the Baptist Minister's Union of Ft. Worth/Tarrant County and Vicinity,"[48] according to his vita.

His message in the 125th anniversary memorial is one of assurance. "As you turn the pages of this book, we pray that you will see more than pictures and prose. We trust that you will see ordinary people, who by the grace of God accomplish extraordinary things."[49] He includes himself—an ordinary man. But his 600 congregants see an extraordinary man who continues to accomplish great things.

■   ■   ■

Mount Gilead Baptist Church—1876

Dr. Lacey K. Williams, revered pastor of Mt. Gilead, credited religion with undergirding his race's great singing, oratory and faithful church-going. "Negro Baptists outnumber all the combined branches of denominations,"[50] he declared. Indeed, there are more historic black Baptist churches in Fort Worth than all other historic black denominations combined. Mt. Gilead is one of the oldest.

Thousands of motorists on the North-South Freeway daily glimpse the imposing brick structure at Fifth and Grove Streets. Few know the history of the building or the congregations that have worshiped there. Carol Roark included Mount Gilead in *Fort Worth's Legendary Landmarks*. "The two-story church has a raised basement and a pedimented entrance portico supported by six massive Tuscan columns. Stained glass windows were added after the original building was completed, many honoring the families who made them possible. . . . When it opened in 1913, the church boasted a sanctuary seating 2,000, a day nursery, sewing room, labor bureau, public baths, gymnasium, roof garden, and swimming pool. During the early years the church also ran a business school and operated a hospital next door to the church."[51] In the days of racial segregation, churches often provided these secular programs as

Mt. Gilead Baptist Church 600 Grove St.

part of their ministry to members denied access to such services in the larger community.

In 1913, the *Star-Telegram*, in its mammoth section on churches noted, "The Mt. Gilead congregation is the oldest in the city and is the largest (N)egro church of any denomination in Texas. All the (N)egro Baptist churches in Fort Worth and Tarrant (C)ounty have gone out from it.

"It has in its membership a large part of the hard-working, substantial (N)egro citizenship of the county. For thirty years," the reporter continued, "the superintendent of its Sunday school has been Prof. I. M. Terrell, who also is head of the (N)egro schools of the city. Prof. Terrell has served longer in this capacity than any similar officer of his race anywhere."[52]

Over the years, from its congregation came two presidents of the National Baptist Convention, three presidents of the state convention, three college presidents, numerous state and national officers, plus hundreds of local educators, doctors, lawyers and businessmen. Yet the church had an humble beginning.

Reverend C. A. Augustus called fifteen Baptists together in September 1876 to organize a church for people of color. The first site was at Crump and E. Thirteenth Streets, in the heart of "Hell's Half Acre," but that did not keep the church from prospering. Augustus led the flock of forty until 1878 when a series of ministers followed in his footsteps.

Lillian B. Horace's book *Crowned with Glory and Honor* included an historical account of Mt. Gilead. She wrote that the Reverend W. W. Hay "served the church acceptably and well for twenty dollars per month."[53] Next came S. H. Smith, under whose leadership the congregation increased to 500 members. In May 1888 the *Fort Worth Daily Gazette* reported, "At 4:00 this afternoon 40 colored men and women will be immersed in the Clear Fork near the ice factory. A protracted meeting has been going on at Mt. Gilead Baptist Church for over a week and the number of conversions is the result."[54]

Horace described Reverend John H. Baptist as one who "came preaching in the wilderness of Judea." Reverend C. P. Hughes, greatly beautified the building in those early days. The Reverend J. Francis Robinson saw an increase in membership before he and some of those members left to establish the Greater St. James Baptist Church. (See page 140)

A. R. Griggs, President of the National Baptist Convention, gave up a higher paying position as state superintendent of missions to accept the call to preach at Mt. Gilead. Horace noted, "He built up the morale of a divided group, cleared the church of indebtedness, remodeled the building, and set the stage for the church's eighth pastor. . . ."[55]

The dramatic Reverend Prince Jones, described as colorful as a cowboy on Main Street, was an eloquent preacher. He pushed the congregation to secure funds for the building of a new sanctuary, but poor health kept him from seeing his dream realized. Shortly before his death in 1909, he recommended Lacey K. Williams of Dallas to the deacons as his successor. The church was about to see the beginning of its golden age.

Lacey as a lad was sailing rocks on the Chattahoochie River in Alabama about the time Mt. Gilead was established. His parents, freed slaves, were leaders in the Thankful Baptist Church. He received his first religious education in its old, weather-beaten, unpainted frame structure. His family moved to Central Texas when Lacey was in his teens. For two years he taught school at Cookespoint in Burleson County. There he gained a reputation as a thinker and speaker, qualities that would serve him well in his later career. Williams earned a Bachelor of Theology from Bishop College and was ordained to the ministry in 1894. Later he graduated with a doctoral degree from Selma University in Alabama. In 1927 Bishop College granted him an honorary Doctor of Laws. At one time Williams held the chair of theology at I. & M. College in addition to his pastoral duties.

When called to Fort Worth he was president of the Baptist Missionary and Educational Convention of Texas, and a vice-president of the National Baptist Convention. As a first task at Mt. Gilead, Williams needed to convince the reluctant members of the church that moving to a new location would be advantageous. He used the pulpit to persuade. "For morning service he preached from the text, 'Our Fathers Worshipped Here.' The genius of the sermon was to prove that because our fathers worshipped 'here,' there was no reason why they should be tied permanently to the spot; for the night service he preached 'The Land Is Mine; Let Us Go up and Possess the Land,'" Horace wrote. The sermons won over the reluctant ones and he raised $4,200 for the new site.

The desired location at Fifth and Grove Streets cost $10,250. The treasurer wrote a check for $250 and made a note for $4,000, to be paid in ninety days. "In a rally May 10, 1910, the membership brought in at one time $3,050, the largest published amount to be raised by any Texas church group up to that time. . . ."[56] according to Horace. Williams donated $1,000 cash, sold his Dallas home and loaned the proceeds to the church. It was not all smooth sailing. Some white people living near the site feared their property values would drop and offered to buy the lot. Williams offered to sell it to them—for $10,000. There were no takers. The finished structure mollified them.

August 24, 1913 was both a sad and glad day as members left the old church and its memories. "With pennants unfurling, and banners streaming in the gentle breeze, a happy membership trudged the nine blocks to a building, so beautiful, so exquisite, so fine that entering it as a church home was a Cinderella experience,"[57] Horace wrote. Williams' preaching attracted such large crowds that soon a sanctuary, which once seemed too large, filled to overflowing. Chairs were set up in every available space.

On the occasion of the church's thirty-sixth anniversary Williams paid tribute to those who had passed on. "Let us take up the work where they left off; prove ourselves worthy of all they have done for us,"[58] he said.

Seven years of plenty passed quickly and in 1916 the rumors of the popular preacher's leaving were confirmed. Lacey K. Williams accepted the call from Mt. Olivet Church in Chicago and eventually rose to national denominational prominence. Lacey K. Williams died in a plane crash October 29, 1940. Dr. A. L. Boone, his closest friend for more than twenty-four years, delivered the eulogy.

During Dr. Boone's tenure, in 1926, a massive pump organ was installed. He pastored Mt. Gilead from 1919 to 1931 when his son, Theodore S. Boone took over the reins of the church. Sioux Campbell of the Writer's Project noted, "The chorus of Mt. Gilead has been such an outstanding feature of the church service that it has brought great renown both to the church and itself."[59] The pastor, (the younger) Dr. Boone, is the director of the chorus and is also an accomplished musician. He plays all string and wind instruments, but is especially talented as a trumpeter. Boone and the choir traveled throughout the Midwest giving concerts. Locally they sang at the First Baptist and First Presbyterian Churches.

From 1933 to 1935 Rev. Boone preached weekly over radio station KFJZ. He later became historiographer of the National Baptist Convention and penned *Lord! Lord!*, the biography of Lacey Williams.

C. C. Harper pastored the church for 27 years, from 1937 until 1964. He led the flock during World War II, the Korean Conflict, and the Civil Rights Movement. Momentous years indeed.

Dallas native Dr. Cedric D. Britt left a four-year-old church in Gary, Indiana to come to one-hundred-and-four-year-old Mt. Gilead. Prior to accepting the call he spoke with Dr. Milton K. Curry, president of Bishop College, and learned of the history of the church and Dr. Harper.

Britt said his mother maintains he started preaching at age three, taught Sunday School at age thirteen, and was licensed at age seventeen. A graduate of Bishop College and Southwestern Baptist Theological Seminary, Britt holds an honorary Doctor of Divinity degree as well. He was attending a Progressive National Baptist Convention in California when a mutual friend introduced him to Robert Evans. Deacon Evans said Mt. Gilead was looking for a minister and the friend recommended Britt.

The church invited Britt to preach the second Sunday in October 1979. They liked his beautiful singing voice and the dramatic delivery of the young preacher. The leadership extended the call. Remembering that time, Britt said, "I felt that it was God's will and a divine assignment that I come to Fort Worth from Indiana."[60]

Common to other downtown churches, Mt. Gilead's membership dwindled as parishioners moved out of the immediate area. The North-South Freeway decimated what had been known as "Baptist Hill." Now Reverend Britt would like to see the church again have a radio/television ministry to reach a broader segment of the population.

Since he began his ministry Mt. Gilead twice has been remodeled, once in 1984 and again in 1996. Asked what is special about the church, he mused, "Nothing is special about any church unless she is a body of Christ. The building, age, does not make her special, but her love, adoration of the Word of God, for the Lord Jesus Christ, and for the people of God make her special in His sight."[61] As they near their 130th year, thousands who have called Mt. Gilead home would agree.

■   ■   ■

Broadway Baptist Church—1882

Should the congregation of Broadway Baptist care to, they could celebrate two organizing dates—the first in 1882 when a group of nine lay Baptists formed the South Side Baptist Church, and in 1883 when these same folk with the addition of a preacher formed the church again. James Leo Garrett, Jr., in *Living Stones*, a two volume history of the church, explained the dilemma. A schism arose and certain members left First Baptist. "Nine of these members, without church letters and with no minister present, met on Dec. 31, 1882 and organized the South Side Baptist Church."[62] The following year, in a revival meeting led by Major W. E. Penn, they voted to annul the previous action and abide by Baptist procedures. Fifty years later Mrs. Emma Florence Bogart reminisced about that beginning. "'One of the keenest disappointments of my mother's life,' Mrs. Bogart said, 'was her failure to be present at the signing of the charter of the church. She was ill. She was present, however, when the first organization steps were taken in a tent in which a revival was being held on the Texas and Pacific Railway reservation.'"[63]

John Gillespie was called as pastor, which in actuality was a continuation since he had ministered to the group since its beginning. But now they were in good standing with the West Fork Baptist Association. In 1885 South Side reported a membership of 121 worshipers.

After much prayer and deliberation, the congregation undertook a debt of $4,000 for the construction of a frame building. "Dime sociables" and a Saturday market, where women sold baked goods, helped pay the debt. On Sunday, November 21, 1886, the proud parishioners dedicated their new building. Located on what was called "Tucker's Hill," the building was equipped with pot-bellied stoves and hard-as-rock pews with a seating capacity of 400. Women sat on one side and men sat on the other. Carpeted aisles led to the pulpit and baptistery.

After they bought the lot on the southwest corner of Broadway and St. Louis, Methodists and Presbyterians bought lots so close members feared the congregations' singing would disturb each other when the windows were raised in summer. This may be the source of the story making the rounds among clerics wherein on different corners one could hear "When We All Get To Heaven," "Will There Be Stars In My Crown?" "No, Not One." Evidently the singing was not a problem, and soon the Jewish community bought a lot nearby. The area became known as "Holy Hill."

In 1890 the flock changed the name to Broadway Baptist. Six ministers, in addition to Gillespie, pastored the early growing church. Garrett characterized each:

> Anderson E. Baten, the Organizer, 1890-1893
> William O. Bailey, the Eloquent, 1893-1894?
> Augustus J. Harris, the Beloved, 1895-1896
> George Samuel Tumlin, the Shepherd, 1897-1901
> John Wm. Gillon, Jr., the Evangelist, 1901-1905
> Clarence A. Stewart, the Builder, 1905-1906

The editor of *The Texas Baptist* in 1884 wrote of Gillespie, "He is clear in exposition, fervent in spirit and his sermons are truly eloquent."[64] For these eloquent sermons the congregation paid him $600 a year, or "as much as possible." By contrast, G. Morgan Wells of First Church received an annual salary of

$2,500. Gillespie resigned in October 1889 due to old age (he was 69) and increasing deafness.

Alabama born Anderson E. Baten led the church as it became fully involved in denominational associations. He frequently spoke and wrote on moral issues. Baten condemned theater-going and was vociferous in denouncing the activities in "Hell's Half Acre," the city's "Den of Sin." He resigned the pastorate to devote full time to evangelism.

Baten's successor was forty-three-year-old William O. Bailey. Minister for only a year, he is remembered for his powerful oratory. The fourth man, and first native Texan to pastor Broadway Baptist was Augustus J. Harris. Known as the "Cowboy Preacher," he rose from an orphaned childhood to prominence in the denomination. Harris accepted a call from the First Baptist Church in San Antonio in 1896.

George S. Tumlin practiced law in Georgia before surrendering to the ministry. A parishioner described his preaching as "logical, forcible and earnest,"[65] according to Garrett. Tumlin's strength as a spiritual shepherd was in the realm of visitation. In 1901, after being confined to quarters for two weeks after a sprain, he preached with even greater conviction on the merits of visiting the homebound.

When Tumlin moved to First Church, Brenham, Broadway called John William Gillon, Sr. A strong supporter of Baylor University, he railed against "football in our Christian colleges" when not preaching evangelism.

A hundred years later, when the Baylor Bears were experiencing a miserable season, Broadway minister Brett Younger, with tongue firmly in cheek pondered why he had never been asked to pray before a football game. He had a prayer all ready. "God, we give you thanks that football is just a game—only in part because we're not good at it. On occasion, our defense parts like the Red Sea, and our quarterback's passes are not always as true as David's sling . . . . We ask only that you help the Baptist boys play so well that the ones who are not Baptist will wish they were."[66]

In 1901 Gillon came to a city of 26,688, according to the 1900 census. "It was still a cowboy's town, but like any town of Mid-America it also had dignified residential sections where quiet, tree-lined streets were appropriate to the new era."[67] His pastorate was marked by an increase of 500 new members.

This upsurge led the congregation to consider a new and larger sanctuary. In 1904 they voted to build on the same site. They moved the 1886 frame building to a vacant lot four blocks away and the congregation worshiped there until the new sanctuary was ready. But it would be left to a new minister to move into it.

Clarence A. Stewart, in 1905, followed Gillon at Broadway. "The major accomplishment of Broadway Church during Stewart's brief pastorate was the erection and dedication of a brick church edifice on the southwest corner of West Broadway and St. Louis. . . ."[68] He left to pastor a church in Kansas.

Prince E. Burroughs telephoned the chairman of the Search Committee on July 11, 1906 to say he accepted the invitation to Broadway. His ministry was uneventful until 1909 when he was summoned home from a tour of the Holy Land. Told that boys playing with matches started the worst fire in the history of the city, he had the unhappy task of ministering to a congregation whose sanctuary, and in some cases whose homes, went up in a spectacular conflagration. The Sunday *Star-Telegram*'s forty-eight point headline on April 4, 1909 screamed, "FIERCE FIRE SWEEPS SOUTH SIDE; SEVEN ENTIRE BLOCKS BURN; LOSS OVER $2,000,000. . . . Three handsome churches, the Broadway Baptist, the Broadway Presbyterian and Swedish (Methodist) church. T & P Roundhouse. Fully 100 residences."[69] Broadway Baptist's loss was placed at $47,000 to $50,000.

To help raise money to rebuild, the women of the church sponsored a spelling bee between Fort Worth lawyers and school teachers. The names of the winning team have been lost in the passage of time, but one can conjure up the image of teachers, red grading pencils in hand, intimidating the attorneys.

A week after the congregation met in the rebuilt auditorium, Burroughs tendered his resignation. A prolific writer, he spent the next thirty-three years writing for the Southern Baptist Sunday School Board.

John Robert Jester, who followed Burroughs, accepted the changes brought about by "modernism," but with stipulations. For example, he allowed, for the first time, the auditorium to be used by a member for a piano recital, ". . . with the understanding that she would have no applause."[70] During his leadership 883 new members joined the church and more than $80,000 went into the church coffers for "the Lord's work." He resigned in 1915 to become Field Secretary of the denomination's Foreign Mission Board.

Historian Garrett summarized, "Through the first one-third of Broadway Baptist Church's first century it had not had a long pastorate. . . . But the church's tenth pastor, Forrest Smith, would be Broadway's under shepherd for more than fifteen years—a period that began prior to the involvement of the United States in World War I and extended until after the beginning of the Great Depression."[71] Smith, a native of Tennessee, began his ministry in 1915.

In addition to caring for his flock, Smith argued forcefully with city officials for the extension of street car lines south to the campus of Southwestern Baptist Theological Seminary.

In 1917 two events occurred which brought major changes to the city. In addition to the impact of a nation at war, North Texans experienced a boom following the discovery of oil in nearby Ranger. With the enormous influx of new residents, Broadway continued to grow and Horace Stephens, the first educational director was hired. Within a year, Sunday School attendance averaged between 500 and 600 members weekly. On Smith's watch, the congregation dedicated a four-story education building. It featured a roof garden "indirectly lighted so as to eliminate the nuisance of bugs," with a seating capacity of 1,000. The congregation, remembering the tragedy of 1909, made sure this structure was fireproof.

But not all services were held in church buildings. Brush arbors had given way to huge tents pitched in a central location. These spring and fall tent meetings had the same social and spiritual fervor as the earlier frontier ones. Smith was one of the organizers who brought Baptist icon George W. Truett to Fort Worth in September 1928. Truett, pastor of Dallas' First Baptist, preached nightly for two weeks at the corner of Henderson and Texas Streets.

Smith also led in fund raising for the building of the present sanctuary. Designed by W. G. Clarkson & Co., the Sunday School part was completed in 1932, and used as the church until the rest of the building was completed in June of the following year.

In February 1931, after conducting a funeral service and grave side service in frigid weather, Smith fell ill of influenza which turned into pneumonia. He died at the age of sixty-three. "His unexpected passing was a great shock to the Broadway congregation and to Baptist leaders as well as his family,"[72] according to historian Garrett. An estimated five thousand mourners paid homage to the beloved pastor and denomination stalwart.

W. R. White, son of a Henderson County farm family, accepted the helm of the church at a time of low morale and high debt, yet he encouraged the flock to look for a brighter future. In 1933 he presided over the grand opening of the new sanctuary and the fiftieth anniversary celebration. He wrote of the new auditorium, "It is both beautiful and spacious. The poor will feel perfectly at home. The most exacting will be pleased. . . . It is for all peoples, a house of prayer, worship and above all a spiritual haven for the hungry hearts of humanity."[73]

The Great Depression cast a pall over his four year ministry. One man in the congregation who in the 1920s had been worth $750,000, was forced to borrow money from the preacher to attend the out-of-state funeral of his brother. White resigned in 1935 and moved to First Church in Oklahoma City.

Over 1,500 attended Sunday School on April 12, 1936, the day thirty-year-old W. D. "Doug" Hudgins, Jr. preached his first sermon. His youthfulness alarmed those uncertain about him until he preached. Then the doubters became supporters. Yet he was best known as one who had extraordinary recall of people's names. After six years at Broadway, Hudgins resigned to accept a call from First Church of Houston.

Just weeks after Hudgins left, Forrest C. Feezor came in January 1943. Born into a home lacking spiritual observances, and into poverty in North Carolina, young Forrest did not see a daily newspaper until he was in college. Educated in a one-room log elementary school and a country high school not much bigger, he attended Wake Forest College on borrowed money. For three years he taught Bible at William Jewell before he began his ministry. After leading and comforting the flock during wartime, Feezor resigned in October 1946 to become pastor of Waco's First Baptist Church.

Garrett summarized the sixteen years of White, Hudgins and Feezor as a time of growth in numbers and stature in the community and in denominational circles for Broadway Baptist.

H. Guy Moore, the next senior minister, could talk to teenage boys in his congregation about horsepower—literally. As a farm boy in Illinois, he rode a horse to school. Following graduation from DuQuoin High School he attended a revival conducted by Billy Sunday. It changed his life. He pastored churches in Kentucky and Indiana while pursuing a seminary education. Prior to accepting the invitation to Broadway, Moore led several congregations in Missouri. Of his preaching style, historian Garrett noted, "He has a voice which is clear and powerful, and a pulpit manner without affectation or mannerism. His sermons are clear, pointed and persuasive."[74]

On Easter Sunday, April 13, 1952, Moore preached in the new sanctuary, the fourth in the church's seventy year history. During the dedication week of the $1,000,000 house of worship, ". . . denominational leaders will join the 4,600 member congregation in praise to God for his many blessings in making the beautiful structure possible,"[75] Cullum Greene wrote in the *Star-Telegram*. The building ". . . consisted of a 1,700-seat auditorium, with the pastor's suite adjoining; a 250-seat chapel with an adjoining family room for funerals; and a 600-seat dining hall with adjoining kitchen facilities, parlor, stage, and classrooms."[76] Of modified Gothic design, the auditorium featured a Gothic floor plan in the shape of a cross, and thus with transepts and a narthex, vaulted ceiling and arched doorways. The divided choir loft could seat eighty persons. Below the choir and to the right was the console of the $75,000 Casavant organ and above the choir the tile baptistery. The stained glass windows are fully described in the booklet *To The Glory of God*. Greene noted, "The spire, which rises 165 feet from the street, is topped be a six-foot cross, which will be lighted."[77]

John and Gayle Wilson watched the construction with a special interest. The certified public accountant and county extension agent changed their wedding site—Broadway was still a hole in the ground— when they married at the Chapel in the Woods in Denton. Gayle, who worked at the courthouse, remembered Moore as a good Bible scholar who was influential in getting several judges to attend Broadway.

Moore came to Fort Worth in 1947 and stayed for fifteen years before he resigned to become president of William Jewell College, his alma mater. During the years of his leadership, in addition to the major building campaign, Broadway became one of the top five churches in the Southern Baptist Convention in giving to world missions.

"On 6 January 1963 William B. Henderson as chairman of the pulpit committee presented to the Broadway congregation a recommendation that J P (sic) Allen, pastor, First Church, Alexandria, Virginia, be called as Broadway's fifteenth pastor,"[78] according to Garrett. By 1964 the church building, which covered an entire block, parsonage, and a fifty-two acre camp site at Eagle Mountain Lake were valued at over $3,000,000. The Fleming Memorial Chapel accommodated 250 persons, and the Fellowship Hall large enough for 600. Allen preached in an auditorium that seated 1,700. He would be remembered for his memorial service following the assassination of

Broadway Baptist Church 305 W. Broadway Ave. Courtesy Broadway Baptist Church

President John F. Kennedy, had it not been for breaking news. The sermon, titled "The Nation in Grief," was scheduled for nationwide telecasting by the American Broadcasting Company, but the shooting of Lee Harvey Oswald by Jack Ruby pushed the sermon off the air.

Allen left in 1969 to join the Southern Baptist Convention's Radio and Television Commission.

Kentucky native John R. Claypool filled the pulpit from 1971 to 1976. During his tenure the morning worship service, especially the sermon, attracted hundreds of visitors to the sprawling South Side church. So popular were Claypool's discourses, they were recorded on cassette tapes. Tapes and an additional 12,000 printed copies of sermons were being mailed weekly according to Garrett's history of the church. In the autumn of 1976 Claypool resigned from the 5,000 member church to take a position in a much smaller church in Jackson, Mississippi. He explained a desire to have time to write as his reason for leaving.

C. Welton Gaddy was the product of a devout Baptist home. During his senior year in high school the youth declared his intention to go into ministry. After graduation from Southern Baptist Theological Seminary Gaddy pastored an American Baptist congregation in Indiana.

In June 1977 he began his association with Broadway. Member Nancy Thurmond recalled his sermons as being intelligently written and beautifully delivered. Gaddy served until 1983 before going to Washington, D.C. as Executive Director of the Interfaith Alliance. "He works with Baptists but this is an ecumenical group,"[79] according to Broadway's Nancy Thurmond. A prolific author, he wrote three books while serving on the SBC Christian Life Commission.

Cecil Sherman, pastor from 1983 to 1992, incorporated Baptist history into his sermons, wanting the congregation to know the background of their theology and how it fit into the present day. In addition to mentoring his flock, he energetically participated in denominational activities. That interest led him to leave Broadway to head the Cooperative Baptist Fellowship, a moderate Baptist organization based in Atlanta.

Steve Shoemaker, who came to Broadway in 1992, has been characterized as a giant pulpiteer among giants. Religion writer Jim Jones quoted a member

of Broadway who described the new minister as ". . . an excellent combination
of preacher and pastor."[80] Shoemaker earned a master of divinity from Union
Theological Seminary in New York City and a doctorate from Southern Baptist
Theological Seminary.

The North Carolina native took an active part in the social ministry of
the church and advocated for racial justice. He raised eyebrows by forging a
relationship with the Rev. Michael Bell, an outspoken critic of the Fort Worth
school district, but that relationship allowed Shoemaker to mediate an agree-
ment which ended years of acrimony. As he left for Myers Park Baptist
Church in his hometown of Charlotte, North Carolina, Shoemaker praised
Broadway as a vital center-city congregation representing the fullest cross
section of people, from the richest to the poorest and everything in between.

That very conglomerate attracted Brett Younger, Broadway's minister since
2001. "The church is both an old downtown church and an inner city church;
that combination means on a Sunday morning we worship in a cathedral and
on Thursday night we feed over 200 homeless people at a sit-down dinner in
the fellowship hall,"[81] he told an interviewer.

Broadway has long had a vital social ministry. In addition to helping the
homeless, they maintain a clothing room, a partnership with a neighborhood
school, and after- school programs for latch key children. Much of this work
emanates from the Gene Thompson Center, named for a retired associate
pastor. As a new pastor Younger said he was startled to read in the church
newsletter "Gene Thompson needs green beans."

Music has always been an integral part of worship in Baptist churches.
Long-time members John and Gayle Wilson consider the music ministry as
one of the treasures of the church. In *Why We Love Broadway: A Patchwork of
Words*, several members cited the music program. Dick Nelson told of the
"Best of Broadway's" condensed versions of popular shows such as *The Sound
of Music, Music Man, Phantom of the Opera, Fiddler on the Roof* and *Guys and
Dolls*. Proceeds from the shows helped finance the music ministry, including
a trip to England by the Chancel Choir. The wide range of musical offerings
inspired Tiffany McClain, in writing why she loved Broadway, to note ". . .
nowhere else do I get a classical concert during worship."[82] Billie Edwards
declared, "Its music has filled my life with beauty that I believe is unmatched

in any other place. Our magnificent organ and tremendously gifted organist are superior gifts to our congregation—to the glory of God!"[83] The Rildia Bee O'Bryan Cliburn Organ ensures that this rich tradition will continue into the next century,"[84] according to the booklet *Celebrating the Glory of God*.

In an interview Thompson recalled the many other past and present civic leaders who have contributed to the ministry of Broadway and the city as a whole. William Fleming funded the building of the Southwestern Baptist Theological Seminary library. Motivated by the last wishes of her son, who died at age seven, Mrs. Lena Pope started a ministry to homeless children. Aided by members of her Martha Sunday School Class, and from a beginning of fourteen children, the Lena Pope Home in its eighty year history has helped hundreds of thousands of youngsters.

Dr. Younger, who holds an undergraduate degree from Baylor University and graduate degrees from Southern Baptist Theological Seminary, wants to build on the successful programs already in place and lead the congregation to a deeper personal faith. As Broadway continues this ministry, its steeple is clearly seen from the downtown freeways. "Our steeple at night looks like a lighthouse on the shore," said a member. Perhaps he was thinking of Matthew 5.14.

■   ■   ■

Corinth Missionary Baptist Church-1886

In the spring of 1886 the Harrison Thompson family, the Guerrys, the Loyds, and the Chaneys and others met to form a new congregation. Rev. C. P. Hughes of Mt. Gilead helped the fifteen pioneers get the church established. Hodge Station in the 1880s was a main stop on the Fort Worth and Denver Railroad and just at the edge of town. The small flock held their first service in the Hodge Station school. "Reverend John Bell was called as its first Pastor (sic). Reverend Brooks served as associate pastor,"[85] according to Shirley Abram *et al* in *Corinth Baptist Church: 1886-1986*.

Harrison Thompson conveyed a half acre, which he wanted to donate, but the congregation insisted on paying him $50.00 for the property. In 1986 State Representative Garfield Thompson, a direct descendent of Harrison Thompson, joined in congratulating the church on its centennial celebration.

The years between were busy ones. Initially the men built a brush arbor, and later a one-room building, known as "The Old House," on the land. This was their church home for six years. After thoughtful discussion the congregation selected the Riverside neighborhood as the new location.

Deacon Gid Hooper wanted a church and school in the area. He took his concerns to Judge Booth, a realtor. Booth donated the land on Ennis Avenue. In 1892 Hooper and Bill Mathes mounted "The Old House" on a horse-drawn wagon and moved it to the present site of Corinth Baptist Church. Hooper hired Reverend Hardeman, who like Jesus was a carpenter, to make any necessary repairs. The site, Tarrant County, Martindale Addition, City of Fort Worth, Lot No. 8, Block No. 1, was officially recorded on April 2, 1906.

During those first years Rev. J. P. Phillips led the congregation for a number of years. Tall and slender, gray-haired Phillips in a long frock coat was the picture of serenity. After his resignation the congregation called Rev. A. J. Robinson, who served only six months. Rev. Phillips returned and stayed until he left to establish Ebenezer Baptist Church in Fort Worth's Stop Six area.

Reverend E. M. Clemons, a big man with a ready smile, followed Rev. Phillips, and in turn was followed by Rev. J. A. Farley.

During these pastorates the congregation continued to grow. By the time of Rev. B. B. Johnson's call from a church in Stephenville, they were ready to expand "The Old House" into a larger one. On April 9, 1922 the new church, furnished with new pews, was dedicated. "Additional property was purchased on November 25, 1925, which is the location presently of the 'B. B. Johnson' Fellowship Hall,"[86] as stated in the centennial history. A photograph, dated 1930, in that history shows the congregation, standing five deep and spread twice the width of the frame church.

Rev. Johnson led the congregation for thirty-four years, from 1919 to the time of his death on November 29, 1953. During this time two buildings were erected, the first a frame sanctuary, the second, the yellow brick one used today, described as "his major and final effort." Clear varnished knotty-pine wainscoting and soft white walls and ceiling lend a feeling of airiness to the sanctuary. Light oak pews with deep red cushions will seat 400. A mural of a flowing blue river provides the backdrop for the baptistery. In May 1954 at a memorial service for the beloved pastor, a portrait was unveiled and hung in the main foyer.

Associate minister Rev. W. M. Glenn who served as interim pastor for fourteen months, saw the addition of many new members. On January 11, 1955 the church called Rev. C. C. Cyphers from Dallas. He was large in size and large in ideas. Under his leadership the congregation erected a modern educational building adjoining the sanctuary. After fifteen years, Rev. Cyphers resigned to return to Dallas to lead Union Baptist Church.

All of these preachers had the support of a dedicated congregation. From charter members "Aunt Polly" Burns and Mrs. Delio Thompson to the current W. M. U. Matrons, the women of the church helped make it thrive. Pioneers such as the Koontz, Sessions, and Spinks families gave time and money for the ongoing band of worshipers. During Rev. Cypher's ministry, the adult choir numbered more than thirty singers. One of them, Mrs. Jimmie Mae Bluitt, had a program sponsored by the Pet Milk Company. A highlight of her career was the meeting of the famous spiritual singer, Mahalia Jackson.

A new era began in late 1970 with the ministry of Rev. L. B. Adams, the eighth man to pastor Corinth Missionary Baptist Church. It was a homecoming

Corinth Baptist Church 2704 Ennis Ave.

of sorts. Rev. Adams grew up on "Baptist Hill" and graduated from Fort Worth Colored High School, which later became I. M. Terrell.

To help pay for his education young Adams worked weekends and summers at the Jeffery Ice and Wood Yard. Among his customers were Dr. and Mrs. Talley. Dr. Talley was pastor of St. John Baptist Church. When Bishop College offered full four-year scholarships to one hundred top black students for an initial payment of $50.00 it seemed Adams would be left out. His father didn't have $50.00. The women of St. John's sold hamburgers and catfish dinners and raised the money.

L. B. Adams earned a degree in history. Upon graduation he taught in Sweetwater, El Paso and Fort Worth. "He admits that like Jonah, he tried to run and hide and deny his future."[87] He committed himself to preaching at Mt. Gilead in 1942 and with the support of his wife, Fern, he prepared to enter the ministry.

At Bishop, Adams attended the L. K. Williams Institute. (Rev. Williams for a time pastored Mt. Gilead Baptist in Fort Worth and is best known for his denominational leadership. See page 113) Rev. Adams recalled his seminary days, ". . . as being long and hard and because of segregation, classes for Blacks were held in the basement. For three years, L. B. attended Bible Conferences and Seminars at Howard Payne University in Brownwood, Texas,"[88] according to a biographical profile.

Ordained in 1949, he led congregations in Texas and New Mexico, including seventeen years at Second Baptist Church in El Paso. On Sunday, November 15, 1970 he formally became pastor of 300 member Corinth Missionary Baptist Church. In an interview with the *Star-Telegram*, Rev. Adams said, "We believe the church should be the focal point for the entire family—such as a day care center, assist existing agencies in training people for better job opportunities and working with the needs of the community."[89] Rev. L. B. George of Mt. Zion Baptist Church (see page 136) preached the installation sermon.

Rev. Adams cherishes his long association with the Original West Texas District Baptist Association, Inc. where he has served as dean and moderator. Other memberships include state and national Baptist conventions. His past and present community life affiliations include "Rio Grande, Inter-racial

Ministerial Union. . . Director of Community Action Agency, Board of Directors of Riverside Community Development (and) served three years on Mayor Bob Bolen's Council, and President of the Ministerial Alliance of Fort Worth."[90]

In a recent interview he admitted to being a "young man of ninety-seven years," who cares deeply about his church and denominational business. He credits those who laid the foundation and left a legacy as the reason he came to Corinth Baptist, and with what he has tried to do over the years. After fifty-three years in the ministry, thirty-three at Corinth, where he is described as energetic for his age, he declares "God isn't through with me yet."

■   ■   ■

North Fort Worth Baptist Church—1890

In the 1880s the area north of the Trinity River was known as Marine Community and later North Fort Worth. There were ten houses and a schoolhouse in 1888 when Confederate veteran W. H. Rowland came by horseback from Azle to preach in the little school. With a capacity of twenty, it soon became too small for services. M. G. Ellis donated land at Ross Avenue and Twenty-third Streets and Dr. B. H. Carroll preached to the crowd gathered in the shade of a large oak tree. Buoyed by Dr. Carroll's sermon, Rev. A. P. Collins of South Side (later Broadway) Baptist presided over a meeting April 20, 1890 in which the North Fort Worth Missionary Baptist Church was organized. Eleven charter members, Rev. W. W. Odum, Frank Cross, Mr. and Mrs. Ernest Haywood, Mr. and Mrs. Sherman Horn, M. B. Kirvin, Thomas Manning, and Mr. and Mrs. Henry Springs joined Collins in forming the first church of any denomination on the North Side. W. W. Odum, the first minister, received $154.00 annually in salary. He led the flock until his health failed. He died in 1904. His obituary in the *Fort Worth Record* noted, "He was born in Georgia about eighty years ago . . . . He began preaching over fifty years ago. In his prime he was a powerful revivalist. He conducted not hundreds but thousands of successful revivals. He converted and baptized thousands and even tens of thousands. . . . The funeral will take place from his late residence at 416 North Pecan Street at 5 o'clock this afternoon."[91]

In September 1891 the Tarrant County Baptist Association welcomed its newest member. By 1893 it was determined the location was too far from the center of the town of North Fort Worth, but a $300 debt still hung over the small congregation. The estate of Louis Wetmore, one of Major Ripley Arnold's dragoons, and father of Mrs. Haywood, provided the money to clear the lien. "Lots 21 and 22 of block 180, located on East 20th Street, were purchased from the Fort Worth Stock Yards Company for the new location,"[92] so states church historian John Deets.

Most of the early pastors served five years or less. In addition to W. W. Odum, 1890-1895, T. N. Rhymes pastored a short time in 1896 before accepting a call from a church in Galveston. J. R. Goode, 1897-1900 saw attendance rise to an average of sixty parishioners. In the new century the following pastored the church: W. E. Dear, 1901-1902; Walter T. Hillsman, 1903-1904; Endorus Neander Bell, 1905-1907. The church incorporated under Hillman's leadership.

In 1904 the church purchased property on Circle Park Boulevard. A few months into Rev. Bell's ministry, Sunday evening, May 21, 1905, a violent windstorm destroyed the sanctuary. The *Telegram* told of the Carlson family who were just about to exit the sanctuary. "It struck the church fairly on the side, picked it from its foundation and moved it several feet to the south. The north side of the building was crushed in like an egg shell, the south wall was pushed outward, the vestibule was blown away and Mr. Carlson was lifted from his feet and carried a distance of two hundred feet. Finally falling against a fence, his flight was checked."[93] A neighbor, J. C. Shelton, who was in his back yard milking his cow, was unharmed.

The rebuilding started immediately. Only a week later, June 8, 1905, Rev. Bell wrote in the *Baptist Standard*, "Let me say to God's people that the frame of our new building, to take the place of the one wrecked by the cyclone, is up and our little band are working heroically to complete this building for God."[94] The double "L" shaped church housed the congregation until 1925.

A throat ailment cut short Wilson C. Rodgers's 1908 ministry. Other ministers following Bell were Eli F. McDonald, 1909-1910; and Walter W. Rivers, 1910-1913. Rivers, "a home-grown preacher boy," rejoined his church after graduating from Decatur College. J. F. Huckleberry, 1914-1915; and

Z. C. O'Farrell, 1916 pastored between the two pastorates of Rivers. The flock called him again in 1917 and he served until 1925.

In December 1925 the church called J. C. Boyd of Comanche, Texas, as pastor. Under his leadership a budget of $12,000 passed and negotiations for a larger building to replace the 1915 one were begun. A three-story cream-colored brick building, measuring 99.5 by 64 feet, at a cost of $55,000 was erected on the back of the church property. Boyd resigned in 1929 to accept a position as superintendent of Fort Worth's Baptist Hospital.

Rev. Carl Hereford held the congregation together during the hard times of the stock market crash and the early 1930s. He is remembered for the night he baptized eighty-four new members. Hereford accepted a call from Waco's Columbus Avenue Baptist in 1932 and Kermit Melugin pastored North Fort Worth from 1933 to 1935. Perry Evans served a few months in 1936. Forrest G. Rogers ministered to the declining church from 1937 to 1939. Times were hard and membership dropped from 1568 to 891.

Stability in the form of twenty-five year-old James N. Morgan's ministry began on December 9, 1939. He would lead the flock for the next quarter century. A native of Whitney, Texas, Morgan graduated from Baylor in 1936, and Southwestern Baptist Theological Seminary in 1941. Both Baylor and Howard Payne bestowed honorary doctorates on the popular preacher. North Fort Worth Baptist, he told a reporter in 1964 ". . . emphasizes evangelism, missions and education in ministering to its membership, its community . . .and the world."[95]

In 1941 work began on a new sanctuary. With 1634 in attendance, the flock dedicated it December 7. Those who read the *Star-Telegram* prior to going to church may have prayed that the envoy President Franklin Roosevelt sent to Japan would be successful in averting war. It was not to be. As the congregation made its way home that fateful day, Pearl Harbor blazed, and member Don Boydstun went down with the battleship *Arizona*.

Morgan made history on November 11, 1951 when he preached the first Fort Worth televised sermon directly from the church over WPAB TV Channel 5. In 1965 he began a regular radio program called "Wonderful Words of Life" on WBAP 820.

In 1967 he resigned his pastorate to accept a call from the First Baptist Church of Hurst. During his years at North Fort Worth he nurtured more than fifty who later went into Christian ministry, and welcomed almost 10,000 into church membership, according to church records.

A recurring vocal cord problem led to his giving up the Hurst church in 1971. He formed the Jimmy Morgan Evangelistic Association and continued his radio ministry which was heard over fifty stations in the 1970s.

In December 1967 D. L. Lowrie moved from Lubbock to pastor North Fort Worth. During his tenure the congregation voted to spend $225,000 to remodel the auditorium. An elevator was installed, and new carpeting, sound system, pew cushions and improved lighting gave the sanctuary a sparkling fresh look. Strains from a new Hammond organ, donated by a parishioner, added to the March 9, 1969 celebratory dedication. In 1971 Lowrie oversaw fledgling ministries to the hearing impaired and to Spanish speaking Northsiders. He ministered to the flock for ten years before he left for First Baptist of Texarkana, Texas.

Reverend Gerald Tidwell served as senior minister from 1978 to 1980. A Space Study Committee, active since 1976, considered relocation. During Tidwell's pastorate the Long Range Planning Committee recommended buying twenty acres at I-35W just north of Watauga-Smithfield Road. The church approved. On May 14, 1980 they held a "Nothing Is Impossible"

North Fort Worth Baptist Church 5801 N. I-35W. Courtesy North Fort Worth Baptist Church

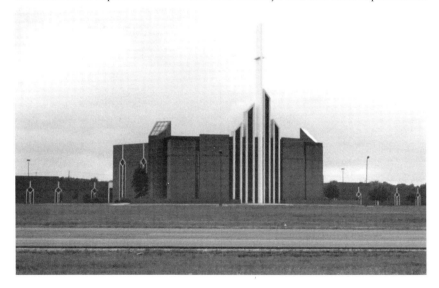

banquet at Birdville Coliseum. Fifteen hundred members, former members, including Reverends Jimmy Morgan and D. L. Lowrie, and friends gathered for the fund raiser.

Rev. Tidwell was credited with keeping the planning committee alive, but he left the church in August 1980 to lead the congregation of First Baptist in Durant, Oklahoma. Overseeing the building of the complex would be left to the next minister, Dr. Jim Futral. Ground breaking was held September 25, 1983. The modern styled church stretches out, rather than up, symbolic of the congregation's out stretched arms, welcoming both parishioners and visitors.

For the church's centennial celebration in 1990 Rev. Futral, from his pastorate in Broadmoor Baptist Church in Jackson, Mississippi, wrote of his fondness for the church and the congregation. Alluding to the coming century he challenged them saying, "As desperately as the frontiersman of Fort Worth needed the gospel. . . a hundred years ago, the well-to-do suburbanite needs Christ now."[96]

Rev. John Redfearn preached his first sermon to his new congregation on August 25, 1986 and served until 2001.

In January 2002 Rev. James Bond came as interim minister. The next pastor, unknown at press time, will find an active congregation that will give support and strength just as they have done throughout North Fort Worth's more than 100 year history.

■   ■   ■

Mt. Zion Baptist-1894

On Christmas day, 1894, Reverend Frank Tribune, state evangelist for the Baptist Missions and Evangelism Convention of Texas, and five others met to form a new church for people of color. It became   ". . .the first large black church on the south side and the second largest black church in Fort Worth,"[97] Mt. Zion's 1975 history committee noted. Lee and Ella Brooks, of 708 E. Rosedale, hosted the founding group. It would be the last one organized by Rev. Tribune before his death three months later. He named it Mt. Zion, "the mountain of the Lord." Katie Patterson, Laura Purvis and Josephine Wells, along with the Brookses, became the charter members. All were former members of Mt. Gilead Baptist.

Following the death of Rev. Tribune, the Convention sent Rev. A. Dupree to work with the fledgling church. A 1975 history states "Dr. A. R. Griggs. . . Superintendent of Missions of the State of Texas, came to Mount Zion and held it as a Mission (sic) station until the membership increased enough to support a church."[98] The small congregation purchased a lot on the corner of Rosedale and Louisiana Streets, but it would be several years before they could build a sanctuary. In the meantime, "Sister M. S. Jones organized auxiliaries such as the Mission Society, Star Light Band and B. Y. P. U."[99]

During the first two decades of its existence, Mt. Zion welcomed three more pastors. Rev. J. B. Bell led the church in 1907 and during his tenure a frame structure was built on the Rosedale site. Rev. J. D. Jones came in 1908. Rev. J. H. Reeves pastored the church from 1910 until 1912. Membership grew to twenty-five congregants.

Rev. L. W. Mackey succeeded Reeves in 1912. The church continued to grow and in 1915 bought property costing $1,800 at 1101 Evans Avenue. "A tabernacle was built. . . and the members remained there until 1919 when Reverend M. K. Curry was called,"[100] historian Y. C. Shamblee wrote. For the next two years the congregation moved back to the old property as Curry oversaw the digging and equipping of a large basement and auditorium on the

Mt. Zion Baptist Church 1101 Evans Ave. Courtesy Mt. Zion Baptist Church

first floor. The finished structure included a raised choir loft with a stained glass window behind it, seating for 500, electric lights and ceiling fans.

The neoclassical Palladian influenced sanctuary is of earth tone brick. Its gleaming dome can be seen from blocks away. Steps on both the front and north sides lead up to the auditorium. The basement, which formerly served as the sanctuary, now houses class rooms for Sunday school.

Members donated pews and approved the expenditure of $900 for a church bell. The bell, on a brick foundation, is now located on the lawn facing Verbena Street, near the church's historical marker. This entire project cost $70,000 at a time when that was a tremendous amount of money. When Rev. Curry left in 1924 the congregation had repaid $20,000 of the debt.

That same year, Rev. A. W. Pryor began a twenty-five year ministry at Mt. Zion. During those years the church paid off its mortgage, swelled its membership to 1500 and reorganized the Sunday school. Changes to the building itself included a new kitchen and banquet room. New pulpit furniture and stained glass windows were installed.

Reverend S. T. Alexander led the congregation in the post World War II period and they continued to upgrade the facility with new paint throughout the existing structure and erecting a $102,000 educational building. The sanctuary was carpeted and removable pew cushions were installed. A stunning landscape painted on the wall behind the baptistery immediately catches a visitor's eye. "The first church organ, a Hammond, was also purchased during Reverend Alexander's administration,"[101] the 1975 history noted. Despite all the progress made, Rev. Alexander's later ministry was marred when he and his flock differed on matters of finance and church policy.

Rev. L. B. (Louis Belvet) George came in 1969 to heal the troubled congregation. He was born in Pittsburg, Texas, the son of a minister. After graduating high school in 1939, L. B. attended college in Austin, then transferred to Butler College in Tyler to major in religion. He later returned to Butler and earned a degree in English and did graduate study at Southern Bible Training School in Dallas and at Southwestern Baptist Theological Seminary in Fort Worth. Rev. George pastored churches in Texas, including thirteen years at Mt. Zion in Amarillo. He came to Fort Worth from Second Baptist Church in Vallejo, California.

By the 1970s the remodeling done during Alexander's pastorate needed updating. Rev. George oversaw the staining and refurbishing of the pews, and attaching book racks to hold the newly purchased Bibles and hymnals. The choir loft and rostrum were enlarged. Modern light fixtures and air conditioning were added in both the sanctuary and educational wing. Next, they turned the basement area into a lounge for the youth of the church. A parsonage in the Rolling Hills neighborhood provided housing for the minister's family.

In the education building contractors remodeled the pastor's and secretary's offices, adding a library and an office for the educational director. The congregation purchased property on Verbena for parking and built a ramp to enable handicapped parishioners easy access to the sanctuary. In addition to the building campaign, Mt. Zion began a bus ministry for those who needed transportation services.

Rev. George participated in community activities and soon gained the respect of the city. He chaired the Civic Committee of the Baptist Minister's Union of Fort Worth and was president of the local Interdenominational Ministerial Alliance. He served on the boards of several youth organizations, Tarrant Bank, and the Fort Worth Public Library. "He is a 33rd degree Mason; a member of the NAACP and Alpha Phi Alpha Fraternity,"[102] according to his vita. The 108th anniversary program stated, "Under his leadership Mt. Zion gained local, state, national and international recognition."[103] Rev. George retired in 1995 after twenty-six years of ministry in Fort Worth.

Described as a dynamic speaker, logical thinker, and capable theologian, he also loved to sing. As late as 2003, well into retirement, his steps have slowed, but he returns to Mt. Zion and sings his favorite hymns in a voice that is still strong.

Following L. B. George's pastorate, Rev. Daniel B. Keys left the Payne Avenue Missionary Baptist Church in Knoxville, Tennessee to lead Mt. Zion until 2000.

Rev. Kendall R. White became the fifteenth pastor of Mt. Zion in January 2001. He had previously served in Lawton, Oklahoma. Pastor White's general focus goes beyond teaching and preaching God's word; he believes a comfortable physical environment enhances spirituality. Like his predecessors George and Alexander, he oversaw renovation of the sanctuary and the Eula

Henderson Fellowship Hall. Also like Rev. George, Rev. White uses his singing voice to convey his message—which is "God owes us nothing, but gives us everything."[104]

Mt. Zion's social ministry includes leading fund drives for college scholarships, sponsoring YMCA and YWCA camp scholarships, encouraging voter registration, and holding First Aid workshops with the Red Cross. They have won awards from the NAACP for their participation. The church is affiliated with the National Baptist Convention USA, Southern Baptist Convention, Galilee Griggs Memorial and the Texas Baptist Convention. Many of the church's members have become prominent in lay and religious organizations.

About the future, the 108th anniversary program proclaimed, "The torch that was lighted during the 19th Century by five charter members has burned through the 20th Century and continues to burn in the 21st Century."[105]

■   ■   ■

Greater St. James Baptist—1895

Greater St. James had its beginning in a tent as a mission of Mt. Gilead, but soon became prominent in its own right. At one time the membership list of Greater St. James Baptist Church read like a "Who's Who" of the Black community. A state representative, city councilman, a president of the local NAACP, the first black administrator at Bell Telephone, the first supervisor at Convair (now Lockheed Martin), and the first mayor pro-tem were all members. Too many educators and business leaders to count worshiped at the massive red brick church on Harding Street. Three elementary schools, Maude Logan, Maudrie Walton, and Versia Williams, bear the names of women who devoted years of service to the children of Fort Worth and especially to Greater St. James.

Maudrie Miller Walton was typical of the dedicated members that helped propel Greater St. James to leadership in the community. The daughter of Deacon Herbert Miller, she joined the church in 1917 when she was nine-years-old. The Greater St. James congregation was still worshiping in a tabernacle, and thus her baptism took place at Mt.Gilead. "As a child and as a teenager, she participated in all activities and programs in the church. As an adult she became one of the leading soprano soloists in the senior choir,"[106] according to *100th Church Celebration; Greater Saint James Baptist Church; 1895-1995.*

Maudrie graduated from I. M. Terrell in 1925, earned a B. A. Degree from Bishop College, and M. A. from Teachers College-Columbia University. She did graduate study at the Universities of Colorado and Michigan. For twenty-seven years she taught elementary school, and was principal of Rosedale Park (now Maudrie Walton) Elementary for twenty years. After retirement, she served eight years as a trustee on the Fort Worth School Board. During World War II she spent thirty-two months in the Women's Army Corp. Mayor Bob Bolen declared November 21, 1983 "Maudrie M. Walton Day" in recognition of her many contributions to the city.

While making an impact in her professional endeavors, Walton held leadership positions in her church throughout her long life. Before to her death in 1998 at age ninety, she was the oldest active member of Greater St. James, both in years and in membership.

In 1895, thirteen years prior to Maudrie Walton's birth, Reverend J. Francis Robinson and thirty charter members organized Greater St. James Baptist Church. They were former members of Mt. Gilead Baptist Church (see page 113) During the early years, in addition to Robinson, J. A. Fisher, W. F. Lawson, J. P. Pruitt, J. B. Slaughter, W. H. Burroughs, and W. M. Conner ministered to pioneer congregants. Hyler L. Dixon and Fannie Mae Heath, authors of "Historic Sketch of Greater Saint James Baptist Church," described all as great pastors.

In 1911 Dr. J. H. Winn began a ministry that lasted until 1940. He led the congregation in establishing a "Mission Station" in Liberia. (Liberia, the oldest black republic in Africa, was settled in the early nineteenth century as a haven for freed American slaves.) In addition to the religious component, a number of Africans received scholarships for an education in the United States.

Closer to home, Dr. Winn oversaw the development of a divinity school at the church. Several alumnae later pastored churches in Fort Worth. According to Dixon and Heath, "The vocational school—On the Job Training Program for Blacks—was held in the lower level of the church."[107] This program was a partnership with the Fort Worth Public Schools.

In 1918 the congregation, numbering about 3,000, moved into its present location at 210 Harding Street. At a cost in excess of $150,000, the late Gothic Revival church was the largest facility available for use by Afro-Americans in the days of racial segregation. For many years nearby I. M. Terrell High School held graduation exercises there.

After thirty years, Rev. Winn left to lead the Fifth Street Baptist Church in Oklahoma City.

Kerven and Lela Carter joined Greater St. James in 1921. Two years later Kerven, Jr., who says he was "born into the church" began an association with the church that has lasted more than eighty years. "I slept in every area of the church,"[108] he teased in an interview. Mrs. Carter took young Kerven, Jr. with her to choir practice, committee meetings, and of course, worship services. As a youth he led the various activities for his age group; as an adult he was announcing clerk of the church for thirty years. Like his mother before him, he sings in the choir.

He recalled the days before air-conditioning. "People came early to get a choice seat beside an open window."[109]

For fifteen years Carter served as superintendent of the Young People's Department. This was a natural role for the dedicated educator. After graduation from Wiley College he taught school, retiring as principal of Eastland Elementary. His graduate studies were at the Universities of Southern California, Denver, Wyoming, and Harvard University.

Carter also remembered that during the pastorate of Dr. Warren S. Brent, World War II servicemen were always welcome at Greater St. James. After the war, when materials again became available, Brent oversaw the installation of a new roof and new floor coverings. Updated electrical and plumbing fixtures made the building appealing to the congregation. The Brent family moved into a new two-story brick parsonage at 1303 E. Terrell. Then trouble arose over policies related to the treasury. Rev. Brent resigned, and accompanied by 200 members, formed Antioch Missionary Baptist Church.

Rev. O. P. Felder ministered to the church for a year. In 1952 Rev. C. A. Holliday began a tenure that lasted until 1978. Holliday, a chaplain during the war, received a citation for meritorious services prior to his discharge. He taught at Butler College in Tyler, and was a trustee of Bishop College. In

1954 the Huntsville, Texas native served as editorial associate to the second assembly of the World Council of Churches at Northwestern University.

The well-respected cleric made headlines in 1963 when Gov. John Connally appointed him to the State Board of Corrections. He was the first Afro-American named to the board that supervises the state prison system. A unit of the prison now bears his name.

In 1968 Holliday said of the church with its membership touching 2,000, "It sounds almost fantastic that a church   . . . with only 30 humble charter members could amass such temporal and spiritual power with so little at its command,"[110] according to Gracie Bonds Staples' newspaper article.

Poor health forced Holliday to curtail his activities and in 1978 he was named pastor emeritus. He died in 1986.

Rev. Bobby G. Webber combined church and state by being both a man of the cloth and a state representative. He served Greater St. James for three years, then established the First Community Baptist Church in Arlington. Rev. Jerry W. Dailey led the flock until 1985 when he answered the call to go to Macedonia Baptist Church in San Antonio.

Reverend R. C. Johnson, a member of Greater St. James since 1953, became pastor in 1986. Prior to entering the ministry he held church positions such as deacon, van driver and director of the Baptist Training Union while

Greater St. James Baptist Church 210 Harding St. Courtesy Greater St. James Baptist Church

working at the General Motors plant in Arlington. Active in the United Auto Workers, he rose to vice-president of the local organization. That office, and his work as a Democratic precinct chair earned him a ticket to a breakfast he will never forget. On that rainy November 22, 1963 morning, he joined others in welcoming the President of the United States, John F. Kennedy. The tragedy in Dallas that same day changed his high spirits to what he recalled as "the saddest day of my life."

Rev. Johnson's organizational and people skills learned as a union official prepared him to deal with church committees and his congregation when he assumed the pastorate of Greater St. James. In addition to Bishop College, his seminary training came from Southern Bible Institute in Dallas.

He has seen his church, like others on "Baptist Hill" suffer from the loss of neighborhood due to the construction of freeways. He ministers to a congregation numbering about 400 who come from all over the area to renew their ties and faith. Rev. Johnson sees a great future due to the area being revitalized. Along with that renaissance, Greater St. James' planned activity center will offer young families wholesome recreation, just as it did in years gone by.

■   ■   ■

Travis Avenue Baptist—1908

Fredona Baker, author of the first two chapters of *Mighty Works of Grace* wrote of Travis Avenue's simple beginning. "When the Payne children skipped happily from their home at 2733 Travis Avenue to the little mission Sunday School at Biddison and Travis, one of their greatest incentives for attendance was the hedgeapple fight that was sure to ensue before their return home."[111] The Sunday School, held in the Prairie Chapel school house, was the work of two families from College Avenue Baptist, the Rosses and the Buells. In 1910 people traveled down Biddison, a dirt road between Hemphill Street and Silver Lake, to get to the school.

Twelve charter members met in November 1910 and organized the South Side Baptist Church. They called Rev. R. W. Langham as their first pastor. The following year they built a small frame building on the corner of Lipscomb and Biddison Streets. It cost $250. In 1912, the growing church purchased property at their present site on Travis Avenue, and with volunteer labor, built another small sanctuary. During the next ten years six men held the office of pastor. J. L. Price served in 1912; J. L. Mahan, from 1914-1915; W. W. Barnes, 1916-1917; S. H. Frazier, 1918; A. S. Harwell, 1919-1921, and C. E. Matthews beginning in 1922.

By then the church listed twenty-eight officers and teachers, with a membership of 318. Under the capable twenty-four-year leadership of Charles E. Matthews the membership grew to over 6,000 in 1946. He resigned to become the first secretary of evangelism for the Baptist General Convention of Texas Home Mission Board, and the following year for the Southern Baptist Convention. Rev. Matthews died of a heart attack at age sixty-nine. Much has been written about the Baptist leader, and biographer C. E. Wilbanks summed up the life of the beloved minister in the following obituary:

"MATTHEWS, CHARLES EVERETT (b. Gasconade County, Mo., Mar. 23, 1887; d. Marshall, Tex., Oct. 5, 1956). Businessman, pastor, evangelist, denominational leader, and author. Orphaned by his father's death when he was 11 months old and his mother's death when he was 16 years old, Matthews attended rural schools and Tipton High School in Missouri and was graduated from Hill's Business College in St. Louis. For 15 years he was employed by Simmons Hardware Co. and Swift and Co. Converted at the age of 27 in the First Baptist Church of Fort Worth, Tex., Matthews later served that church as financial secretary and educational director. Ordained to the ministry on Sept. 28, 1921, at the age of 34, he served as pastor of Birdville and Hurst Baptist churches simultaneously and Travis Avenue Baptist Church, Fort Worth, 1922-46. Matthews received his theological education at Southwestern Baptist Seminary, where he studied for three semesters. Later he served as a trustee of that institution for 16 years, serving 10 years as vice-president of the board and two years as president."[112]

Dr. Ellis L. Carnett became pastor in 1946. The son of a Baptist preacher, Carnett had a thriving insurance business, but the call to religious service could not be ignored. At first he believed that calling would be in music. He studied at the Chicago Conservatory and Southwestern Baptist Theological Seminary. From 1921 to 1933 he taught music at the seminary. He was leading the music at a revival when he felt the call to a preaching ministry. Gambrell Street Baptist ordained him to the ministry.

Like in the days under Rev. Matthews, with Carnett's ministry the progress of the church continued. Returning World War II servicemen and their wives were starting families. This meant a burgeoning Sunday School enrollment. Buildings "A" and "B" were constructed during Rev. Matthews' pastorate, and Dr. Carnett oversaw the erecting of building "C" and the reorganization of the Sunday School departments.

The post-war sense of optimism and vitality which permeated the mood of the community was personified in the character of Dr. Carnett. Joy Howington wrote regarding the minister, ". . . words such as warm-hearted, loving, jovial, optimistic were expressed."[113] Sadly the church accepted his resignation in June, 1952.

Dr. Robert E. Naylor left the prestigious First Baptist Church of Columbia, South Carolina in October, 1952 to became pastor of Travis. He knew of the church from his association with Rev. Matthews, but at first did not want to leave Columbia. Helen Yeatts quoted from an oral tape made by Naylor. "He (Matthews) talked about Travis, its history, its evangelistic heart, its leadership in the Convention. . . as only a man that loved it, could discuss it,"[114] Matthews urged him to pray about it, and the result was Travis gained one of their most outstanding preachers, and ironically the very one Rev. Carnett secretly predicted would succeed him.

"Bob" Naylor, born and reared in Oklahoma, graduated from East Central Teachers College in Ada. During his senior year he determined the pulpit rather than the classroom was where he should be. In 1929 he was ordained in the First Baptist Church of Ada, Oklahoma. Three years later he earned a Master of Theology from Southwestern Seminary. He served churches in Arkansas and his home state before going to South Carolina. While at Arkadelphia, Arkansas, Ouachita College presented him the honorary Doctor of Divinity in 1941.

Dr. Naylor's influence beyond Travis included the presidency of the Fort Worth General Minister's Association, a director of the Southern Baptist

Foundation of that convention, and first vice-president of the Baptist General Convention of Texas. His radio and television ministry reached thousands. In 1955 his book *The Baptist Deacon* was featured at the opening of a St. Louis Baptist book store.

In the summer of that year, a major change occurred at the church. Prior to central air conditioning, the congregation made a choice—sit near an evaporative cooler (Grimes Fortenberry called them swamp coolers.) and be relatively comfortable, but unable to hear Dr. Naylor's strong voice, or sit where one could hear the sermon, but suffer from the summer heat. Catering businessman Walter Jetton, who gained fame as President Lyndon B. Johnson's favorite barbecue man, came to the rescue. Jetton led a drive to raise $200,000 for central air. They rushed to get the air conditioning installed before Rev. Naylor left for a Baptist World Alliance meeting in London. Workmen installed the units on a Saturday night and turned them on. But there was one little problem. They had not installed the thermostats. It got cooler and cooler and colder and colder. "I want you to know we met in the coolest auditorium that anybody in that church ever imagined for a June morning,"[115] Dr. Naylor recalled.

By the mid 1950s the need for a new auditorium was apparent. Ground breaking ceremonies were held on a rainy day in October of 1957. Rev. Naylor lifted the first shovelful of dirt, then handed the muddy shovel to Walter Jetton. Progress was halted in March 1959 when a storm, some believed it to be a tornado, ripped sixty percent of the tiles off the almost completed building. Fortunately insurance covered most of the financial loss and the contractor hired extra help to get back on schedule. Eighteen months after the ground breaking, construction on the 3,280 seat auditorium was finished. For comparison, Fort Worth's Bass Hall seats about 2,000. If the pews were laid end to end they would stretch a mile. At that time it was the largest sanctuary in the Southern Baptist Convention.

Festivities filled the week of April 26, 1959. The $500,000 Georgian Colonial sanctuary of red brick and light gray limestone with hand-carved stone columns was ready for occupancy. Fortenberry commented, "The eight-foot bronze cross, with its top 168 feet above ground level, could be seen for miles."[116]

Dr. Naylor attended the ceremonies, but as a former minister. The vacancy caused by the sudden death of the Southwestern Theological Seminary president in April 1958, was filled when trustees named Dr. Robert Naylor to lead the seminary.

The pulpit committee asked Dr. James E. Coggin, pastor of First Church, Texarkana, to preach September 20, 1958. His stirring messages on Sunday morning and Sunday evening resulted in thirty additions to the church—an unheard of response to a visiting preacher. Immediately the committee tendered an invitation. Dr. Coggin, the eleventh pastor and only the fourth since 1922, accepted and led the congregation for the next twenty-four years.

James Earl Coggin, the youngest of ten children, was born near Tupelo, Mississippi on September 11, 1921. When he was five the family moved to Mobile, Alabama. After high school and Howard College (now Sanford University) he earned a Master and a Doctor of Theology from Southwestern Seminary. Young Coggin decided at age fifteen he would enter the ministry. He preached his first sermon in a small Alabama church, and later pastored churches in Oklahoma, Tennessee and Texas before coming to Travis Avenue.

One of his first duties was to speak at a dinner attended by over 1,200 members. He used statistics to tell the story of their church. "There were 221,391 square feet of space and 1,995 light globes in the church buildings; (annually) 30,000 pieces of literature were distributed in Sunday school and training union; 500,000 people entered the various buildings for activities and worship services; 500 meals were served to 50,000 people; and 166,000 pieces of mail were sent from the church."[117]

After six years of devotion to his duties, the popular minister faced a near career-ending crisis. On June 21, 1965 Dr. Coggin and his family were in an automobile accident. Mrs. Coggin, their two children and her mother received minor injuries. He suffered a broken neck. Months of recuperation and rehabilition followed. By 1966 he could preach on a limited schedule and within a year resumed his regular duties.

One such duty was to oversee the 1967 "Forward Program of Advance." This called for the completion of the banquet hall, purchase of additional property, and construction of adult and youth education facilities comparable to the church sanctuary. Rev. Coggin also nurtured the congregation during the 1960s' years of domestic upheaval. He commented, "This sociological change produced the greatest strain and demand on Travis that she had ever known."[118] As the neighborhood changed, Travis changed. Dr. Coggin introduced bus and ethnic ministries. The Sunday school benefited and in an article in *Christian Life Magazine* in 1969 was ranked thirty-second largest in average attendance among all denominations in the United States.

Dr. Coggin announced his retirement in 1982 after twenty-four years as senior pastor. The previous year he had been treated successfully for a malignancy, but he felt a new pastor could better lead the congregation as it entered into yet another building phase. Rev. Jimmy Allen, president of the Southern Baptist Radio and Television Commission served as interim until the search committee recommended Dr. Joel C. Gregory.

Born and reared in Fort Worth, he already knew much of the church's history and mission. A graduate of Baylor University, Gregory earned a Master of Divinity from Southwestern Seminary and a Ph.D. from Baylor.

He came with a reputation as an unusually gifted biblical expositor. This was a major prerequisite for the committee and congregation. After "Gregory preached tremendous messages on Sunday morning and Sunday night,"[119] according to *Mighty Works of Grace*, the membership voted unanimously to call him to their pulpit.

Rev. Gregory's successful pastorate at Travis became over-shadowed by his stormy tenure at Dallas' First Baptist. In his own words, prior to W. A. Criswell tapping him on the shoulder, "I was up to my eyeballs at the Travis Avenue Baptist. . . . The church had thrived and now had eight thousand members. It was in my hometown, enjoyed about as much peace with its pastor as a big Baptist church can enjoy, and appeared to be a place to retire. We were on television locally and nationally."[120]

On more than one occasion men of the Dallas search committee visited Travis Avenue. Although they infiltrated the congregation, he knew they were there. "No member of the Audubon Society searching for a rare bird is keener-eyed than a visited preacher surveying the congregation for a pulpit committee,"[121] he recalled. He worried about leaving the church since he had led in the campaign to start a $7,000,000 building program. Still, when

First Baptist pressed, Gregory agreed to preach in view of a call. He asked
Dr. Coggin and Dr. Naylor to substitute in the Travis Avenue morning and
evening services. They agreed.

Some members were outraged that he should consider leaving. "I would
get visits, letters, and remonstrations that I had 'promised to stay.' Travis
Avenue had not lost a preacher to another church since the 1920s. That a pastor would leave . . . to go to another church just was not thought to be a way

Travis Avenue Baptist Church 3041 Travis Ave. Courtesy Travis Avenue Baptist Church

things were done,"[122] he wrote. Other members believed he had become too close to "fundamentalists" and did not regret his leaving.

In *Too Great a Temptation* he described his exodus from Travis Avenue and later from First Baptist. Gregory's ministry in Dallas was so clamorous that he gave up the pulpit and went into the private sector.

Michael Dean became pastor in 1991. His preaching style, punctuated with hand gestures, is unpretentious. One parishioner described the senior minister as a people person who uses visuals for dramatic effect. He gave an example. "One Sunday he had a table on the steps leading up to the platform. A cloth covered it, so we couldn't see what was on it. He preached about 'big shoes to fill,' then removed the cloth to reveal three pairs of shoes." The preacher explained that one pair belonged to a long time deacon who recently died. "'These are big shoes to fill,' he said. He held up a pair of ladies' shoes that had belonged to a devoted church worker. 'These are big shoes to fill.' He did the same for the third pair of shoes, making his point in a way we would remember."[123]

In his early years at Travis Avenue Baptist, Rev. Dean led the church in paying off massive indebtedness. Now he leads a debt free congregation, mindful of its history and hopeful for its future.

Chapter Six

THE METHODIST
CONGREGATIONS

The Methodist Church is an outgrowth of a movement within the Church of England. John Wesley, the son of a rector and a pious mother, sought to find peace of mind through devotion to God by strict discipline and observance of church ritual. At a prayer meeting at Aldersgate Street in 1738 he felt the tug of the need for an intimate relationship with God. He began to preach on the necessity of personal conversion, freedom from sin as taught in the Bible, assurance of salvation, and holiness of life.

From England, Methodism spread to Ireland and then to America. It thrived and grew as the nation matured, and ". . . some have said that Methodism has been 'the most American of all churches,'"[1] according to William B. Williamson. Especially suited to frontier life, the movement crossed the continent with the people, including the settlers of Texas.

First known in the United States as the Methodist Episcopal Church, the denomination split in 1845 over the slavery issue. It took almost a century, until 1939, for the Methodist Episcopal Church, South, and the Methodist Protestant Church to become the Methodist Church at the Uniting Conference in Kansas City in 1939. However, Fort Worth Methodist congregations united prior to the national movement, and that fueled the tremendous growth of the city's First Methodist Church.

In a "Sketch of History of Fort Worth Methodism" W. E. Williams penned, "The ubiquity of Methodist preachers is shown by the story of the man from the east who hated them and determined to go so far west that there would be none and who after going to the farthermost west, was greeted first by one, and then declared it was no use to try to get out of their reach, and then joined the church and became a preacher himself; it well exemplified the effort of Methodist preachers to reach the first settlers in Fort Worth and vicinity."[2]

Governed by the General Conference, most Methodist congregations follow a simple form of liturgy which includes hymns, prayers, Scriptures, creeds (usually the Apostles' Creed), a sermon and a benediction. Methodism had its beginning in Fort Worth soon after the fort became a village. Circuit riders preached to the faithful at the Masonic Lodge, then moved on to the next village.

To Methodist ministers "IBM" doesn't refer to a NYSE listing. To them it means "I've been moved." In keeping with Wesley's philosophy that each minister has a unique gift to be shared with different congregations, Methodist clergy regularly serve many over the years of their ministry. At annual conferences bishops attempt to meet the needs of both parishioners and ministers with proper assignments, and often it involves a new location. Therefore the churches profiled in this chapter were blessed by multiple ministries, supplied by pastors too numerous to name them all.

"Twenty years without a home is the early history of Methodism in Fort Worth. As early as 1855 Methodist preachers were here,"[3] a Writers' Project historian wrote.

■   ■   ■

First Methodist—1874

Twenty-six-year-old John Wesley (a common name for Methodist males) Chalk waited anxiously to hear his first assignment that late December day in 1852. Only a week earlier he had been admitted on trial into the ministry of the Methodist Episcopal Church, South. Bishop Robert Paine at last called out "Red Oak Mission—John W. Chalk." Red Oak, a small settlement about twenty miles south of the village of Dallas, became his home base. Chalk rode horseback from village to village, house to house in Denton, Ellis and Tarrant Counties, preaching wherever he could find a welcome.

Before the formation of churches, worshipers called themselves members of a "Methodist society." Each society kept a register and records show John Chalk received members from Fort Worth during 1853. From this sprang a church that reached gigantic heights in the denomination.

Fort Worth became a district in 1856 and Fountain P. Ray pastored the mission. A year later Bishop Robert Alexander wrote, "Fort Worth is now a nice village and is improving in a very substantial way."[4] Despite these activities, the Methodists did not erect a church building until 1874. Prior to this time the flock met in homes or in the Masonic Lodge. In 1873 the Central Conference appointed R. H. H. Burnet to the Fort Worth Station. The small congregation had already organized a Sunday school and named George Mulkey its superintendent.

"In December, 1873 the first property to be owned by the church was purchased for a parsonage on East First Street,"[5] according to a Writers' Project history. Rev. Burnet was the first occupant. The leadership also purchased a lot at Fourth and Jones Streets for the first Methodist church building. Old records reveal a stipulation that construction would not begin until five people subscribed $100.00 each.

W. J. Boaz, Hugh Davis, S. H. Mulkey and J. C. Terrell (a member of the Christian Church), put up their money. Still shy of the required five, George Mulkey, who worked at a planing mill, told them his worldly assets amounted to only $25.00, but he would give $100.00 worth of labor. George Mulkey, one of the first members, for fifty-seven years energized and supported the church. He co-founded what would become Mulkey Memorial Church (see page 175).

On May 15, 1874 the Methodists began the construction of their first church building. In 1876 the bishop appointed M. D. Fly to pastor the church for the next two years. Fly resigned before his term was finished, saying ". . . he could not live on $275 a year."[6] H. G. Wells served the church in 1879 and John R. Allen came in 1880. By this time the pastor's salary had risen to $600.00 a year. In 1881 Pastor John A. Murphy reported membership reached 275.

The year 1887 saw the end of a two-year drought, the worst in the history of the state to that time. Thousands of settlers left the area and many churches disbanded. Bucking the trend, that year the Fourth Street congregation decided to take another step forward. They moved the frame building that had housed them for thirteen years to the back of the lot. They erected a new brick $16,500 structure. Described as a "very imposing structure, having two inspiring spires which reached toward heaven,"[7] Williams quoted a source. Now minus the "two inspiring spires," and roofless and windowless, nevertheless, the walls of that building still stand, complete with its historical marker.

In 1890 the conference approved the official name change from Fourth Street to First Methodist Episcopal Church, South. The establishment of the Missouri Avenue (see page 181) and Mulkey Memorial (see page 175) Methodist Churches prompted this action. In other business they approved the charter of Polytechnic College (now Texas Wesleyan University) with W. F. Lloyd, pastor of First Church, elected one of the trustees.

During Lloyd's tenure the growing congregation added two rooms to the back of the brick church. As the membership increased, 700 in 1894, so too did the pay of the minister. Horace Bishop received an annual salary of $2,300, the largest paid to any minister in the conference that year.

Up to this time bishops appointed ministers to one to two year pastorates. E. D. Mouzon, the first to serve four consecutive years, made such a favorable impression that ten years later he was elected to the episcopacy.

First Methodist continued to grow. Rev. Alonzo Monk preached to a flock numbering more than 900, and his successor, Rev. H. D. Knickerbocker's congregation rose to 1101. They needed to consider a new, larger sanctuary. A building committee bought a lot on the corner of Seventh and Taylor Streets for $18,000. They sold the Fourth Street property for $10,000 and erected a two story, light colored brick and stone facility. It had a balcony on each side in the sanctuary, and one in the back, which they used for a choir room. There were eight class rooms on the upper floor. The first floor sanctuary provided seating for 800, and church offices were at the rear of the building.

"Occupying an important corner in the very heart of the business center of the city, the new church could hardly be more conveniently located, and the new site promises to prove more advantageous than that of the forsaken building at the corner of Fourth and Jones Street,"[8] a reporter noted.

Leaders of both the city and the denomination attended the March 8, 1908 grand opening. The decade to follow saw the growing influence of the downtown church. It took twenty-eight years for the congregation to surpass 1,000 in Sunday school enrollment, but only eleven years to reach the 2,000 mark. This happened under the leadership of Rev. Frank P. Culver in 1920.

With the advent of World War I, many First Methodist boys trained in camps all over the United States. Other Methodists left their home churches to train at Camp Bowie. In 1917 John R. Nelson raised $40,000 to provide spiritual services for the soldiers stationed in Texas. According to the September 16, 1917 *Fort Worth Record*, "'Amusement Row' was organized and opened by First Baptist, First Methodist, and First Presbyterian churches for Sunday matinees for the soldiers of Camp Bowie. Musical numbers and motion pictures were included in the programs."[9]

Technology came to First Methodist on May 3, 1922. WBAP, the pioneer radio broadcasting station, aired a sermon by Rev. J. W. Bergin. Churches in far flung areas took advantage of the opportunity to worship via radio. Williams quoted a letter Bergin received from a listener. "I take pleasure in informing you that a congregation of more than two hundred enjoyed the services of First Methodist recently. The service came in clear, pleasing and elevating."[10]

Builders of the Seventh Street Church envisioned it being adequate for at least fifty years. They miscalculated. Within twenty years skyscrapers encroached upon the church grounds. Membership ballooned so rapidly it became necessary for the church to rent office space in one of those skyscrapers. A 1928 building committee tried unsuccessfully to buy the remainder of the block. As a next option they found a site at Fifth and Florence large enough to accommodate the flock. They sold the Seventh Street property for $360,000 and used the money to purchase the lots. The committee raised an additional $300,000 toward the eventual $1,000,000 facility.

Rev. E. B. Hawk laid the corner stone October 5, 1930. On Friday, October 31, 1,200 parishioners attended the door-locking service at the Seventh Street church. Twenty-seven years of religious services had come to a close. Dr. Hawk handed a key to board chairman E. J. White. White locked the doors. Rev. Hawk, taking a sentimental last look through the beveled plate glass, saw someone move. Tom Hood, the custodian since 1914, was about to be locked inside. White opened the door, re-locked it, and closed that chapter of First Methodist's history. Dr. Hawk became Dean of Southern Methodist University's School of Theology—later named Perkins School of Theology.

The congregation marched to the Fifth Street site. The old key is included in a framed picture of the old building, preserved with the church records. As described by a member of the Writers' Project, "Among the church building, the First Methodist Church has given to Fort Worth a religious monument of outstanding beauty and architectural grandeur. Located at 800 West Fifth Street, this edifice covers practically a full city block. It is of modified Gothic design, and is topped by twin towers that stand out against the city's skyline. Housed in these towers are the celebrated sixteen cylinder deagan chimes."[11]

Well-kept houses surrounded the church's new 1930 home. John Peter Smith Elementary School, two blocks to the north, was the only nonresidential building in the area.

After worshiping for months in Wesley Hall, the congregation held the grand opening Sunday June 14, 1931. On Friday, June 12 the *Star-Telegram* devoted an entire page to the upcoming festivities. Ninety members of the Board of Stewards signed a tribute to Dr. Hawk. It said in part, "WE PAY TRIBUTE to Eugene B. Hawk, our beloved pastor since 1925 and the moving force behind the wonderful progress of the . . .Church. . . ."[12] The tribute went on to note his birth on a Tennessee farm, education in Virginia, and law practice in Oklahoma before he devoted twenty-two years to the ministry. He served First Methodist Church six years.

Dr. J. N. R. Score led the congregation during the dark days of the Great Depression. With money not so tight, in 1940 the flock purchased lots across Fifth Street in front of the church for parking space. Two houses on adjoining lots to the west became available. Dr. Judge Lyle (see *A History of the Fort Worth Medical Community*) bought one and donated it to the church. Merchant Marvin Leonard and Dr. Lyle each contributed $5,000 toward the price of the other. The houses were moved, resulting in additional parking space.

Dr. Score completed eight years at First Methodist before he accepted the presidency of Southwestern University in Georgetown.

The Conference appointed Arkansas native Dr. Warren Johnston to the church in 1942. He served nine years. He earned both bachelor and master degrees from Hendrix College in his home state. "Hendrix awarded him an honorary doctor of divinity degree in 1941,"[13] according to the *Star-Telegram.* Leading the congregation in the dedication of the new building he deemed to be the highlight of his pastorate. An average of 350 persons joined each year of Johnston's tenure and membership increased to the point that First Methodist became the tenth largest church in United States Methodism.

Author, scholar, world traveler, and native West Texan, in 1952 Gaston Foote began a long and illustrious tenure in Fort Worth. The son of a Methodist minister, the youth preached his first sermon at age fifteen. After gaining experience in small churches by helping his father, Gaston Foote went on to pastor large congregations in Montgomery, Alabama and Dayton, Ohio. He attended Clarendon Junior College, and graduated from Southern Methodist with bachelor of divinity and master of arts degrees. He earned a doctorate in theology from Iliff School of Theology in Denver, Colorado. Rev. Foote also held a doctor of divinity degree from Miami University in Oxford, Ohio. And—the lanky West Texan played the piano.

Prior to coming to First Methodist he had traveled extensively in Europe, Africa and the Far East. His books included *Keys to Conquest*, *Just Plain Bread*, and *Lamps Without Oil*. As guest chaplain, in 1950 Dr. Foote led the United States Senate in prayer.

Rev. Foote, during his time in Dayton, wrote sermonettes for the local newspaper. He continued this practice and soon these words of inspiration appeared regularly in the *Star-Telegram*. Widely praised, he told reporter Frances Edwards, "Some of my most prized notes of appreciation have come from persons of the Roman Catholic and Jewish faiths."[14] The newspaper published fifty of the sermonettes in a book entitled *Footnotes, Sidewalk Sermonettes for Saints and Sinners*.

Barely settled into his office, the new pastor soon learned what the officials of the church considered their major problem. Even with ninety-two rooms, First Methodist was bursting at the seams. With growth from 3,000 in 1931 to 4,400 in 1951, it became evident they needed more space. They built a youth center, Epworth Hall, in 1955. A three story brick and stone structure, the architect designed it to harmonize with the sanctuary, historian Williams wrote. "On the first floor was a four lane bowling alley, a clothing bank, teen club rooms for youth activities, a Jamboree Room, kitchen, game room for ping-pong, hobbies, a small gym, and a snack bar."[15] The second floor contained offices and classrooms, a gymnasium complete with lockers, showers and dressing rooms. The third floor was devoted to the (James R.) Hill Memorial Library, a craft shop and a four-room apartment used as living quarters by one of the staff members.

Almost no public buildings were air-conditioned when the congregation built its sanctuary back in 1930. They included an open court with a stone pulpit built into the exterior wall. For many years they placed folding chairs in the courtyard and held summer evening services outdoors. With the arrival of air-conditioning, they seldom used the space until 1956 when Rev. Gaston Foote transformed the open court into the Garden Garth. A gift from Mrs. B. S. Walker provided for landscaping in keeping with the Gothic architecture.

One of the most interesting events in the church's history occurred in 1956. Twenty-eight children presented a musical program. Unique, because they came from *Casa Materna* in Naples, Italy, the only link between American and Italian Methodism at the time. While in Fort Worth the youngsters got a taste of Texas, riding horses and eating a chuck-wagon supper at parishioner Ray Smyth's ranch. Without the support of the Methodists, these and hundreds of other Italian children would be homeless.

Adding more international flavor, in 1957 Rev. Foote traveled to Moscow, Russia as the only local minister to participate in the world conference sponsored by the *Christian Century*, a nondenominational Chicago weekly. In his absence Congressman Jim Wright and Brooks Hayes, president of the Southern Baptist Convention, filled the pulpit.

At the April 1958 General Conference the leadership changed the official name of the denomination to the United Methodist Church and First Methodist became First United Methodist. That same year Texas Wesleyan College honored Dr. Foote with the doctor of literature degree.

Following Dr. Gaston Foote's pastorate the bishop assigned another powerhouse of preaching, Dr. Barry Bailey, to the flagship church. Bailey grew up in Sheridan, Arkansas and graduated from Hendrix College. He earned a B.D. at SMU's Perkins School of Theology. Graduate studies took him to Edinburgh, Scotland, Frankfurt, Germany, and Jerusalem. Centenary College and Southwestern University awarded him honorary doctoral degrees.

A prolific writer, Dr. Bailey authored four books: *Especially for You, We Are Not Alone, Living with the Unexpected,* and *A Picture of God.* He also reached out to thousands through First Methodist's televised ministry. He is best remembered for his persuasive preaching.

Rev. Wayne Day came to Fort Worth from St. Paul United Methodist Church in Houston, a congregation in the Rice University area he helped revitalize. "He was also the founding pastor of Klein United Methodist Church in suburban Houston, which for many years was the fastest growing church in that region,"[16] the *Star-Telegram's* Jim Jones said of the spectacled minister. Religionists praised Day for his ability to bring healing to a troubled church. He needed this skill in 1995 because the congregation still reeled over the resignation of Rev. Barry Bailey.

At first, Rev. Day kept the severely divided church alive, but later in his ministry divisions arose over the music program and staff layoffs. Sunday, February 23, 2003 all seemed well behind the high Gothic towers. Dr. Wayne Day preached his prepared sermon. The congregations sang "Let There Be Peace on Earth," little realizing the fragile peace of First Methodist would soon be broken. "Later the same day, Day delivered a shocker,"[17] according to the lead story on page one of the local newspaper. He announced his resignation.

Citing the stress of leading a large church, (First Methodist counted a membership of 11,000), the fifty-seven-year-old man of the cloth indicated he might even retire from the ministry. "I've served large churches for almost three decades, and there are a lot of problems involved," he told Jim Jones. "I'm ready for a rest and to explore some new directions."[18]

First Methodist Church 800 W. Fifth St. Courtesy First Methodist Church

One of the problems concerned terminating the church's TV broadcasts. "For 27 years, the 9:30 a.m. Sunday service at First Methodist Church has been a staple for many TV viewers in the area,"[19] John Gutierrez-Muir reported. Belt-tightening, combined with increased costs of air time, caused church leaders to switch to the Internet and free videos as substitutes. Disagreements over the direction of the music program added to tensions within the church.

Rev. Day pointed to his revitalizing and expansion of programs for children and youth as his greatest achievement at First Methodist. However, in resigning he said, "I feel I can no longer be an effective leader and a healing force. . . in part because of many of the divisions in the church. . . . It's a great concern to me that the stress has begun to affect my emotional and physical health."[20]

He called for a healing shepherd. On July 8, 2003 the church ushered in a new era with the naming of Rev. Tim Bruster of Georgetown as the senior minister. "I'm excited about being appointed to First United Methodist Church,' Bruster wrote in an e-mail to the *Star-Telegram* from England."[21] He returned to Texas in time to preach his first sermon September 7, 2003.

Tim Bruster, born and reared in Louisiana, brought twenty-five years experience to the pulpit of First Methodist. He graduated from Centenary College in Shreveport with a bachelor of arts in religion in 1981. His master and doctor of divinity he earned from Perkins School of Theology in 1985 and 1991. Bruster led churches in Tyler and Houston before his most recent pastorate, First United Methodist Church of Georgetown. Bearded and mustached, his youthful appearance and youthful approach to church activities attracted him to First Methodist's staff and lay leadership. "He draws energy from working with people,"[22] a former associate said of him. Another recalled, "He brings a lot of personal warmth and also he is a great mender of fences,"[23]

Rev. Harvey Ozmer, superintendent of the Central Texas Conference's Temple District praised Rev. Bruster's preaching style. "Tim is a marvelous preacher. He has great spiritual depth and sound theology that is deeply rooted in United Methodism."[24] That will be needed as he follows in the footsteps of preaching giants at First Methodist. His congregation wishes him well.

■   ■   ■

Saint Paul Methodist Episcopal Church
1877 to 1930

(This history is taken from *The First One Hundred and Twenty Years of the First United Methodist Church of Fort Worth*, written by J. D. F. Williams, D.D.)

The conflict between the northern and southern branches of Methodism led to the Plan of Separation in 1844. In Fort Worth the two merged in 1930. They sold St. Paul's property to the First Methodist Church and many of the parishioners joined that church. The events leading up to that time are told below as they were written.

"Saint Paul Methodist Episcopal Church takes its place along with the other church buildings which were homes of the First Methodist Church congregation,"[25] Williams wrote. He quotes from a history in the Dedication Souvenir booklet, dated February 24, 1924, furnished by Mrs. Kate Looney, a former member of St. Paul's and later a member of First Methodist.

"St. Paul's Methodist Episcopal Church was organized December 4, 1877, with thirty charter members. . . . The first service was held in the old Masonic Hall on East Belknap Street, and in January, 1878 the lots at Ninth and Main Streets were purchased on which the parsonage and church were erected, the first service being held therein on May 4, 1878. In 1884 the building became too small to accommodate the membership and was enlarged by the addition of two wings and a tower with an eight-hundred pound bell, and the auditorium was reseated with opera chairs.

"In the year 1887, under the pastorate of the Rev. J. P. Dimmitt, a wonderful revival was conducted in the Church by the Pastor, and nearly three hundred conversions occurred, and the membership of the Church was largely increased.

"The construction of the Church at Seventh and Lamar Streets was begun in the year 1899; the cornerstone being laid on the 12th day of May, 1890, the building was two years under construction. It was dedicated by Bishop John Waldon. This building was used by its membership until its destruction by fire on February 8, 1920. Following the fire, the membership worshipped in the Y.W.C.A. Hall on Main Street, until the completion of the temporary buildings at the present location at Tenth and Burnet Streets, which were occupied in the month of April, 1920.

"During the pastorate of Rev. J. F. Boeye a mortgage on the property at Seventh and Lamar Streets, which had been such a heavy burden upon the membership, was paid off, and at a Jubilee service, held on November 13th, 1910, the mortgages were publicly burned, amid the rejoicing of the membership.

"Ground was broken for the present new building on July 20, 1923, and on September 3rd the corner stone was laid. The plans for the completed Church call for additional wings in which will be ample Sunday School rooms, gymnasium and club rooms for the young people, the erection of which in the near future is the hope of the membership. . . ."[26]

An article in the July 4, 1890 *Fort Worth Daily Gazette* told of Bishop Godsell's donation of furnishing the altar, pulpit, furniture, chiming bells and organ, as a memorial to his mother.

When Rev. J. W. Bergin pastored the church, St. Paul and First Methodist held a series of united open air services. These meetings led to the unification of the two. "Out of the equity from St. Paul property, the parsonage of 1111 Elizabeth Boulevard was bought,"[27] Williams noted. For a complete listing of the ministers who served St. Paul Church see the Williams history.

Following the merger the St. Paul building housed the Little Theater, and later the People's Museum. The building also served as a rallying point for a number of evangelistic campaigns. A small article in the *Star-Telegram* on June 23, 1938 served as the historic structure's obituary. "Demolition of the old St. Paul's Methodist Church Building at Tenth and Burnet Streets, to begin in a few weeks, will mark the final chapter in what is probably the most colorful and unusual history of any church ever established in Fort Worth."[28] A parking lot serving the Medical Arts Building and the United States Courthouse took its place.

■   ■   ■

Allen Chapel African Methodist Episcopal Church—1870

George Richard Allen withdrew from St. George Methodist Church in Philadelphia in 1787 and started worshiping in an old blacksmith shop. He established Bethel Church and became the first bishop of the African Methodist Episcopal Church. Following the 1865 news of the emancipation of Texas slaves, AME circuit riders spread out from Galveston to establish churches, including Allen Chapel. "The oldest and largest African Methodist Episcopal Church in Fort Worth, the congregation was organized about 1870 by the Reverend Moody, a pioneer circuit rider, and five area settlers,"[29] Clyde McQueen recorded in *Black Churches in Texas*. They named the Fort Worth church in Allen's honor. Congregant Joe Standifer in 1982 compiled the Elm Street church's history.

"Among the five who gathered with Rev. Moody was Mrs. Emily Patterson, grandmother of Mr. Elvis Guinn and great-grandmother of Dr. James E. Guinn III and Dr. Edward W. Guinn (see *History of the Fort Worth Medical Community*), both of Fort Worth. Mrs. Patterson's daughter, Emma, was married to Professor James E. Guinn. Both were pioneer black teachers in Tarrant County, and James E. Guinn Elementary School was named in honor of Professor Guinn, who also served as its first black principal."[30]

The small flock met in members' homes until facilities were built at the present site. "The first formal meeting place was a one-room house located in the 1000 block of East Second Street. A few months later the meeting place was a shanty with boxed-in walls and a cobblestone floor. In 1873 a small one-room brick building was the place of worship." Professor Henry H. Butler, for whom the Butler Housing Project was named, charged ten cents a day for students to attend his classes in the church building. "The membership increased, interest in the church mounted, and a larger red brick building became the place of worship,"[31] Standifer wrote. Deed records dated March 2, 1878 record the sale by L. A. Cannon of a tract of land fifty by one hundred feet on the west side of Elm to trustees R. Lawson, George Reed and H. Thomas.

The congregation began a major construction project in 1887. Hard financial times caused the leadership to plead for a miracle. It came in the person of Margaret W. Peltz, who paid the lien and helped the church avoid foreclosure. From those first buildings, two others—including time in a tent during construction—housed the flock until they erected the present sanctuary at 116 Elm Street.

"There was a prevailing conviction in the mind of the founders of this church that eventually a majestic, imposing structure would be its permanent place of worship. With this thought in mind, the members decided to raze their place of worship, . . .and build a new church in that location,"[32] according to Standifer. They moved into the new one in 1912.

Rev. S. R. Jenkins proposed yet another church be built. More than one hundred parishioners pledged financial support. They were not looking to become a part of history, but their names are inscribed on a marble slab in the north vestibule. Those who donated $25.00 had their names etched in the art glass windows. Erected on a "pay as you go" plan, they finished the $20,000 facility in 1914. The yellow pressed brick sanctuary seated 1,350. Dr. James Guinn, in a 1991 interview recalled the days when "you had to arrive as much as 30 minutes early to be seated."[33] The church is of particular significance because William Sidney Pittman, son-in-law of Booker T. Washington, designed

Allen Chapel AME Church 116 Elm St. Courtesy Allen Chapel AME Church

the handsome Gothic Revival building. It contained a main auditorium with a three-quarter balcony, a gallery, basement and classrooms. "The dining room and kitchen in the basement were originally used as an economic department for training people for the solution of the strained servant problem existing in Fort Worth at that time. The basement also had a day nursery, where children could be left while their parents 'worked out,'"[34] Standifer noted.

The congregation first installed the memorial altar furnishings, the brass candelabra, and altar cross. Next they purchased a silver communion service, thanks to a donor. "A beautiful lectern and pulpit, designed to match the other church furniture, was placed in the building. The pipe organ is one of the most beautiful musical instruments in this country, consisting of many sets of pipes, sounded by compressed air and played by means of several keyboards. It is a fitting addition to this beautiful church, for after all no church as lovely as this is complete without an appropriate organ,"[35] the historian concluded.

The joyful congregation dedicated the modified Gothic structure July 22, 1914. "The cornerstone ceremony was conducted on the church grounds, and the cornerstone was laid by the most worshipful Prince Hall Grand Lodge, Free and Accepted Mason, jurisdiction of Texas."[36]

According to Standifer, "The church has been known by three names. Deed records indicate the original name of the church was The African Methodist Episcopal Church of Fort Worth. The Fort Worth city directory of 1894-1895 lists Rev. C. A. Harris as the pastor of the African M. E. Church. The city directory of 1896-1897 names it Allen's Chapel A. M. E. Church. In subsequent issues of the Fort Worth city directories the 's was omitted and thus the name Allen Chapel AME Church came into use as it is presently."[37] Since the historian wrote his account, the church has taken on another designation, the Historic Allen Chapel. In 1984 the National Register of Historic Places included it in that select group.

Through all these names the church on the northeast edge of downtown has been a grounding place for generations of African-American Methodists. Dr. Daryl B. Ingram led the church for eleven years before his elevation to Presiding Elder of the Conference.

Dr. Gregory H. Kimble came to Allen Chapel in 2002. Had he lived in another time, he might have been a military advisor to warrior King David since his first career was as an army officer in armor and infantry divisions. Following his service Kimble attended Southwestern Baptist Theological Seminary, earning a master of divinity and master of religious education. Kimble also holds a doctor of ministry from Howard University in Washington, D.C. He now preaches about King David to a congregation numbering about 500. Prior to his assignment in Fort Worth, he pastored a church in Sherman and was an army chaplain for five years.

In 1982 the congregation refurbished the interior of Allen Chapel to its original luster and in 2003 senior minister Dr. Gregory Kimble is hard at work to see that the exterior is restored to its former glory. He spoke in a reverential voice when describing the member's unbounding love for their church. His goal is to work with them as they seek to regain the prominence they had in the past.

■   ■   ■

Morning Chapel Christian Methodist Church—1873

The Colored Methodist Episcopal Church in America was organized in 1870. An 1868 report listed fifty colored members in the Fort Worth circuit. "The Colored Methodist Espiscopal Church has since changed its name to the Christian Methodist Episcopal Church. While it is an autonomous Church, it still holds fraternal relations with the United Methodist Church,"[38] according to historian J. D. F. Williams.

A document dated 1985 gave a history of the Morning Chapel CME Church. December 15, 1870 the essayist wrote,

". . . will always be an historic day for our Church. It is its birthday. Jackson, Tennessee and Liberty C.M.E. Church, of which the Reverend Issac Lane, later to become the fifth Bishop of our Church, was Pastor, will always be historic, for it was in the above named city and church that the organizing General Conference of our Church was held. Some people think the name 'Liberty' was prophetic. It was here that a great step toward liberty, freedom and dignity was taken by the C.M.E. Church, with blessings and help of the Southern Methodists."[39]

A few faithful and illustrious pioneers joined Anderson Caville and H. C. Williams in organizing the Morning Chapel Colored Methodist Episcopal Church in 1873. Caville paid Stephen Terry $150.00 for a lot at Sixth and

Crump Streets. Caville built the first structure, but it fell. He raised more money and began to rebuild. He and Tom Mason carried the financial load for the new church, and without the assistance given by fellow Methodist George Mulkey, the church would have failed from the start. Ten years later, under the leadership of Rev. H. A. Booker, the congregation moved into a new, stone edifice at Fifth and Crump Streets. In 1907 the Cotton Belt Railroad bought the church property. Rev. G. H. Harlee and his flock moved two blocks north to Third and Crump. The city condemned that structure and Rev. Alfred F. Johnson preached to his congregation ". . .in the upstairs auditorium of the K of P Hall on East Second and Crump Streets,"[40] according to an 1977 history. Under the leadership of Rev. George A. Simpson, who served from 1934 to 1936, the church was razed and rebuilt in its present architectural stone structure. A mural painting by Mrs. Pauline Belew depicted Christ praying in a wilderness setting. The vivid blue of the sky immediately draws the eye of the worshiper to the magnificent scene set above the choir loft. New pews made

Morning Chapel CME Church 903 E. 3rd. St. Courtesy Morning Chapel CME Church

for comfortable seating. "A new Hammond Church Organ and Chimes were installed, lending much grace and spiritual fervor to the worship services,"[41] the historian noted.

Rev. M. E. Bradley pastored the church during 1949 when the worst flood in history devastated the city. He "worked untiring transporting people in his car from the flood area, wading in water up to his waist line for about eight hours helping victims to safety. He opened church doors not only for his members, but for everyone. Others caught the spirit and food and clothing came from everywhere, the victims had a place to stay, food and clothing. This was his contribution to the needy with no compensation attached,"[42] according to a church history.

The death of beloved minister Rev. George Simpson saddened the congregation in 1948. Funeral services were conducted at the church, then about thirty cars and two bus loads of mourners made the trek to Gainesville for burial.

As Methodist custom dictated, several ministers led the historic church over the years. Under the supervision of Rev. J. C. Darden, who served from 1952 to 1959, the congregation erected the H. P. Porter Education Building. Rev. Lindsey Rucker, Darden's successor, preached in the newly air-conditioned sanctuary during his 1959 to 1966 tenure. Rev. William A Schultz in the late 1960s witnessed the remodeling of the sanctuary and education building. "The church sanctuary has taken on a new look," according to the church history, "with new windows, new doors, bamboo wall-paneling, new cushioned pews, wall-to-wall carpeting, new lights, mural in choir loft refinished—changing the image of the church to an edifice of spiritual beauty and comfort."[43] They also installed a new Hammond organ and pianos.

In 2003 the church proudly displayed a banner proclaiming its 135th anniversary. Rev. Manuel Henderson preaches with a strong voice. "Do I have a witness?" he asks and the congregation supports him with affirmations as they participate in another spirit-filled service.

■   ■   ■

Handley United Methodist Church-1877

All around the red brick, modified American Gothic style church on Forest Avenue, street signs designate the area as "Historic Handley." Streets such as Craig, Kell and Routt are named for founding members of the Methodist church when it was in the town of Handley. Five generations of the Routt family have worshiped at Handley Methodist.

In 2002 the congregation celebrated its 125th anniversary by recalling its past. Frances Brewer evoked memories of her days as a five-year-old in Sunday School at the original church. "Mrs. Howell was the Superintendent, and she always wore big, beautiful hats."[44]

Charles Whittle wrote that his "... was a "there" family- when the Church met, we were there." Rosa Lee Weiler recalled, "In the basement of the 'old white church,' there were the times as a preschooler, I watched the ladies quilt and can cakes to sell, and there was a carnival/party where several Methodist men stood behind a sheet with their pants legs rolled up while their wives tried to identify their husbands."[45]

Robert C. Warden wrote of his early ministry post there, and then the growth he experienced. "Serving Handley was one of life's culminating events for me. Handley, for better or worse, helped mold me into much of

Handley United Methodist Church 2929 Forest Ave. Courtesy Handley United Methodist Church

what I am today. The experiences, the ministry, the pastoral and support team, the laity, and the Fort Worth East Side community fed me in ways too numerous to describe."[46] Major Warden is now an Army Chaplain stationed at Ft. Jackson, SC.

Mrs. Billie Brown, in an essay, noted that a hundred years ago, "The preacher spent his life traveling. He lived with the people who were members of the various charges. . .. Horace Bishop speaks of having fourteen regular appointments and preaching twenty-four times a month. He never took break-fast and dinner at the same place except on Friday. That was laundry day. . . Mrs. Philpott looked after his laundry and mending. He kept his wardrobe in one of the his saddle bags, and his books in the other."[47]

A Rev. Womack (first name unknown, perhaps Drury, but J. B. Womack was in charge of the Fort Worth Mission at the time, so it is probable this is the one) and a few residents of Handley organized a church in November 1877 as the Handley Charge of the Arlington and Village Creek Circuit, Fort Worth District, North West Texas Conference. Rev. J. J. Cannafax, also the first school teacher, preached in a small school house located in the 100 block of Forest Avenue. The school had a door in each end and two windows on opposite sides. The building lacked a proper foundation, and hogs fre-quently rooted in the cool dirt beneath the floor until Rev. Cannafax shooed them away.

In 1882 a group, ecumenical by necessity, came together to build Union Church. The Methodists used it two Sundays a month, the Baptists one, the Presbyterians one, and others held services occasionally in the afternoons. This arrangement worked until 1907 when the Methodists and Baptists with-drew and built their own churches.

In Handley UMC archives, historian Elvie Walker recorded the story of the old church bell as told to her by Katie Garrett. "Her grandfather, C. W. Wilson, and another man took a team of horses and the wagon to downtown Fort Worth early one morning to get the bell. It was difficult getting the wagon up the hill on Lancaster to Fort Worth on the old sand roads. Now think about it. I really hadn't thought of that being a hill to downtown. Coming back was even a greater chore. The wagon sunk into the sand and the men didn't get back until after dark."[48] At the 1907 division of the property, Alexander McBee asked for and received the bell. It is now part of a memorial on Handley Drive.

Following J. J. Canafax, the Central District assigned many preachers, usually for one or two years.

The first Methodist church, built in 1908 on the southeast corner of what is now Church and Forest, had fifty members. Rev. W. T. Jones, the first full time minister, came in 1916. In 1922 Rev. W. C. Hilburn's family received "modern" renovations to the parsonage—an indoor bathroom and natural gas piped into the house.

The congregation had outgrown the church plant by the 1920s, and under the leadership of Rev. Hilburn, they enlarged the sanctuary and put the bell in a tower beside the church. "Mrs. Flora South, a long time teacher in Sunday School, would come early each Sunday and ring the bell,"[49] Brown noted.

In 1942 Rev. A. W. Franklin rejoiced with his flock as they celebrated paying off the building debt. That same year, in the midst of World War II, they bought an army barrack for use as additional classrooms. The war over, the congregation began plans for a new, enlarged church.

Under the leadership of Rev. J. D. F. Williams, pastor from 1946 to 1948, they bought a lot on Forest, the present location of the sanctuary. Rev. Hubert Crane continued the movement as they started a three stage building program. The congregation moved into its new home, valued at $180,000 in 1954 dollars, and on July 11, Rev. Fred Benkley preached the first sermon there. Located two blocks north of the original church, the new one had an open court garden in the center where they held summer services and socials. "The structure   . . . has classrooms for all departments of the Church School, a fellowship hall serving as both sanctuary and banquet hall, a modern kitchen . . . offices, a library and church parlor,"[50] according to a *Star-Telegram* description. For the second unit, Bishop William C. Martin, and District Superintendent Rev. Hayden Edwards joined Pastor Nick Kupferle at the March 27, 1960 ground breaking ceremony. Miss Maggie Smith, the oldest member of the flock, joined the dignitaries in turning a spade of dirt.

Veteran member Betty Bryan remembered Rev. Kupferle's tenure as one of growth and outreach. "His sermons were excellent. He could call everybody by name and involved the whole congregation in activities. We had musicals with the youth, and dinners for all ages,"[51] she said.

The congregation and Pastor John Wesley Ford consecrated the third unit, the Educational Building, on April 12, 1970. Counting property bought and donated, the church now owned most of the block bounded by Handley Drive, Routt, Forest and Craig. At this time membership exceeded 1,600 and their property was valued at well over $500.000.

A series of ministerial assignments marked the passage of the 1970s and 1980s. In the 1990s in keeping with the movement to advance women in ministry, Rev. Ann Stevens served as senior minister. Described as an excellent preacher, the congregation readily accepted their first female senior pastor.

"She made this church a family church," according to Betty Bryan. Stevens organized activities for all ages and interests. Soon parishioners could join a Bible study class, a diet group, or learn to line dance. She and Mr. Stevens entertained at their Springtown home. "She (Rev. Stevens) would say she was going to the farm for the weekend and I imagined a modest country house. The first time we (our seniors class) saw it, it just blew us away it was so beautiful,"[52] Bryan recalled with a chuckle. Rev. Stevens retired in 2000.

Rev. Gus Guthrie likes the friendly small town atmosphere of the Handley community. In his third year there he said, "It may be part of Fort Worth, but it doesn't know it."[53] The narrow streets and third generation families remind him of small towns where he grew up. A "preacher's kid," Guthrie lived in several places, but considers himself a West Texan. He earned a degree in accounting at McMurry, a Master of Divinity at TCU's Brite Divinity School, and a Ph.D. in marriage and family counseling at Denton's TWU.

On the day of Pentecost, "And suddenly from heaven there came a sound like the rush of a violent wind, and it filled the entire house where they were sitting," according to Acts 2:2. On April 16, 2002 suddenly from the west there came a sound like the roar of a freight train and a violent wind and it tore the roof off Handley United Methodist Church's sanctuary. The tornado damaged the educational wing to a lesser degree, and fortunately the church records were spared.

As an example of the friendliness of the community, Guthrie said neighbors as well as congregants helped clean up the debris. After getting a new roof and interior repairing and painting, the hundreds of volunteers celebrated with a "Whirlwind Party." Hamburgers, hot dogs, cold drinks, and lots of fun were the order of the day.

Rev. Guthrie honors the past as he looks to the future. He visits pioneer members, seeks to serve younger ones, and plans for a time when the church will expand its ministry to meet the needs of the changing, but still historic neighborhood.

■   ■   ■

Christ Methodist—1883 (Swedish/Mulkey Memorial/St Mark)

In March 1883, with twenty charter members, the Swedish Methodist Episcopal Church became the second oldest Methodist church in Fort Worth because Handley Methodist was still in the town of Handley. Rev. P. S. Juhline was the first pastor. Later that year Rev. S. E. Carlander, in poor health and seeking a warmer climate, took charge of the church. "He wrote in the *Sandabudet*, a Swedish Methodist paper, about the advantages Texas had over the northern states. These advertisements brought a number of Methodist members from Illinois, Minnesota, and Michigan to Fort Worth," [54] historian Ruth R. Stone recorded.

In 1884 the leadership of Swedish Methodist bought a sixty by one hundred foot lot on Broadway Street from W. H. Nye for $500.00. They erected a frame sanctuary and parsonage. All went well until the great fire of 1909 (see page 71). Following the devastation the parishioners rebuilt and in 1914 the Ilseng family donated a piano, comfortable pews and invited the members to a banquet. Bishop W. O. Shapard dedicated the new building. Services were in the Swedish language until 1920, and in 1924 the parishioners changed the name to Broadway Methodist Episcopal Church.

"September 5, 1930 the trustees of St. Paul's Methodist Episcopal Church of Fort Worth merged with Broadway Methodist Episcopal at the Southern Annual Conference,"[55] according to Stone.

Meanwhile, another Methodist church congregation which would become Mulkey Memorial Methodist, matured in tandem with the Swedish Methodist Church. By 1888 the First Methodist Episcopal Church needed to start mission churches in the southern edge of the city. The leadership established Missouri Avenue (see page 181) and Mulkey Memorial.

As a young man George Mulkey made $1.00 a day riding the pony express route between Fort Worth and Waxahachie. With that he fed himself and his horse. He moved to Fort Worth in 1862 and became the first district clerk of Tarrant County, the first police and fire commissioner, and vice-president of the old Traders National Bank. A devout Methodist, he wanted to do something to honor the memory of his parents. His father, Rev. William Mulkey served the Methodist denomination more than fifty years as a minister and evangelist. George Mulkey accepted Bishop Joseph S. Key's suggestion that a church in their memory would be fitting.

At its first organizational meeting, twelve people convened to form Mulkey Memorial Church. In November 1890 sixty-four charter members welcomed Rev. John M. Barcus as their first pastor. They met in the afternoons in the Swedish church until their sanctuary was ready. Under the leadership of Rev. H. A. Boaz, the membership grew to 350.

In 1907 the congregation moved into their new church located on the corner of St. Louis and Cannon. The building, sixty feet wide and forty feet long, had a seating capacity for 500. Designed like European cathedrals, its high ceiling provided a wisp of coolness in the Texas heat. Mulkey Memorial, like the Swedish Methodist, Broadway Baptist, and Broadway Presbyterian went up in flames in the great fire of 1909. And like the other congregations, Mulkey Memorial immediately began to rebuild.

For the next thirty years the churches ministered to separate congregations, but in 1939 Bishop Holt appointed a district conference committee to consider merging the two. Laymen from each congregation approved the merger and in November 1940 the conference officially linked them. They took the name Broadway-Mulkey Methodist Episcopal Church, South. At that time Mulkey had 299 members and Broadway had 106 on their rolls. They sold the Broadway property to Fort Worth Bible Church and met at the St. Louis facility.

"On February 2, 1945 Mel Faulk, county clerk and member of Broadway-Mulkey, instructed Judge G. L. Robertson to prepare an instrument for recording the new name of St. Mark Methodist Church,"[56] Stone noted. In the following years the congregation made improvements, but the building became unsafe for occupancy. The conference offered new sites in the Ridgmar or Hallmark addition. In 1955 the parishioners voted for the Hallmark residential area. St. Mark bought three acres on the South Freeway, broke ground on April 25, 1959, and moved into their new home on June 26, 1960. Pastor Charles Chadwick had the honor of preaching the first sermon there, but former minister Rev. G. W. French received credit for maneuvering the congregation through the relocation process.

A *Fort Worth Press* story captured the emptiness of the old sanctuary. Reporter Seth Kantor wrote of the stillness. "It's been almost 40 years since her most interesting day. She was 31 years old then. It was the day Ormer Locklear was buried."[57] He explained that Locklear was the toast of the movie world, both as star and stunt flyer when he died in a plane crash. Charlie Chaplin, Mary Pickford, Tom Mix, Fattie Arbuckle and Buster Keaton sent floral offerings. "Half the people of Fort Worth, 50,000 of them, lined the streets to see what may have been the longest funeral procession in the city's history." People came in horse-drawn buggies and cars to travel the route from St. Mark's to Greenwood Cemetery.

On October 3, 1983, the congregation celebrated its 100th anniversary. They received proclamations from the Fort Worth Chamber of Commerce, the Tarrant County Commissioners court and Mayor Bob Bolen read the city's congratulation in person. Former parishioners renewed ties with old friends. Eight former ministers—V. Cyrus Barcus, Charles Chadwick, G. W. French, William L. Hankla, Bob Messer, W. T. Reynolds, Roy Roland and Paul Sandstrom—joined the well-wishers. The church adopted the challenge "Moving into a second century of service."

Still another move occurred when St. Mark chose property further to the southwest. In 1984, when they considered moving, the graying congregation felt the need to attract younger members. To do so they needed to build in newer neighborhoods, away from the increasingly commercialization of the freeway. They found the Meadowcreek area the ideal location and purchased five acres near McCart Avenue. With their new home, they took a new name. On October 18, 1990 the flock chose "Christ," rather than "Harvest" or "Southwest." The red brick facility, completed in 1992, is of modern eclectic design in its use of elements. Stained glass windows and a cross mounted on the high-peaked roof give it an identity. In the Fellowship Hall, a full size quilt depicts the history of the church. Hundreds of thousands of loving stitches made needlepoint pictures of the three churches, and squares embroidered with names of members complete the wall hanging. Outside, three large wooden crosses on the front lawn, which represent the crucifixion scene, are visible from Sycamore School Road.

Rev. Bruce Baker led the church during the transition period. Rev. John Robbins succeeded him and today another Baker, no relation, leads a congregation composed of the desired mix of veteran members and new families.

This Baker would make an interesting subject for "Trivial Pursuit." Which Methodist minister was raised a Presbyterian? Which Methodist minister did the Texas House of Representatives in the seventy-seventh Legislature declare "Minister of the Day?" Which Methodist minister pastored a United Methodist church in Dublin, Ireland? Which Methodist minister is studying for a second doctoral degree, this one from the University of South Africa in Pretoria? The answer is Vaughn W. Baker.

The amiable minister graduated from Miami University in Ohio, and earned Master and Doctor of Theology degrees from Southern Methodist. In the United States Dr. Baker served four churches in Texas, the most recent in

Christ United Methodist Church 3301 Sycamore School Rd. Courtesy Christ United Methodist Church

Weatherford before he came to Christ United Methodist in January 2003. Here he appreciates both the history and the future of the church. "The people have received us very warmly and they are hungry to go forward. This is a small church, but the potential is great,"[58] he told an interviewer. "We are prayerfully seeking God's mind as to what we should do," he added.

Rev. Baker recalled he once pastored a church that had the option to adopt the name "Christ" which was his first choice. The congregation selected another name, but now he is at Christ Church. Coincidence or fulfillment of the adage "All good things come to those who wait?" Whichever, both he and the members of Christ United Methodist Church feel blessed by their association with each other.

■   ■   ■

St. Andrews—1888

Rev. James W. Moore, with fifteen charter members, organized St. Andrews United Methodist Church. At first the congregation worshiped two Sundays a month at Morning Chapel C. M. E. (see page 168) Rev. Moore secured property on Ninth Street, then called "Ham Branch," and met there. He built the first church. The Bishop sent a Reverend Ford and he, because the small group had little money, preached for a year without pay. By the time Rev. D. C. Lacy came, things were better, and was the the first to use the three-room parsonage.

Rev. J. M. Wormley pastored when the congregation bought property on East Terrell and moved the church building there. Trouble awaited. "It was blown from it's foundation and a heavy debt incurred trying to build a more substantial foundation,"[59] In 1917 they worshiped in the "big South Main Street Methodist Church" historian Natalie Johnson wrote. Later they worshiped at an East Rosedale Street sanctuary. They bought their present home, the former Missouri Avenue Methodist Church at 522 Missouri, in 1950. For a time, on school days, the Southside Public School met there.

Carol Roark in *Fort Worth's Legendary Landmarks* offered this description of the historic building. "The asymmetrical yellow-brick church has a sandstone base and a steeply pitched hipped roof. Square towers—the main belfry tower is taller—with pyramidal pressed-metal roofs flank the curving entrance portico. The diverse design draws inspiration from the intricate ornamental detailing of architect Louis Sullivan in the terra cotta frieze bands and from the forms of the Prairie School in the extreme roof overhangs and general massing of the building. Fine stained glass windows, both Gothic-arched and rectangular, further enliven the facade. A three-story rectangular education building was built on the west side of the church about 1915."[60]

Over the years in these sanctuaries, many men of the cloth preached to sometimes large, sometimes small, congregations. After Rev. Moore got the church organized, between 1889 and 1905 the bishop assigned five ministers to the growing church. Rev. M. L. Kirkpatrick, 1904-1905, became the first minister to live in the parsonage. Another milestone, noted in Johnson's history, also occurred in 1905. During the pastorate of Rev. F. L. Thompson, the church hired their first organist, Miss Jimmie Norris. Until the congregation could buy one, she played on an organ loaned by Mrs. Madie Johnson.

From 1908 to 1915, under the guidance of Reverends A. Brown, Moses Smith, and I. H. Wyatt, the congregation "prospered financially and spiritually" according to the historian. The West Texas Conference listed the church as one of its largest. Rev. A. L. Cooper, from 1917 to 1921, preached at the Main Street church.

St. Andrew's United Methodist Church 522 Missouri. Courtesy St.Andrew's United Methodist Church

To pay for expansion, the women of the church raised substantial sums of money through bazaars. "At one time," Johnson recalled, "Sister Callie Cawthorne, a parishioner, raised six hundred dollars."[61] That was a lot of money in those days. With money on hand, the congregation purchased pews, a pipe organ and pulpit furniture.

Throughout its history, many outstanding preachers led the church. Rev. R. M. Davis pastored when the conference named St. Andrews ". . . the most esteemed rank in all around report to the District Conference as well as the Sunday School and Epworth League Conventions,"[62] historian Johnson wrote.

In addition to its exceptional preaching, for years Fort Worth citizens of all denominations heralded St. Andrews' music program as superb. Old timers recall the occasion when a choir concert, from anthems to spirituals, filled the Will Rogers Memorial Auditorium.

In 1939 the congregation changed its name from Methodist Episcopal to Methodist, and in 1968, as did other churches of the denomination, became known as United Methodist. Through the Great Depression and World War II years, St. Andrews provided spiritual and social services to the community.

Many community leaders have worshiped at St. Andrews. Congregant Edward J. Briscoe devoted his life to the children of Fort Worth. An elementary school is named for him. "L. Clifford Davis, one of Texas' premier civil-rights lawyers, is best known for spearheading the legal battles to desegregate the Fort Worth school district and to dismantle the Jim Crow public accommodation barriers,"[63] according to the history. Clifford L. Davis Elementary School is named in his honor. (For more on Judge Davis see *History of the Fort Worth Legal Community.*) Dr. R. A. Ransom, Jr. renown roentneologist, like those listed above, drew spiritual strength from membership in this vital church.

The post-war period saw changes in the old, near south side neighborhood. Young white families bought homes in newer sections of the city. Missouri Avenue Methodist membership dropped from 323 to 169 in a six year period. A 1950 story by reporter Mack Williams revealed that only fifty-one members lived near the church. After much discussion, sometimes heated, that congregation voted 42 to 25 in favor of selling the property to St. Andrews.

The new owners undertook a remodeling project that changed the sanctuary to a more conventional arrangement by taking out a movable wall. They held the first services on May 20, 1951. The 2003 era sanctuary features three sections of maple pews, fitted with hunter green cushions. Three large stained glass windows give both light and beauty to the worship center. Over the choir loft, etched in gold tone parishioners are reminded "The Lord is in His Holy Temple let all the earth keep silence before Him." Ministers at the Missouri Avenue sanctuary included Reverends J. H. Carruthers until 1956, L. L. Hayes, 1956-1971; Eric C. Purnell, 1971-1984; Patrick Williams, 1984-1987; Doyle R. Allen, 1987-1993; and Georgia M. Allen, 1993-1998 who became pastor of Polytechnic United Methodist (see page 185). Reverends Alfred G. Sanford and Chauncey S. Nealy pastored until the turn of the new millennium. Of this group, Rev. L. L. Hayes, in addition to being a powerful preacher, led in civil rights and education movements.

Dr. Luther W. Henry spent much of his ministry in administrative positions. He led the Council on Ministries as associate director, then director, and was district superintendent for many years. During this period in his ministry the Henry family attended St. Andrews and his being named minister became a homecoming of sorts. Prior to this assignment he served as associate pastor at First United Methodist Church.

"St. Andrew's had been the flagship church in the Central Jurisdiction,"[64] he said in a recent interview. He accepted the challenge to help the historic South Side church regain its prominence as an important downtown congregation. To do that he reaches out with new programs and emphasis on attracting young families. Those young families joined many whose membership covered decades on an autumn Sunday in 2003. They heard Dr. Henry, in a distinct, but gentle voice encourage his congregants to "look at the life of Jesus to understand suffering and fairness."[65]

Issues of fairness and suffering are of traditional importance to Afro-Americans, and at St. Andrews, in addition to the United Methodist hymnal, parishioners sing from *Songs of Zion*. It contains both contemporary and traditional music, including songs classified as "Spirituals." Some musicologists contend Negro spirituals and New Orleans jazz are the only genres indigenous to the United States. Spirituals emanated from the hearts of the pre-Civil War slaves as potent outflowings of religious and social passion. They were the music of the "invisible church." These churches were secret places where the slaves held worship services. "In the preliterate era of slavery, the fuel of the 'invisible church' was the musical expression constantly fed by oral tradition,"[66] according to an essay in *Songs of Zion*.

The songs also aided field workers in productivity. The rhythm of a lively tune encouraged faster picking of cotton or doing whatever the task at hand. Also they allowed slaves to communicate in "secret code" without arousing white overseers's suspicions.

The majority of the words came from the Old Testament of the Bible. Its stories of Hebrews in bondage spoke to the oppressed people. "Go Down, Moses" and "Didn't My Lord Deliver Daniel?" had special meaning for them. From the New Testament they sang of Jesus' death in such songs as "Were You There When They Crucified My Lord?" and "He Nevuh Said a Mumblin' Word."

The conditions in which slaves lived influenced other texts. These songs spoke of life and death, suffering and sorrow, and grace and hope. "Deep River" tells of the slaves' yearning for freedom from worldly cares through death. "Swing Low Sweet Chariot" expressed the same theme.

Words to "De Gospel Train"—"Git on board, little children/ Git on board, little children/ Git on board, little children/ Dere's room for many a mo'" gave more than a hope for eternal life. At times they signaled that the Underground Railroad was active in the area.

"Wade in the Water" had a duel message. "Wade in the water/ wade in the water, children,/ wade in the water/ God's a gonna trouble the water," told runaway slaves to go into a river to foil bloodhounds picking up their scent.

The disruption of families and longing for tribal relatives were poignantly expressed in "Sometimes I feel like a motherless chile/ Sometimes I feel like a motherless chile/ Sometimes I feel like a motherless chile/ A long ways from home/ A long ways from home." The second refrain says "Sometimes I feel like I'm almos' gone," with the last part being, "Then I get down on my knees an' pray/ Get down on my knees an' pray."

Hope is revealed in a song such as "Balm in Gilead." The Promised Land, Heaven, and "over Jordan" were thought of as actual places, places of refuge.

The most important element of the song was the human voice. It provided contour, rhythm, texture, melody, tempo and text. Oft times the clapping of hands or tapping of feet provided the only accompaniment. Improvisation became one of the main stylistic features of this folk music and explains why today some singers improvise when performing songs such as the national anthem as well as spirituals.

The singing of these songs continued beyond the days of slavery. "In the 1870s, with the Fisk Jubilee Singers of Fisk University. . . the early spiritual went through an artistic metamorphosis that not only changed its form and appearance, but also helped make it a permanent American musical art form,"[67] the essayist in *Songs of Zion* noted. From these came gospel, blues and country—all songs telling stories of human emotion.

Today, through its music, preaching, and service to society, St. Andrews blends its proud heritage with ambitious plans for the future.

■   ■   ■

Missouri Avenue Methodist Church 1889-1950

As Methodists, and others, moved to the southern boundary of the city, the need for neighborhood churches developed. A few "south siders" from First Methodist organized Missouri Avenue Methodist in 1889. Originally they met in an old schoolhouse, then in 1895 built a sanctuary on property on the southeast corner of Missouri Avenue and Annie Street. When that property burned, they purchased three lots on the northwest corner from the old site. In 1904 they hired architect James Flanders of Dallas to design the sanctuary.

For almost fifty years the church provided spiritual nourishment to surrounding Methodists. However, as the neighborhood matured and the young people moved away to start families elsewhere, the Missouri Avenue church felt the decline. As stated above, the congregation voted to sell the property and erect a new church in the Morningside area. At a May 8, 1950 meeting of the Quarterly Conference, J. M. Dickson moved "that the cornerstone of the Missouri Ave. Methodist Church be placed in a prominent place in the new building."[68] The motion carried. With the end of one phase of history, many of the longtime members joined in the formation of Morningside Methodist and began a new phase in their spiritual lives.

Polytechnic Methodist—1892

Polytechnic United Methodist Church has had from its beginning a close relationship with Texas Wesleyan College. In 1881 the Methodist Church's Northern branch chartered the first college of that name, located in a rented downtown building. Later it became known as Fort Worth University. Historian C. C. Bock wrote of the Southern branch's efforts to establish their own institution. A committee led by Bishop Joseph Key selected a site on a hill four miles east of Fort Worth. "The chosen name, 'Polytechnic,' was a popular one for colleges in the period 1850-1900. It comes from the Greek *polytechnos*—skilled in many arts." In 1891 they constructed a two-story brick building with a high mansard roof, and until demolished a century later it was the oldest college building in continuous use in Tarrant County. "It was in this building that the Polytechnic Methodist Episcopal Church, South, was organized on January 3, 1892."[69] Rev. C. A. Evans presided.

"We organized a church with thirty-six members and more to follow, at the Polytechnic College last Sabbath. This membership consists largely of the faculty and students. . . . . The religious atmosphere which pervades there is an adequate reason for expecting an increase in membership by the conversion of sinners. To come in contact with such influence is to be convinced of the truth, and impressed with the beauty of Christianity,"[70] The Church Visitor noted January 8, 1892, only one week after the event.

Rev. Evans held services for eighteen months in the college building until a 50' x 80' church was erected on the southwest corner of the campus. Historian JoAnn Jenkins recalled, "Known as the 'Old House,' it was built in the style of rural churches of the day, with separate entrances for men and for women."[71]

By 1894 the bishop upgraded the church from its mission status, and Rev. E. V. Cox divided his time between it and a church ten miles north of the city. In 1896, Polytechnic, with 234 members, gained a full-time minister, D. C. Stark.

Felix M. Bransford joined the church as a student. Fifty years later he recalled, "(in the area) there were only 30 houses. In between there were farms and pastures and . . . cattle ranches. Neighboring towns of Handley and Forest Hill were hours away by the only means of transportation available at the time.

"For several years the church had no parsonage and for 15 years the church had no building of its own, during that time using the college chapel as a place of worship. In 1899 when I came to the college the parsonage was located on a corner of the present site of the William James School."[72]

The building about which Evans wrote belonged to the college. In 1909 both institutions were growing. It was time to build a "real" church. The school administration gave permission to erect a sanctuary on what is now the northeast corner of East Rosedale and Wesleyan Streets. The college would retain ownership of the land, but the church would have title to the building,"[73] historian Monette Fugate wrote.

Known as the second church, the two-story rectangular structure featured a hipped roof and orchre brick with contrasting yellow brick pilasters and quoins. At a cost of $30,000, the large pedimented front entrance with paired Ionic columns flanking the doors' arch created a grand entrance portico. "Come unto me" was inscribed over the entrance. Rev. E. B. Hawk preached, as a pot-bellied stove furnished heat in winter, and worshipers used cardboard "funeral home" fans in summer to augment whatever breeze might enter through the open windows. Hawk became dean of Southern Methodist University's Perkins School of Theology.

Fugate recorded some memories of the second church. "Forrest Markward can remember sitting in the unfinished basement and wriggling his bare toes in the dirt. Martha Hall Locker remembers Brother Mussett, a Civil War veteran, who was deaf and had a wooden leg. He would sit on the front pew and every now and then let out a loud shout." This frightened Martha and her sister, Margaret, until Mrs. Hall explained Mr. Mussett was shouting for joy. "Hugo Brandt, a lifetime member of this church, said his mother thought this was the grandest and most beautiful building she had ever seen."[74]

In 1920 the college bought the building. It is now the Nicholas Martin Hall, part of the Performing Arts Department.

The congregation made plans for the third church, located across the street west of the campus. The cornerstone carried the date 1921, but the construction lasted until 1926. A large handsome building, it was faced with polychrome brick. The three door front entrance, which looked to the east, was reached by a broad flight of steps. Above the doors, carved in Gothic letters, was "Polytechnic M. E. Church South." This alluded to its membership in the Methodist Episcopal branch of Methodism. Three-story stained glass windows depicted Latin crosses. Quoins of white smooth-cut limestone adorned the east and west walls.

The sanctuary followed the "Akron" plan. This style stressed the importance of the pulpit and the communion table—the places where the Gospel was preached and the Lord's Supper sacrament observed—with concentric seating facing them. Miss Willie Fayette Montgomery recalled an unexpected difficulty Rev. C. Q. Smith encountered. In 1926 he began the task of fitting the straight pews from the second church into the curved spaces of the third church. This required much skill in measuring and splicing, probably something not taught in seminary.

In memory of their son, Sam, pioneer grocer S. S. Dillow and his wife donated a large painting of Christ praying in the Garden of Gethsemane. It hung at the back of the pulpit.

After World War I, Fort Worth experienced a growth spurt that spread to nearby towns. In January 1922 the city annexed the City of Polytechnic, leaving the church and neighborhood to bear the name. Both survived the Great Depression and in 1941 the congregation made plans for a fiftieth anniversary celebration with a new name, Polytechnic Methodist Church.

Silliman Evans, to honor his father's memory, donated chimes. The plaque reads:

EVANS MEMORIAL CHIMES

THE CHIMES IN THE BELFRY OF THIS

CHURCH ARE IN MEMORY OF THE

REVEREND COLUMBUS ASBURY EVANS

1851-1922

WHO ORGANIZED THE POLYTECHNIC

METHODIST CHURCH JANUARY 2, 1892

AND WAS ITS FIRST PASTOR

Following World War II, returning servicemen and their young families settled in the Polytechnic neighborhood. Many of them were Baptists or Methodists. In 1947 the Polytechnic Baptist Church held its first services in the Austin stone building directly west of the Methodist church. Detroit turned out new cars to fill the void of years of shortage during the war, and Polytechnic Baptists and Methodists bought them by the hundreds. "With so many Methodists and Baptists arriving at the same time, all parking spaces were quickly filled,"[75] Fugate noted.

Membership in Polytechnic Methodist grew. People whose ages ranged from toddlers to those old enough to remember the "first church" were crowded into every nook and cranny. High schoolers met in a building across Ave. E.

Rev. Hayden Edwards, described as diplomatic, versatile and dynamic, began his ministry there in 1947. He immediately formed a committee to study the problem of overcrowding. After considering several options, it recommended selling the third church to the Baptists and building a new one. Wesleyan President Law Sone agreed to convey a part of the campus for the new structure in exchange for the use of classroom space during the week. A formula agreed to by both entities called for sharing the cost of utilities and maintenance.

Ground breaking ceremonies for the proposed $500,000 building at the corner of Collard and Rosedale were held Sunday afternoon, December 24, 1950. It was a festive day. Rev. Sid Anderson, missionary to China offered the prayer. Dr. P. E. Riley, first minister to preach in the third church reviewed the history of the congregation, and documents and coins were removed from the old cornerstone.

Throughout the construction phase, parishioners watched. A steel shortage during the 1951 Korean Peace Action led the builders to use pressed, laminated wood in the sanctuary's trusses. To save money they used natural limestone rather than the more expensive manufactured stone, and opted not to have a steeple on the chapel. At one time the magnificent east rose window almost felt the budget cutter's red pencil, but Mr. and Mrs. Clarence Epperly came to the rescue, and through the years the window has inspired worshipers with its multicolored beauty.

Jenkins, quoting from the Tarrant County Historic Resources Survey, wrote, "The new church complex consists of the main sanctuary, and a connected education wing and chapel. This simple, but finely detailed, Gothic Revival ensemble forms a U shaped, central court plan. The buildings are of warm, cream brick with limestone trim. The gabled main sanctuary has a central entry with corner buttresses framing three tall, pointed arch windows, notable for their stained glass and Gothic tracery. A tall bell tower with finely proportioned corner buttresses rises at the intersection of the main sanctuary and the education wing."[76]

Despite cost overruns and bad weather delays, after two years workmen completed the air-conditioned fourth church. The auditorium could seat 900. The first floor housed a large fellowship hall, library, parlor, and offices. The second and third floors contained classrooms for older children and adults, with the nursery and kindergarten rooms on the first floor. Classes and individuals donated money and valuable items to furnish their new home.

A symphonic carillon with 100 bells plus eleven bells for the Westminster strike, sounded throughout the Poly community on Sunday August 24, 1952. Members first met in the old church, then carrying small items—Bibles, class pictures, even chairs from the nursery—they walked across the campus to their new home. Willard Barr, trustee, and later mayor of Fort Worth, joined other parishioners as they listened to church organist Donald W. Bellah, chairman of the college's Fine Arts Department, sound the opening anthem. Professor James H. Kincaid, TWC choral director, led the song service. Newly appointed Rev. H. Brown Loyd preached. Among the many visitors sat Rev. Edwards, now superintendent of the newly created East Fort Worth Methodist District.

Polytechnic has called thirty-seven ministers in its long history. Most served for one to two years. Several, such as Hayden Edwards, 1947-1955; H. Brown Loyd, 1955-1960; Maggart B. Howell, 1960-1964; C. C. Sessions 1966-1970; Gilbert Ferrell, 1980-1985 pastored for a longer period.

Rev. Frank Leach, 1989-1995, led the congregation in celebration of its 1992 centennial. Aware of the legacy that was theirs, he and the congregation raised $386,000 and refurbished the entire building. They installed new heating and air-conditioning systems, applied fresh paint, and reworked the north entrance.

At one time Polytechnic counted 3,123 members. However, as young families moved to newer neighborhoods and the pioneers died out, the church declined in numbers, but not in vibrancy. Today dedicated longtime members drive past their neighborhood churches to worship in the place they've known since childhood, which after 1968 was called the Polytechnic United Methodist Church. They listen attentively to Rev. Dr. Georgia Allen, whose delivery style is reminiscent of the late Congresswoman Barbara Jordan.

If one were to call the Allen home and ask to speak to the minister, the response would be "Which one?" Both Dr. Allen and her husband are clerics.

She taught school before obtaining a Master's Degree from Brite Divinity School and a Doctorate in Ministry from Perkins School of Theology. After pastoring in several cities, she came to Polytechnic in 1999. When asked why this church, she replied, "It's so open and loving. It's really what a church ought to be. The people are warm and inviting." She also expressed a concern. "People look at this big Gothic building and feel intimidated. It says 'Don't come in here,' but the membership is screaming "Come, we love you.'"[77]

She would like for the community to feel welcome at the special Christmas Eve candle light service. "It's beautiful! We come from whatever we're doing—knowing how busy Christmas Eve is—but we take the time to give honor and praise to the Lord. We remember it's His birthday."[78]

Polytechnic has a wide range of social services, such as English as a Second Language (ESL) classes, a Job Bank to help people find work, and membership in the Poly United Center and SEARCH agencies that assist the needy. They partner with the Boys and Girls Club across the street. "These efforts are the church's way of saying 'God bless you, and we love you.' We hope that even if they choose not to come to our big building that they will know they can go somewhere and find the love of God. That's very important."[79]

In its more than a century the church and the college, now Texas Wesleyan University, have collaborated in providing educational and spiritual leadership. In 2003 the church donated the building to the university. They will share space on the first floor, use the second floor for faculty and staff offices, and use the third floor for multiple activities. Of their new office mates, Dr. Allen said, "It's a great relationship that God has blessed us with and we're delighted to renew that partnership."[80]

Chapter Seven

THE EPISCOPALIAN CONGREGATIONS

On September 25, 1838, the Episcopal church in the United States sent a foreign missionary to the Republic of Texas.

"The Episcopal Church in Texas, unlike the Methodist, Baptist and Churches of Christ, is eminently one of cities and industrial towns,"[1] Driskill and Grisham wrote in *Historic Churches of Texas.* On October 14, 1860 Bishop Alexander Gregg visited Fort Worth and held services in the Masonic Building, but it would be a decade later before the Episcopal movement took hold.

For non-Episcopalians some definitions are in order. A "station" refers to an unorganized mission: a place which has only an occasional visit and church service by a passing minister. A "mission" is a congregation organized with a warden, a secretary and treasurer of the bishop's appointment. It is ministered to by a missionary appointed and sent by the bishop, and supported in part by moneys secured elsewhere by the bishop or "missionary board."

A "parish" implies self-support and self-government, under the oversight of a bishop, conformity to the doctrine, discipline and worship of the Episcopal Church. A "cathedral" pertains to the church in which is the bishop's seat, or the head church of a diocese. A "diocese" refers to a bishop's jurisdiction.

In the Episcopal Church a "bishop" is a high-ranking clergyman with authority over a church district. A "priest" is a clergyman ranking below a bishop and authorized to administer the sacraments and pronounce absolution. Priests generally are addressed as "Father." A "rector" is a minister in charge of a parish. A "vicar" is a person in charge of one chapel in a parish, or as deputy to another minister. A "warden" is a lay officer appointed by the bishop who attends to the secular affairs of the church.

■   ■   ■

St. Andrew's Episcopal Church—1876

A twentieth century reporter, Sioux Campbell, characterized St. Andrew's as a church which

"... surrounds its communicants with the objects of its teachings, either in sculpture, statues, or pictured windows, and the whole of the interior of the church represents the drama of the life of Christ. Beginning with 'The Annunciation,' and the subsequent birth of Christ and culminating in the stupendous spectacle of Christ's Ascension into Heaven, the storied windows of St Andrews (sic) preach a wordless sermon that touches the heart and lifts the soul to heights of sacrifice. But a happy note, too, is struck, for in three beautiful embrasures the triumphant days of the Savior's earthly ministry are told."[2]

She goes on to describe the Nativity, Entry into Jerusalem, and the Call of St. Andrew in the rose window. But like the stained glass windows of other Fort Worth churches, neither words nor photographs adequately convey their beauty.

St. Andrew's owes much of its history to the dedication of Bishops Alexander Gregg and Alexander Charles Garrett. In 1859, then Rev. Gregg, rector of a church in South Carolina, was elected the first resident missionary bishop of Texas. A year later Colonel Nathaniel Terry and other pioneers welcomed the new bishop to Fort Worth. Conducting the first Episcopal service, he administered Holy Communion to five people. Bishop Gregg licensed William Hudson, one of those in attendance, as lay reader for both Fort Worth and Birdville. Records of Mr. Hudson's work are lost.

In 1872 Reverends Thompson L. Smith and Nelson Ayers held services in the court house. George Jackson, a cashier at the First National Bank, worked at the station as warden.

By this time the population had grown to the point where the Dallas diocese, headed by Bishop Gregg, needed division. In 1874 the General Convention approved the Missionary District of North Texas.

Garrett was named the new bishop. He was born in Ireland in 1832, just four years before Texas won her independence from Mexico. He graduated from Trinity College in 1855. As an ordained priest, he came to America in 1860. In his adopted country the Irishman won acclaim for his missionary zeal, scholarship, and power as a preacher.

On a blustery day, March 17, 1875, to be exact, now Bishop Garrett made his first visit to Fort Worth. A year later he established St. Andrew's Mission and placed Rev. Edwin Wicken, at a salary of $300 a year, in charge of the ten members. After serving in Fort Worth, Wicken helped organize churches throughout the state. He returned in 1913, and died in 1918. His headstone at Mt. Olivet Cemetery reads, "Diligent in Missionary service of the church. . . His works do follow him, and he being dead, yet speaketh."[3]

Next, Rev. T. J. Mackay, the First Missionary Priest and First Parish Rector, led services in various places, including the court house. The first year was difficult—at times the small group was unable to pay rent for its meetings. But by June 17, 1877 Garrett noted in his diary,

". . . a Parish meeting at 4 p.m. at which resolutions were adopted of a highly encouraging character. The city has grown immensely. . . . Many earnest people have come in; an excellent feeling now prevails; and I am confident that the days of severest trial are past,"[4] according to Jennifer Morrison in *The History of the Episcopal Church in Fort Worth*. With renewed energy and greater financial resources, the congregation bought a lot at the corner of Bluff and Pecan Streets and built a church and rectory. They laid the cornerstone in 1877, thanks in part to Bishop Garrett's securing additional funds for the structure. The good bishop described it as "very neat and churchly." By 1878, the flock counted sixty-four communicants and the mission status was upgraded to parish.

Rectors following Mackay include W. W. Patrick, 1878-82; W. D. Sartwell, 1882-86; R. H. Prosser, 1886; Joseph DeForest, 1887-89; Varday McBee, 1890-91; Harry Cassil, 1891-96; Bartow Ramage, 1897-1916; Dr. Edward Eckel, 1917-1930; Dr. Halsey Werlein, 1931-36; Louis Martin, 1937-68; John Hildebrand, 1968-89; Dr. Jeffrey Steenson, 1989-2000; Quintin Morrow, 2001 to present.

Soon the first structure became too small and another took its place in 1878. Reverend W. W. Patrick ministered there. His four-year pastorate was one of patient growth. "This building was the one later moved to 10th & Lamar and used as a Church—and later as Parish House,"[5] according to the centennial history. The frame structure, erected at Fifth and Rusk (now Commerce), cost $3,800, according to the *Fort Worth Daily Democrat*, a lot of money at that time. The reporter trumpeted, "It is said to be the most beautiful edifice in northern or eastern Texas."[6]

An 1881 treasurer's report showed donations from "H. L. Bartels—.50; Mrs. M. Williams—1.50. . ." for a total collection of $3.95 on July 17. The unnamed treasurer also noted, "If the Rector & his family are not kept humble it will not be the fault of St. Andrew's Congregation."[7]

Rev. W. D. Sartwell is remembered as a strong force for missions, but his career was cut short when he contracted typhoid fever which left him an invalid. "Rev. Ralph H. Prosser followed, but remained only about a year and then removed to Louisiana,"[8] a *Fort Worth Tribune* feature writer noted.

In 1887, energetic, hard-working Rev. Joseph DeForest led in the construction of a two-story frame building at Fifth and Jones Streets. It served as a rectory until the city bought it in 1914 to be used as a nurses' home for the new City-County Hospital. (Pioneer John Peter Smith had donated a five-acre tract "way out on South Main" for a hospital, but it was deemed "too far from town" and after much controversy city and county fathers built on the property adjoining the rectory.)

After the retirement of DeForest, the next minister could fill in as organist should the need arise. Rev. Varday McBee, trained in music as well as theology, served the flock for about two years. His successor, Rev. Harry Cassil, brought with him many talents. He had been a Presbyterian, a soldier in the Civil War, a printer and farmer, before his calling to full-time ministry. In 1896 he moved to Georgia.

A young man from Tennessee, Bartow B. Ramage, brought the church into the twentieth century in a pastorate that lasted almost twenty years. In the 1890s St. Andrew's parishioners looked southward, bought lots on Lamar at Tenth Street, and started a building fund.

Different components contributed to the new sanctuary. "The young ladies of Miss Furman's class will put in a $500 memorial window dedicated to the class. The Ladies Aid Society will also put in a window," according to a

Writers' Project report. For months the children collected money in jugs. The proud youngsters then donated their gifts for the furnishing of a Sunday School room. The September 30, 1909 issue of *St. Andrew's Call* urged that "Fifty cents per month laid aside each month for a year will pay for one stone."[9] The church vault contains a list of all the members who paid $6.00 for a stone.

Ground was broken in 1909 for architects Sanguinette & Staats' design of the Gothic Revival style sanctuary, which they modified to fit the narrow lot. Carol Roark in *Fort Worth's Legendary Landmarks* described the $120,000 edifice, known as the much longed-for Stone Church. "Built of gray dolomite, a hard limestone from Carthage, Missouri, St. Andrew's is in a cruciform plan, a nave with single side aisles and a single transept . . . crossing."[10] The interior features wood paneling. The rood screen was carved in Italy. "Rood" means "cross," and a cross is at the top center of the screen. "The screen reaches across the Church between the altar and the congregation and signifies 'the gate through which the entrance to heavenly rest is gained,'"[11] according to the historical description. The ceiling highlights exposed wood roof beams and coffers. "The extreme width of the interior, including nave and side aisles, is sixty-two feet; and the depth from the main front wall in the west to the rear wall of the sanctuary will be ninety-four feet,"[12] the church history notes. In addition, two transepts of fifteen feet by twenty-four feet separate the chancel from the nave.

The organ occupies the arch on the Epistle side of the chancel. The whole is reminiscent of an English medieval parish church.

Ramage, rector from 1897 to 1916, led the congregation to their new home on Rogation Sunday, May 12, 1912. The *Fort Worth Tribune* noted, "The Bishop (Garrett) and visiting clergymen of the Diocese conducted the Opening Service, the choir and congregation of Trinity Parish joined St. Andrew's upon this occasion. The church was packed long before the hour for the service to begin, and hundreds were unable to obtain admission."[13]

Crowds came to the night service as well. According to the church history, "Just before the sermon, an old man, tottering with weakness and showing that he had suffered much during some weeks spent in All Saints' Hospital, spoke of 'Looking Backward and Looking Forward.' He told of the early days of the

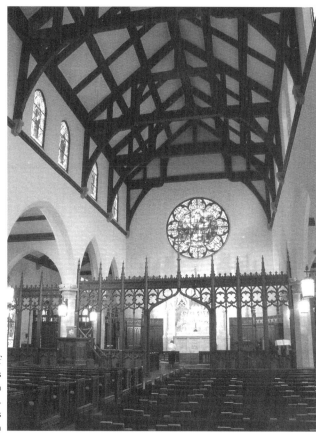

Interior of
St. Andrew's
Episcopal Church
10th and Lamar.
Courtesy St. Andrew's
Episcopal Church

church in Fort Worth."[14] He knew whereof he spoke. It was Rev. Edwin Wickens, the first Missionary to hold services regularly in the city.

Rev. Dr. Edward H. Eckel came at a propitious time—just three years before the Ranger oil boom of the early 1920s—and he retired before the hard days of the Great Depression. Under his leadership the parish grew in numbers and influence.

Rev. Halsey Werlein was called from his post in the Canal Zone to succeed Dr. Eckel. "During his ministry there was renewed life and activity, and as the parish prospered, many windows, Chancel Furniture, and other Memorials were installed,"[15] according to a newspaper account. Remembered as a typical Southern gentleman, friendly and full of religious spirit, Werlein died in his sleep November 27, 1936.

The grieving parishioners welcomed their new rector, plain-spoken Rev. Louis F. Martin in 1937. The young man from Cincinnati, Ohio proved to be an able preacher and financially strong administrator. Yet his arrival created controversy. Hired by the Wardens and Vestry without the consent and blessings of the Rt. Rev. Harry T. Moore, then bishop of the Dallas Diocese, it sparked a rift between the parish and diocese.

Historian Mary Lou Herring remembered Martin as a "turn off the lights when you leave a room" sort of man. His conservation and fund-raising led to the retirement of the debt on the church and the resulting consecration December 31, 1939. For a time Bishop Moore had refused to participate in St. Andrew's observances, but he relented and preached the consecration sermon. In it he noted that St. Andrew's was the only large parish in the diocese free of debt.

During Martin's twenty-one years they added the Ryan Building, and remodeled the parish house and other facilities. "When Mr. Martin retired in 1968, he became rector emeritus until his death December 11, 1987 at the age of 90,"[16] church historian Ted Stafford wrote.

From 1968 to 1989 Rev. John Hildebrand served as rector. Known as a gentlemanly, caring pastor, he nevertheless held strong beliefs. Judy Mayo, staff member and longtime family friend, said, "What some people didn't know was that behind that gentle countenance he had a steel will. He didn't have any problem with saying, 'This is wrong.'"[17]

Hildebrand led the congregation in diligent Bible study and supported their desire to retain the use of the 1928 *Book of Common Prayer*, one of the few churches allowed to do so.

For years the church needed more classrooms, and it was during the later part of Rev. Hildebrand's ministry that the Ryan House became a reality. With the help of the Thomas M. and Helen McKee Ryan Foundation, St. Andrew's built a Guild Room, Youth Room, Multi-purpose Room and Confirmation Room at the south end of the Parish House. For this and as a tribute to his leadership the congregation dedicated St. John's Chapel at Camp Crucis in his honor. After retirement, Hildebrand assumed rector emeritus status. He died in February 2000 after a lengthy illness.

Rev. Dr. Jeffrey N. Steenson, called to St. Andrew's as rector in 1989, obtained his doctorate in early Christian theology from the University of

Oxford in England. A North Dakota farm boy and former Chicago area sports-writer, Steenson advocated traditional Anglican teaching, and played a prominent role in church affairs, including the publication of the *Living Church Magazine*. After ten years, the popular rector tendered his resignation. Of his ministry, he said, "I love being a pastor. I love to preach, and baptize and marry and bury, but I also sense that God is calling me to rekindle this gift of teaching for the sake of the larger Church."[18] Rickey Brantley, senior warden who heads the vestry, spoke for the congregation in saying the scholarly Steenson would be sorely missed.

When Rector Quintin Morrow speaks of an influx of young families to St. Andrew's, he includes his own. Morrow planned to teach American History at the college level, but the pull of ministry prevailed. "I started walking toward the doors and they opened for me,"[19] he said in an interview. After earning an undergraduate degree at Christian Heritage College, the San Diego native studied at Trinity Episcopal School for Ministry in Pittsburgh. He came to Fort Worth in April 2001 following ministries in Southern California.

Having majored in history, it's not surprising that Rev. Morrow appreciates the historical roots of the Fort Worth church, including the use of the 1928 *Book of Common Prayer* and the reverency he finds in the worship services. He cites the continuity of families, such as the Moncriefs, the Ryans, the Tandys, who have supported the church for generations as making St. Andrew special.

Yet his ministry is not solely about looking to the past. St. Andrew's is in transition as a younger segment of the congregation takes on new leadership roles. The church provides lunch and Morrow leads in Bible study for downtown workers who need a spiritual respite from the business day. Other social ministries include support of the Union Gospel Mission and East Door Ministry. They also offer musical events for people throughout the community as a way of opening doors and saying "we're part of downtown and we want to be a part of your life."

Rev. Morrow's sermons are aired on radio station WRR and are available via computer to shut-ins and congregants unable to attend services. These innovations are meshed with the traditional forms of liturgy and provide a depth of worship for those seeking a spiritual experience free of the whim or vagaries of fads or fashion. "This makes St. Andrew's the best kept secret in town,"[20] according to the youthful rector who values the history of the Anglican church.

■　　　■　　　■

Trinity Episcopal-1895

At 4:00 on a Sunday afternoon, November 19, 1893, twenty-one members of St. Andrew's Parish met to establish a new mission church. Named "Trinity" for the river that flows through the city, Bishop Alexander Garret granted official organization status on March 6, 1895. Early parish records show that four days later eight children were confirmed and baptized.

Historian Charles A. Watson, in his comprehensive work, *Trinity Parish: 1893-1993,* cited the unofficial efforts of Maria D. Beggs in the establishment of the new congregation. Unable to serve on the all-male vestry, she nevertheless co-signed the lease for a lot on St. Louis where Trinity's congregation built their first owned house of worship. This lease, dated September 5, 1894 is the oldest document in Trinity's archives. "She was also a founder of All Saints Hospital, originally called Maria Hospital in recognition of her leadership."[21] (See *A History of the Fort Worth Medical Community* for a fuller account of the hospital.)

Headquartered in Dallas, Bishop Garret appointed Rev. J. B. C. Beaubien as Priest-in-Charge of the Fort Worth mission. The small flock held their first services in a rented Swedish church at St. Louis and Broadway Streets.

In ill health much of the time, Rev. Beaubien pastored the mission from March 1895 until November 1896. During his tenure the congregation moved a small structure to the corner of Hemphill and Pennsylvania. J. Henry Bevan gave an organ and other members donated additional amenities.

Rev. Beaubien left for Bonham, Texas, and the Vestry wrote to several prospects. They called Robert H. Cotton, a graduate of the University of London and former curate of All Saints Parish Church in Manchester before coming to America. He began his ministry November 17, 1896 after agreeing to the annual salary of $1,000 and a "free residence." A dispute arose over whether or not this meant "rectory." Church leaders started a rectory fund, but at times used it to pay current expenses. Despite differences over finances among Vestry members and the priest, they constructed a chapel complete with stained glass memorial windows, and a Sunday school building. A money crunch led to cutting Cotton's salary by $18.00 a month. He angered parishioners when he bought some carpeting and did not have enough money to pay for it. The relationship continued to deteriorate. In 1906 Bishop Garret approved the removal of Rev. Cotton after ten years of growth tempered by controversy.

The Rev. C. A. Roth fared better in his nine year ministry. By 1911 the congregation numbered more than 300. Minutes of the June 4, 1914 vestry meeting show the purchase of the 1500 block of Lipscomb for $6,260, but it would be years before they could develop the property.

Rev. F. T. Datson led Trinity for two years, 1917-1919. "He is still remembered for his outstanding work with the soldiers stationed at Camp Bowie and nearby flying fields,"[22] according to Mrs. C. K. Smullen's 1948 history of Trinity. An Englishman, he was especially close to the men in the Royal Flying Corps who trained nearby. These servicemen helped fill the sanctuary every Sunday before Datson left for a church in Wichita Falls.

L. W. Heaton became rector in September 1919. The congregation voted to move the Guild Hall from its Hemphill location to Lipscomb Street. They tore down the old church, and first built a Community Center at the new site, then in 1924 completed the new sanctuary.

Even as the new buildings were in progress and the congregation grew to about 300, storm clouds were on the horizon. Reverend Heaton's sermons on evolution and the Virgin Birth of Jesus raised the hackles of some members. The Vestry rejected a resolution demanding his resignation, but the congregation split over the issue. In 1924 Bishop Harry T. Moore urged dissidents to withdraw from Trinity and form St. John's mission. Concerning the controversy, Watson quoted a New York Episcopal Church publication. "The Ku Klux Klan, J. Frank Norris (see page 96) and the general public also attacked Trinity 'in a centre saturated with the bitterest type of extreme Fundamentalist thought,' . . ."[23] Moore reluctantly dismissed the charges because Heaton's views were shared by some leaders in the national Church. Vindicated, but unable to heal the wounds, Heaton resigned in 1925.

The Reverend F. W. Golden-Howes came in December of that year. His task, in addition to reconciling the factions, was fund raising. Burdened with debt, the Vestry purchased a used Kimball pipe organ and cut the rector's salary. Golden-Howes resigned and accepted a post in Mexico City.

The Vestry called Dr. H. Cowley-Carroll in April 1928. He became the first Trinity rector to air sermons on local radio station KFJZ. These were discontinued in 1929—again due to financial problems. The nation fell into the Great Depression, and Trinity, like other churches, found itself strapped for cash. Rev. Cowley-Carroll resigned in 1931.

Rev. C. G. Fox came in October of that dismal year. He had been a Missionary Priest to the Cree Indians in Manitoba, Canada and a Canadian chaplain in World War I. The minutes for Vestry meetings for the years of 1934 to 1938 are missing, but other records indicate only seventy-six parishioners gave to the church treasury in 1938. Despite this lack of money, Fox remained with the parish until his retirement in 1938. During World War II he again served, this time as chaplain to the Texas State Guard.

By 1939 a reconciliation between Bishop Moore and Rev. Heaton resulted in the pastor again being assigned to Trinity. As the nation's economy improved, he led in a building program and old debts were paid. Shortly before the congregation celebrated its fiftieth anniversary, Heaton resigned.

In December 1943 the 370 communicants called Rev. Miller M. B. Sale as rector. During his tenure the parish experienced a more stable financial footing and they gave him a vote of confidence and appreciation when he left in 1945.

Rev. Hugh Farrell, a convert from the Roman Church, led the congregation for the next two years. He oversaw the purchase of a Hammond organ. The congregation replaced the old oak altar with an elegantly carved walnut one in 1946. The following year, needing to be near his invalid mother, Farrell resigned and accepted a position in San Francisco.

The September 25, 1948 laying of the new sanctuary's cornerstone at Stadium Drive and Bellaire Drive South was the highlight of Rev. William J. Heilman's eight year tenure. He preached his first sermon on Trinity Sunday, June 1, 1947. An innovator, "He instituted the 9:30 a. m. Family Eucharist, after which service coffee, buns and fruit juice were served in the Parish House by members of the Guild,"[24] Watson noted. Heilman and others urged members to consider moving into the Texas Christian University neighborhood.

Although reluctant to give up the place where they had struggled and worshiped, filled with memories of christenings, weddings and funerals— the Parish voted on August 17, 1947 to leave the Lipscomb Street location.

On December 5, 1948, he preached his first sermon in their new home. The sandstone structure retains the look of English village churches. Made of native Texas stone, it is an adaptation of English Medieval style with a single tower, and long nave, divided at the middle to form a cross.

By the end of Rev. Heilman's pastorate, communicants numbered 1,000 and annual receipts totaled about $50,000.

Dr. W. P. Barnds succeeded Heilman. Building continued as the parish added new classroom and office space. They bought "the house next door to the west at 3417 Bellaire Drive South and called it the Sunday School Annex,"[25] according to historian Watson. In 1966 the Rev. Dr. Barnds was consecrated Suffragan Bishop of the Dallas Diocese and elected Rector Emeritus of Trinity.

Reverend Richard Rogers, the new rector, brought new ideas in his 1967 to 1972 ministry. For the first time women were eligible for Vestry membership and the age limit was lowered to eighteen for both men and women.

Trinity Episcopal Church 3401 Bellaire Dr. Courtesy Trinity Episcopal Church

In 1973 David P. Comegys became rector. He restored harmony to the parish following Rogers' at times contentious leadership. Watson wrote "Just when the Vestry thought all systems were running smoothly, the Rev. Mr. Comegys suddenly disclosed that he would soon resign."[26] He left for St. Luke's Episcopal Church in San Antonio in March, 1975.

When Rev. John H. Stanley answered the call to Trinity in 1975, he little dreamed he would have the daunting, but rewarding task of presiding over the 1993 centennial of the parish. The celebration was one of the fondest memories of his twenty-three year pastorate. "We did a lot of remodeling and put in a new organ for the big event," he said in a recent interview.

The friendly, outgoing Illinois native pastored churches in the Midwest before coming to Fort Worth. From the start, he admonished his congregation to "Love God, learn and grow in the Spirit, be committed, be involved,"[27] according to Watson. He put his words into action by serving as president of the boards of the Presbyterian Night Shelter, which he later served as president, and other civic organizations. Stanley led as Trinity entered a period of growth, both in communicants and prestige.

Now retired, he smiled as he related some of what he called "Gracie Allen" stories. For more than twenty years he conducted a Bible Study for a group of "mature" women. After twenty years, they became "very mature." One woman, he diplomatically declined to identify her by name or age, opined that the material had gotten boring. He asked what she would like to study. "The Jewish religion," she responded. They were studying Genesis, Exodus and Isaiah! Another member of the group noted the names in the study, "certainly sounded Jewish." These moments of levity only served to further endear him to his charges.

Following his 1998 retirement Rev. and Mrs. Stanley now have time to travel—they just returned from a trip to Italy when interviewed. And like grandparents around the world, they delight in spending more time with their grandchildren.

The new rector, J. Frederick Barber, "Father Fred," also likes to spend time with children. He proudly announced one of the church's goals is to use recently purchased property at the end of the block to expand their preschool facilities. Another goal is to build bridges between long time members of the congregation and the many new young families. "The older ones are an asset and the young ones are the future,"[28] he said in an interview.

Virginian Rev. Barber holds a master's and doctorate from Vanderbilt University, and despite years pastoring churches in up-state New York, he still retains a bit of the South in his speech. A parishioner described his preaching style as "dynamic," and another described him as "a breath of fresh air." In addition to preaching, with a slight drawl he extols the virtues of Trinity. "It's near TCU and thus serves students, it has a broad mix of people, economically and age wise, and it's home to the moderate Episcopal worshiper."[29]

The church's social ministry includes the "Care Bears" drive for ill children, and sponsoring refugee families. On a regular basis, volunteers provide sandwiches for the Presbyterian Night Shelter and Union Gospel Mission. Trinity volunteers also work with the Aids Outreach Center, Habitat for Humanity, CROP Walk and South Central Alliance of Churches. All this, according to Father Fred, is in keeping with the church's, and his, mission to reach out to the community as he leads the 1,000 or so parishioners in the new century.

Chapter Eight

THE CHURCH OF CHRIST CONGREGATIONS

Allan Carney in his 1934 series on Fort Worth churches wrote, "Churches of Christ represent the conservatives of the Christian faith which in former years were known as Disciples and Christians. In the 1890 census report, the two groups were linked together as Disciples of Christ, but in the 1906 report, the Conservatives were reported separately as Churches of Christ."[1]

In *An Encyclopedia of Religions in the United States: 100 Groups Speak for Themselves*, the Church of Christ is described as a fellowship of autonomous congregations who ". . . believe that the New Testament is complete in revealing God's will to man and that all religious matters must emanate from its message.

"Their worship consists of teaching (preaching and reading Scripture), prayer, singing, communion (partaking of the Lord's Super in memory of his death), and taking an offering. Their singing is without any instrument because they do not find it on the agenda of the New Testament church."[2] It is this last characteristic that most non-members associate with Church of Christ worship.

■   ■   ■

The Southside Church of Christ—1892

The first years of Southside Church of Christ, before the separation from First Christian, have been covered earlier. By 1885 some members of First Christian craved a place of worship closer to where they lived. Major K. M. Van Zandt offered a lot at the corner of Jennings Avenue and Cannon Street for a meeting place. At a cost of less than $1,000 these "southsiders" erected a 40'X 60' frame building. J. W. Lowber (the Church of Christ does not use the term "reverend") was the preacher for the downtown church and also spoke for the south side group until the coming of their first full-time preacher, Ben Hill,"[3] according to their 1972 history.

"The Southside congregation, as an entity of its own, dates to 1892,"[4] according to the 1972 account. In 1895 John E. Dunn was called to preach. T. W. Kidwell served from 1896 until 1901, with H. H. Whitlock preaching from time to time. A total of forty-one men served the congregation in its first 100 years.

In 1898, during Kidwell's tenure, 120 members, including First Christian song leader George Gavin, left that church and joined Southside. Around 1900, the centennial history noted, a significant number left Southside and formed a congregation on East First Street known as Central Church of Christ.

C. E. Wooldridge preached at Southside from 1903 to 1910. Orphaned at an early age, the youth learned the value of self-reliance and hard work—characteristics he carried into adulthood. Not a tall man, he nevertheless presented a striking figure with a shock of dark hair and erect posture. He was the father of four sons and one daughter, and his grandchildren remain active in the Church of Christ today. Elsewhere, sixteen years later, the Central Church of Christ bought a building at College and Leuda Streets. Meanwhile Southside, now located on the corner of Jennings and Murphy, began to worship with Central. "The church incorporated in March 1917, under the name of Southside-Central Church of Christ,"[5] according to *History of Southside Church of Christ: 1892-1992.*

For the next ten years several men preached at Southside, but at times the church had no local evangelist at all. The Church of Christ, more so than some other congregations, depends heavily on leadership from its elders, and when no preachers were available, the elders kept the flock together.

Staff member Dan Leaf explained, "Elders are the congregation's shepherds. They guide and lead spiritually and are responsible for the oversight and nurturing of the congregation."[6] Elder L. G. Lacy resigned in 2003, closing a page of history. He and his father's combined services as elders lasted for seventy years. Lacy, the younger, recalled his college days at Texas Christian University. In his Bible class he was the only Church of Christ adherent among twelve Disciples of Christ followers. "We had some lively discussions,"[7] he said in a recent interview.

John Dickey brought stability to the church, serving from 1926 to 1934. Membership rose from 150 to 576 during that time. A. Hugh Clark preached from 1934 to 1936, and C. A. Norred from 1936 to 1943. During this period Southside enlarged the building at Lueda and College. The 1945 directory listed 1,082 members.

Robert C. Jones preached for ten years, beginning in 1943. Elred Stevens preached from 1953 to 1962. In the 1950s the neighborhood became more commercial and less residential. By 1953 the membership was half what it had been a decade before, but with the arrival of Stevens things were improving. "An invigorating spirit of optimistic vision has replaced defeatism that had become so pronounced. . . ,"[8] according to C. A. Norred's 1954 history of the church.

On June 8, 1957, the elders revealed plans for new quarters. Land was purchased at Hempill and Hawthorne Streets and construction began. The splendid red brick structure blends contemporary with the feeling of classical architecture. The auditorium did seat 1150, but remodeling in 2000 resulted in wider aisles and seating was reduced to 850. The chapel is large enough for 150 worshipers. The building contains twenty-three classrooms, two nurseries, a library, and four offices. It cost $600,000 in 1959 dollars. The congregation held their first service in the new sanctuary May 3, 1959. Today's congregation enjoys worshiping within the serene dove gray walls. The white pews are outfitted with wine-colored cushions to match the carpeting. Six sparkling chandeliers provide light for Bible reading and singing from *Songs of Faith and Praise*.

The decade of the 1960s saw the decline of the neighborhood as more and more people moved to suburbs and newer parts of the city. Membership dropped to 500. "Instead of retreating, the elders of the church made the decision to remain and be a good neighbor in the old neighborhood,"[9] according to the centennial history. Southside marked its seventy-fifth anniversary with a Homecoming celebration on November 5, 1967.

By this time the church counted as members several evangelists who preached throughout the country. One of the most successful of these, Horace Busby, baptized an estimated 18,000 people during his ministry.

In 1968 George Stephenson left after serving for five years. He was succeeded by Wyatt Sawyer of Dallas. In 1973 Hardeman Nichols assumed the
preaching duties. Bob Barnhill served from 1977 to 1982 when John Scott
came to Southside.

Important events occurred during the 1980s. Scott brought with him a
love for the poor and outcast. He led the church in its "Pantry Ministry," and
gave food to hundreds of people in economic straits. That ministry is ongoing.
A daycare facility—the Southside Christian School—cares for infants through
kindergartners. Also during the 1980s the elders saw the need to reach out to
the growing Hispanic community. They hired Roger Munoz as the first
Spanish speaking minister. Armando Marin came in 1990.

Kyle Kiser has been at Southside since 1993.

In 1992 Southside celebrated its 100th anniversary by writing the
church's history, using the motto "Southside 100 Years, Now On to
Completion," meaning that 100 years in God's sight is a short time and the

Southside Church of Christ 2101 Hemphill. Courtesy John Clinton

church's work is on-going. Two years later, Margery (Mrs. O. P.) Leonard, of that pioneer family, unveiled a Texas State Historical Marker commemorating the church's first century. It reads in part, "This congregation, initially led by Dr. I. L. Van Zandt and other elders, was established in a fast growing southern area of Fort Worth in 1892."[10]

Throughout the years, Southside's members have counted it a strength that the same doctrine and order of worship practiced in 1855 by their founders is still advocated and followed, and they look forward to the next 100 years.

■   ■   ■

The North Side Church of Christ-1899

Twelve persons interested in establishing a Church of Christ on the North Side met in the old M. G. Ellis School at 215 N. E. 14th Street in 1899. In 1956, a *Star-Telegram* reporter noted, "The enthusiasm of those original members has been characteristic of the congregation throughout the years and today the North Side Church of Christ, with a membership of 581 persons, occupies property at 2001 Lincoln, valued at $200,000."[11] By 2003 the membership had declined, yet according to Brother John C. Goble, "We are few in number, but our faith is still strong."[12] A visitor to the church today might experience what it must have been like in the days of the pioneers—a small group of dedicated people gathered for a simple worship service.

The first minister, M. H. Moore, also was principal of North Side High School. Moore later served as superintendent of the Fort Worth School District from 1915 until 1931. An elementary school is named in his honor.

The congregation erected its first building in 1903 at 1421 Boulevard. Later the founding members bought an old cleaning plant on N. W. 12th St. and renovated it for use as a house of worship. They met in this facility for five years.

In 1908 the congregation bought property at 14th and N. Houston Streets. They constructed a church with a seating capacity of 125 in the auditorium. As the membership grew, they were forced to expand three times. After forty years in this location, the congregation deemed it more practical to start afresh rather than build yet another wing.

They saved enough money to buy lots just off N.W. 20th Street on Lincoln Avenue and to start the construction. Alas, funds were insufficient to complete the project. Daily after work, the men of the church met at the skeletal building to finish the job themselves. They hung the ceiling tiles, then laid the hardwood floor. The youth did their part by carrying supplies to the men, and the women fed them all.

In 1949, after a year of construction work, they moved into their beautiful new church home at 2001 Lincoln Avenue. At a cost of $110,000, the brick building is of medieval Romanesque design, with prominent fenestration of windows and towers. Steps on two sides of the elevated entryway lead to triple doors giving access to the auditorium. A smooth limestone border, in contrast to the buff brick, accents the doors.

The auditorium, serene in its simplicity, can seat 700 in three sections of dark oak pews. The walls of oak wainscoting and beige upper areas contrast with the deep red carpeting and the red drapes covering twelve double windows. To the north of the sanctuary, twenty classrooms provided space for the 400 or so weekly Bible students. A nursery and office spaces completed the structure.

Brother Waymon D. Miller led the congregation during this phase of expansion. A graduate of Harding College and Quachita College, he first served congregations in his home state of Arkansas. He pastored a church in Lubbock before coming to Fort Worth. Miller left North Side in July 1949 to serve as a missionary in South Africa. He returned in 1954. During his second tenure here he and the congregation rejoiced in paying off the mortgage, and having enough money to air-condition the entire facility.

Brother Roy Cosgrove came from a family of preachers. Remembered for his interest in the youth, he would invite them to his house for informal get-togethers. "I'll just open a can of tuna and some Cokes," he would say. He preached in the time between Waymon Miller and John C. Goble.

After graduating from high school in Nocona, Goble earned both a bachelor's and master's degree from Abilene Christian College (now University). He held pastorates in Maypearl and Gorman, Texas, and in McAllister, Oklahoma before joining the staff of North Side in 1965.

Early in his ministry here he encouraged the congregation to reach out to the Hispanics living in North Fort Worth. "The year 1970 saw the beginning

left: M.G. Ellis School circa 1899. First meeting place of North Side Church of Christ Courtesy North Side Church of Christ

below: North Side Church of Christ 2001 Lincoln Ave. Courtesy North Side Church of Christ

of a new work, fully supported by North Side, *Iglesia de Cristo*, 2001 Prairie Avenue,"[13] according to the 1973 history. They hired Estanislao Castaneda to preach to the Spanish-speaking congregation. This effort to broaden their ministry continues today. The Hispanic flock, numbering about 100, is a vital part of North Side's history. As the mission congregation increased, they became more independent. Today they are no longer governed by North Side's elders. However, Brother Goble preaches, in English, to a second generation of youth who are more conversant in that language.

In looking to the future, Bother Goble would like to form an adult singing group, much like the one the North Side High School Exes had. He recalled that W. C. Ray was a member.

W. C. Ray, a 1935 graduate of North Side High School, has been a member of North Side Church of Christ his entire life. (Legend has it he was born on the second pew.)

Ray and more than fifty other young men from the church joined the military in World War II. When he returned in 1945 he began leading the song service at North Side. He leads the singing even today, in a tenor voice which is still vibrant.

Brother Goble had the Ray family, the Murphy family, the H. C. Fullers, the Smiths, and other families in mind when he praised the congregation for having laid a great foundation of Christian love on which to build the future. And what does the future hold? "An old-fashioned revival in the spring of 2004,"[14] he said. That, combined with Vacation Bible School, regular worship services—and the dedication of longtime members will sustain the church as an important part of both the history and future of Fort Worth's North Side.

Chapter Nine

THE JEWISH CONGREGATIONS

"When 20-year-old Jacob Samuels opened a Fort Worth dry-goods store in 1857, he was the town's only Jewish shopkeeper,"[1] according to Hollace Weiner's essay in *Celebrating 150 Years*. When asked, he told townspeople he, like many of them, was born in a log cabin. He failed to mention the log cabin was in Poland. He also predated the establishment of the city's Jewish synagogues.

Historically, European Jews were forbidden to own land. To earn a living they became peddlers. By necessity, they became "middlemen" offering goods between rural and city dwellers. "In America, many Jews became wholesalers because that was a familiar niche,"[2] according to Weiner. Those who migrated to Texas brought with them this skill. In Fort Worth they established small businesses selling food, clothing, tobacco, and liquor, and when finances permitted, they sent for their wives, children and extended families. "Jacob Samuels opened a trading post in Fort Worth, (when) skirmishes with the Indians were still common,"[3] Ruthe Winegarten and Cathy Schechter noted in their history of Texas Jews.

Although Jews now make up less than one per cent of the population of the city, two vibrant synagogues attest to their commitment to religious life and community involvement.

■   ■   ■

Ahavath Sholom—1892

By the 1890s the town had matured from a stopover for cowboys driving cattle to market into a growing city. Places of worship dotted the landscape, including Ahavath Sholom, the first synagogue, also called a *shul*. It had its beginning in the home of William Jacob Goldstein.

A poor peddler with a shiny patent leather pack on his back, Goldstein came here in the 1880s and made his home at Fifth and Calhoun Streets. On October 30, 1892 he and several friends met to form an orthodox congregation. He was elected president, with Moses Shanblum, vice-president; Joseph Jacobs, secretary; and Jacob B. Colton, treasurer. With officers presiding, for three years they held services on High Holy Days in rented halls. A page from the minutes, dated "Fort Worth, Tex. October 6th 1895," the title in flowing English penmanship, with the actual minutes written in Yiddish, tells of members and their struggling movement. Dues were $6.00 a year, payable at fifty cents per month. Those unable to give cash gave items of equal value.

"Balls, parties, raffles and every type of entertainment was (sic) held,"[4] according to *Congregation Ahavath Sholom: 100th Anniversary*. With enough money on hand by 1893, they paid $500 down for a lot and an additional $500 was paid out in two years. The jubilant congregation erected the first synagogue, a small frame building fifty feet long, twenty-six feet wide and sixteen feet high with a shingled roof at the corner of Jarvis and Hemphill Streets. It cost $640. They purchased an Ark, a special cabinet for the Torah scroll, at a cost of $12.50. It was specially designed and built, prior to the first service. In 1901 they moved the building to 819 Taylor Street.

Membership grew from the original thirty-one men (they did not count women) to one hundred when the first brick building was completed in 1906. One of the members, Philip Dan, came to Texas in 1904. He was traveling from his home in Memphis, Tennessee to San Antonio. "When his train stopped for a layover in Fort Worth, he met a man who convinced him that he should stay. . . and who got him a job as a tailor in the A. & L. August Mens store,"[5] according to the Dan family history. Dan's grandson, Alfred Cohen, is now a member of Ahavath Sholom.

Moses Shanblum deserves much of the credit for the success of the synagogue. The Russian immigrant came to Fort Worth in 1878. First he peddled piece goods and dresses, then opened a fruit stand at Seventh and Main Streets. After getting his family settled here, he turned his attention to the nascent synagogue. "The white-haired, snowy-bearded man plodded the streets, knocked on house doors and rang bells for 62 years in Fort Worth, raising funds and collecting money for the congregation and its auxiliary agencies,"[6] according to the *Star-Telegram*. Shanblum was the force behind the construction of the Hebrew Institute, and the establishment of the endowment that helps underwrite the Hebrew School. He died in 1940 at the age of eighty-seven.

Although some sources name Charles Blumenthal as the first rabbi, the Yiddish minutes reveal that Ahavath Sholom hired Rabbi G. Halpern in 1904. "The minutes credit him, along with the Board of Directors, for getting the Hebrew School off the ground."[7]

Charles Blumenthal was a rabbi who contributed much to the congregation. He taught Jewish children to read and write Hebrew in afternoon classes. In 1945, the eighty-seven-year-old retired rabbi returned to teach grandchildren of those in his congregation forty-one years earlier.

Blumenthal, speaking to *Star-Telegram* reporter Jack Douglas, Sr., recalled that when he first saw the synagogue, ". . . it was well out of the business section and was mainly surrounded by private homes."[8] The Carnegie librarian lived across the street from the synagogue and Seventh Street was residential, the homes adorned with flower beds that would later give way to the offices of the *Star-Telegram*.

The name "Congregation Ahavath Sholom," (which means "Love of Peace") written in Hebrew, stood out against a white frame surrounding the double doors of the imposing edifice. Stone steps led up to the main floor and balcony of the sanctuary. For eight years the basement served as the school facility and the center for various activities. The leadership believed worship, study and fellowship were the underpinnings of a successful synagogue. That led the congregation, in 1910, to build a three-story Hebrew Institute on property in the same block. The Hebrew school, the Sunday school, and the rabbi's study occupied the first floor. On the second floor they built a kitchen and combination auditorium/banquet hall, and the third floor housed the gymnasium, dressing rooms and showers.

Rabbi Abraham E. Abramovitz led the congregation during the 1920s and Philip Graubart came in 1929.

Rabbi Isadore Garsek began a thirty-three year tenure in 1946. He was serving a congregation in Lubbock when he came to a meeting in Fort Worth.

There he met Sadye Mae Carshon. "They married and after World War II the congregation hired him."[9]

Garsek, born in Russia in 1913 and described as a gentle, loving friend who unfailingly practiced the principles of Judaism, quickly endeared himself to his congregation and the city. He became a leader in issues of social justice and interaction with people of all faiths. His activism ranged from comforting the sick to marching in the civil rights movement in Selma, Alabama.

By mid-century businesses surrounded the property. Parking lots abutted the children's playground. The flock, numbering about 300 families, had outgrown its sanctuary. On High Holy Days the overflow met in the Institute. Moreover, in summer with windows open in pre-air-conditioning times, street noises interfered with worship services.

Reporter Douglas wrote, "Buildings, like men, must come to the time when their days of service are gone—and Tuesday that time came for Ahavath Sholom Synagogue at 819 Taylor."[10] A parking lot replaced the forty-five year old structure that had been the heart of the city's conservative Jewish community. "The Hebrew Institute and Ahavath Sholom's Taylor Street shul were razed in 1951 as the congregation readied to move to a spacious synagogue at Eighth Avenue and Myrtle Place,"[11] historian Hollace Weiner recalled.

On Sunday, February 18, 1951, the congregation, led by Harry Rosenthal carrying the sacred scroll, the Sefer Torah, marched down Eighth Avenue to their new location. This Torah, (the five books of Moses) given by the Rosenthal family,   ". . . has been an active part of Jewish communal life and religious observance for 650 years,"[12] according to the centennial history. Songs, prayers and greetings preceded the ground breaking ceremony. Throughout the following months congregants watched the new $400,000 plant take shape. Designed by Charles O. Chromaster, it incorporated the best features of the world's finer new synagogues. At last, on September 11, 1952, 700 people attended the dedication festivities. Nationally known Rabbi Manuel Laderman of Denver, Colorado gave the keynote address.

Another dedication, this one on May 15, 1960, celebrated the opening of new educational facilities. That same day   Rabbi Garsek's alma mater, the Hebrew Theological College of Chicago, awarded him an honorary Doctorate of Hebrew Letters. Visiting Rabbi Oscar Fasman said, "Garsek . . . had a great share in developing the physical beauty of this house of God."[13]

Rabbi Garsek retired in 1979 and assumed emeritus status. The flock called Rabbi Alexander Graubart, whose father, Philip, had been rabbi in 1929.

By the 1970s it was again time to move. Ahavath Sholom paid $100,000, a donation from the Mary Potishman Lard Foundation, for twelve acres at Hulen and Briarhaven. "Ground breaking ceremonies were held September 30, 1979, and construction was begun November 21, 1979,"[14] according to the centennial history. The modern style, featuring a prominent Menorah, reflects a forward thinking philosophy with a history rooted in centuries of tradition. December of 1980 saw multiple celebrations of the dedication of the new building. On December 7, 1980 a procession of leaders carrying the Sefer Torah marched that warm, late fall day. The *mezuzah* was affixed to the doorpost. (A *mezuzah* is a small cylinder containing a rolled-up paper or parchment on which are printed verses from Deuteronomy.) Leo Rosten, in *The Joys of Yiddish* explained, "The *mezuzah* consecrates the home, which is so very important in the life and ethos of Jews."[15]

"Prayers were said, speeches were given, and a new era in Congregation Ahavath Sholom's history had begun."[16]

Congregation Ahavath Sholom 4050 S. Hulen

The city joined Ahavath Sholom in mourning the death in 1985 of Rabbi Garsek. Some 1,000 Jews, representatives from a broad range of other denominations, as well as civic leaders, attended the September funeral service at the *shul*. Rabbi Robert Schur, of Congregation Beth-El, said of his friend, "Garsek was always a model for the Jewish faith. He appeared at all times as a man of dignity and strength." He went on to say, "We were greatly different, since he was very traditional and I'm very liberal, but that never interfered with—in fact maybe spiced—our relationship."[17]

After only two years, Rabbi Graubart left for a California position. Rabbi Jack Izakson succeeded him.

Long time member Alfred Cohen remembered Rabbi Izakson as a friendly "people person." He would inquire about one's family or golf game with equal interest. Fort Worth lost him to a Spokane, Washington synagogue.

On May 14, 1991 the congregation called Sidney Zimelman as rabbi. During his rabbinate the congregation voted to affiliate with the United Synagogues of America and to extend to all members of the *shul*, both men and women, egalitarian rights in religious services. Later, debate over Zimelman's leadership style led to the flock's decision not to renew his contract. Moshe Tutnauer of Israel was interim rabbi until December 1999 when Alberto "Baruch" Zeilicovich came to soothe the troubled waters.

No stranger to conflict, Rabbi Zeilicovich served a congregation in Medellin, Colombia during the worst of the drug wars as well as one in strife torn Israel. In addition to his theological background, he holds a master's degree in psychology.

Argentine-born Zeilicovich, a multifaceted man, brought his love of opera and rock music, and his dedication tempered with humor to the 650 families in need of stability. At his installation he said, "We are here . . .to collect diamonds. But the diamonds we will be collecting will be the moments of love and inspiration that we share with each other. And when we do that, we will be the most brilliantly shining congregation anywhere."[18]

He characterized Ahavath Sholom as significant because of its 110 year history of providing for each generation, the oldest, the present, and the next, with Jewish values and Jewish spirituality. "There is a sense of family that makes this *shul* so special. . . . "[19] He described it as *haimish*, the Yiddish term for warm and embracing.

Zeilicovich lauds the quality and quantity of cultural offerings of his new city. "Considering the size, you have such a wonderful, overwhelming, unbelievable cultural life in Fort Worth that compares favorably with New York and other large centers of culture,"[20] he told an interviewer. In both sacred and secular matters, he praised the spirit of togetherness he found here.

The new rabbi's goal is to unite the congregation, the entire Jewish community and to reach out to non-Jews. Zeilicovich is a member of the Cattle Country Clerics and lectures at Texas Christian University. He is a Rotarian, on the Internal Review Board of Cook Children's Medical Center, a member of the National Conference for Community Justice, and the Interfaith Alliance. Not surprisingly, the guest list at his 1999 installation included Congregation Beth-El Rabbi Ralph Mecklenburger, a neighbor from across the street, and Rev. Ken Horton, senior minister of McKinney Memorial Bible Church, a neighbor just down the block, and Tom Law, a former South American missionary and new chief executive of the Tarrant Baptist Association.

■   ■   ■

Beth-El Congregation—1902

In the early 1900s, Reform Jews, more so than their Orthodox cousins, wanted a synagogue reflecting an expression of civic pride as well as a religious identity. These Jews were proud Americans, some born in Texas, others born in the South, and fourteen born in Europe who considered Texas their home. A group of forty-three men met and established a congregation dedicated to worshiping in the reform style. Hollace Weiner, in *Beth-El Congregation Centennial*, wrote, "It implied a Protestant model of worship with congregants responding in English and listening to an organ and a choir rather than chanting in an ancient tongue."[21]

Pioneer Henry Gernsbacher, one of the state's leading merchants of pots, pans and kitchen utensils, called the meeting to order at 11:00 on Sunday morning, September 21, 1902. Those in attendance were leaders in business, lodge and social activities within the small community of Jewish families. Among the founders were Isidore Carb, Max K. Mayer, the first Jew born in

Fort Worth, and Theodore Mack, the first Jewish lawyer. Mack, during a sixty-year career, argued or briefed 1,500 cases. "He refused to try cases in Tarrant County between 1918 and 1924 because of (Ku Klux) Klan-controlled juries,"[22] according to Winegarten and Schechter's history of Texas Jews. Mack's son, Henry, his grandson, Theodore, and his great-granddaughter Elizabeth, followed in his footsteps both as lawyers and as members of synagogues.

Philip W. Greenwall, another of the founders, managed an opera house famous throughout the area. The Greenwall Opera House, owned by his brother Henry Greenwall of Galveston, hosted such stars as Sarah Bernhardt, Douglas Fairbanks, John Philip Sousa and the Barrymores. In 1936 it became the Palace Movie Theatre.

Visiting rabbi Solomon Philo attended Gernsbacher's organizational meeting in hopes of being hired to lead the new congregants. After selecting the name "Beth-El," which means "House of God," they elected Sam Levy president of the congregation and hired Philo on probationary status. With his waxed mustache, tailored frock coat, and slight British accent, he impressed his charges. But, according to historian Flora Schiff, ". . .his efforts were unsuccessful and his services succeeded in almost disrupting the Congregation."[23] They sent him packing.

In 1904 newly ordained Joseph Jasin became their rabbi. Looking not much older than members of the youth group, he nevertheless doubled the membership, and co-edited the Waco based *Jewish Hope*, a Texas Zionist newspaper. He was a frequent public speaker for Zionism, an unusual position for a Reform rabbi. Four short years later Beth-El lost him to a New York assignment with a national Zionist organization.

During Jasin's tenure, the women of Beth-El, not content to worship in borrowed quarters, did what they did best—cook. Ladies in the Fort Worth National Council of Jewish Women hosted covered-dish suppers at the Fort Worth Fat Stock Show and raised $320. That, along with their twenty-five cent a month dues, formed a building fund. Belatedly, the men joined their determined spouses and in 1906 bought a lot at Fifth and Taylor Streets. The first Temple, a two-story neoclassical stucco and wood synagogue, opened two years later.

George Zepin, as a circuit-riding rabbi, first visited Beth-El in 1904, four years before the congregation welcomed the Russian born cleric as full-time leader. Zepin's interests led him to work with Fort Worth charities, and ultimately to a post as secretary of the Union of American Hebrew Congregations in Cincinnati, the umbrella organization for Reform synagogues. "Good shepherd that he was," Weiner noted, "he found his own replacement, Rabbi G. George Fox."[24]

Fox neither looked nor acted like the stereotypical rabbi. The red-headed Chicagoan shocked the city when he announced his first sermon, "Lincoln's Contribution to the Nation." To his mostly Southern-sympathizing congregation this was an outrage. He preached it anyway.

"Rabbi Fox viewed Jewish prostitution as a disgrace and feared that its existence would tarnish the image of Jews in the community,"[25] Winegarten and Schechter wrote. Determined to act, he insisted on a police raid of several brothels in Hell's Half Acre. They rounded up twenty Jewish prostitutes. Recent immigrants with no means of support, these "fallen angels" Fox told to get a decent job or else. "Or else" meant deportation. When asked why he targeted only Jewish women he responded "I look out for my own. . . . They (Gentiles) could look out for their own."[26]

In a more conventional sense, he is remembered for his efforts in building the second temple. According to an article in the February 28, 1919 *Star Telegram*, "The Temple Beth-El Congregation has purchased property at Broadway and Galveston,"[27] In keeping with then current trends, the building committee envisioned a place for family recreation as well as worship. Due to budget cuts, only a kitchen, dining hall and large meeting room with a stage survived. But at a cost of $140,000 they did not skimp on the main part, the sanctuary. The distinctive front entrance featured sculpted tablets containing the Ten Commandments and twin seven-branched Menorahs. For eighty years Jews climbed the sixteen stone steps and entered through one of three ornate double doors. Up to 850 people could worship in the main sanctuary, and the smaller chapel seated 145. Stained glass windows, the eternal light, and the Ark holding the Torah were integral parts of the sanctuary.

Fox also is remembered for his co-founding and editing *The Jewish Monitor*. Even after he left for a larger synagogue in Chicago, the weekly remained in circulation for another decade.

Fox's successor, Harry Merfeld came to Fort Worth in 1922 and easily made friends with local leaders such as Ben E. Keith, Congressman Fritz Lanham, and merchants Oscar Monnig and Marvin Leonard. Prohibition laws were bent as Merfeld and a priest who had access to sacramental wine often enjoyed an ecumenical glass of fruit of the vine. A man of many interests, the rabbi, trained in law, also enjoyed show business. His home away from home and temple was the Fort Worth Little Theater, where he worked backstage as financial manager. This prompted his trustees to insist he spend more hours at the temple and less at the theater.

The Depression years were difficult for Merfeld. He wrestled with paying indebtedness from the building program while juggling declining revenues and a shrinking membership. At one time things were so bad that when the secretary quit the rabbi answered the telephone and paid the bills, sometimes with postage stamps. After the janitor contracted tuberculosis, the rabbi had to empty the trash. By 1936 when Hollywood's Temple Israel issued a call, the theater-loving rabbi was ready to go. Merfeld held other posts and upon his death at age seventy-two Rabbi Robert Schur delivered the eulogy. Rabbi Merfeld and Amy, his wife, are buried in the Beth-El section of Fort Worth's Greenwood Cemetery.

Rabbi Samuel D. Soskin arrived in Fort Worth about the time Adolf Hitler began menacing Europe. Soskin warned of persecution abroad and spear-headed efforts for greater tolerance of minorities in America. Liberal and idealistic, his sermons rankled some congregants as being "too socialistic." He put his idealism to work after the attack on Pearl Harbor by joining the Navy as a chaplain.

Like Soskin, Eugene Lipman wanted to be a chaplain, but first he had to serve a congregation for a year. While at Beth-El he chaired the National Brotherhood Week Committee and produced an Interfaith Concert of Sacred Music. The program consisted of thirty-two Protestant and seven Catholic choirs in concert with the two synagogues. This broad-based effort proved helpful in his chaplaincy. First in Europe he worked with displaced persons, then served as liaison in Palestine and later as a chaplain in Korea.

"The congregation was displeased about losing a second rabbi to the war effort,"[28] Weiner wrote. They invited Corsicana's Rabbi Ernest Szrulyovics

Grey, a Hungarian emigre and too old for military service, to lead them. They celebrated with him when he earned American citizenship during his tenure. The gentle, soft-spoken cleric at times filled in at funerals and weddings at Ahavath Sholom because their rabbi, Philip Graubart, had joined the chaplaincy. When Rabbi Soskin resumed his Fort Worth pulpit, Rabbi Grey returned to Corsicana's Temple Beth-El.

Beth-El welcomed Soskin after the war, but a rocky road lay ahead. Most women of the temple adored the handsome rabbi, except his wife, Dorothy. She chafed at the role of clerical wife and after failure to resolve their problems, the two divorced.

Then on August 29, 1946 the "unthinkable occurred," Weiner wrote. "After a night of 'nickel' poker sponsored by B'nai B'rith and attended by more than 100 cigar-and cigarette-smoking gents, fire erupted in the basement social hall."[29]

Readers of the *Star-Telegram* learned 125 firemen responded to the three alarm blaze, but were unable to save most of the contents. "Consumed in the fire were . . .the pipe organ, pews and many stained glass windows and a number of large boxes packed with clothing and ready for shipment by the Red Cross to needy peoples in Europe."[30] Custodian Enoch Jackson, among the first on the scene, rushed into the inferno and rescued two Torah scrolls. Also, minutes of pre-1920 meetings, housed in a corner library, escaped with minor water damage. The Steinway grand piano, purchased second-hand during the Depression, suffered only smoke damage and is still used by the congregation.

The congregation faced a big decision—move or rebuild. Energetic former Temple President Isadore E. Horwitz pointed out the difficulty in selling the charred remains. He argued that rebuilding would cost $100,000 less than moving. Eighty-seven congregants voted to stay, eighteen to move. "Rebuilding began December 8, with tiny gold-plated shovels distributed to donors,"[31] Weiner recalled.

Back in 1933, Beth-El opened its doors to neighbor Broadway Baptist when that church was in the midst of renovations. Now, the Baptists welcomed the Jews to their sanctuary while Hungarian designer Erno Fabry oversaw the rebuilding. Fabry, remembering how the Nazis denigrated the Star of David, chose to showcase it as a symbol of pride. Each of the ten stained glass windows was topped with a yellow star. A giant wooden star floated from the ceiling. "The ceiling lights were so high that changing burned-out bulbs required staff to assemble scaffolding and stage periodic 'relampings,'"[32] according to Weiner.

Contractor Harry B. Friedman lovingly put Fabry's design into place. He and his wife Mamie Potishman Friedman donated the marble blocks for the altar wall. They also bought cremo Italian marble for the frame surrounding the Ark,.

Rabbi Soskin stood by his congregation and gave encouragement in the rebuilding, but resigned in 1949 to guide Brooklyn's Congregation Beth Emeth. He entered into a successful second marriage and maintained ties with his many friends in Fort Worth until his death in 1970.

Rabbi Milton Rosenbaum brought the observance of some traditional rituals when he came to Beth-El in 1949. As a first step, he reintroduced the blowing of the shofar on High Holy Days. "In 1902 the congregation borrowed a shofar from Dallas, so we know they initially used a traditional ram's horn,"[33] according to Weiner. She found records from the 1930s indicating payment to a trumpet player for services rendered on Rosh Hashanah and Yom Kippur.

With Fort Worth's post war population booming, Beth-El's Religious School found itself bursting at the seams, but Rosenbaum loved it. Especially close to the children, he pushed for more meaningful religious experiences for them, including bar mitzvahs.

Prior to air-conditioning Rosenbaum wanted to encourage the Sabbath worship habit even in hot Fort Worth summers. He enlisted the aid of Rabbi Abraham J. Brachman. Independently wealthy Brachman, who at age forty-five enrolled in rabbinical school, loved to fill the pulpit on High Holy Days for overflow crowds at Ahavath Sholom. He agreed to lead Friday night summer services at Beth-El. Even when temperatures soared above 100 degrees, thirty to forty worshipers showed up for the rites.

Rosenbaum disliked rented housing and without success he urged the board to buy a parsonage. That proved to be a minor flap compared to the outrage the board felt when in 1956 their rabbi signed a petition denouncing the American Council for Judaism, an anti-Zionist organization. Rosenbaum resigned and moved to a congregation in Detroit. He died in 2002.

Rabbi Brachman substituted after Rosenbaum's departure until Rabbi Robert J. Schur came in December 1956. A new era began for Beth-El.

Praised as a "Renaissance rabbi," Schur served his congregation faithfully for more than a quarter of a century while reaching out to the larger community. Within Beth-El he is remembered for his poetic way with words and a small book of prayers he authored is now a collector's item.

Concern for the welfare of children led to Shur's participation as a state delegate to the 1960 White House Conference for Children. He worked to bring about a diagnostic clinic for children that evolved into the esteemed Child Study Center. For teenagers he organized the Fort Worth Federation of Temple Youth. On a personal level, when he learned that two children in his congregation had witnessed the death of their pet, he provided grief counseling. "When Rabbi Schur put his hands on a child's head, the child felt love,"[34] congregant Margot Schwartz recalled.

Soon after his arrival in Fort Worth he became friends with Congressman Jim Wright and city leaders. A strong advocate of racial equality, Schur joined black ministers in civil rights marches and rallies. Despite criticism, said one minister, "He felt that what he was doing was right in the sight of God."[35]

Schur's civic work caused others to think of him as an "articulate conscience of the community." Another described him as one of Fort Worth's "most active pathfinders." Members of Beth-El honored him on the tenth anniversary of his rabbinate by giving him a comical set of plastic keys. Later in the evening they gave him the 1967 Buick Skylark with a set of real keys. To honor him on his twentieth anniversary, congregants Sol Brachman, Manny Rosenthal, and Martin Siegel paid off the temple's debt.

Before his thirtieth anniversary, his health declined. Diagnosed with Alzheimer's disease, he publicly acknowledged his malady and continued to serve his congregation and community as long as possible. In 1986 Beth-El granted him rabbi emeritus status. A beloved friend of many in Texas, he died February 5, 1994.

Rabbi Ralph D. Mecklenburger, who grew up in Chicago, began his Fort Worth ministry in 1984 as an adjunct to Schur. Mecklenburger and the third temple have much in common. Both combine elements of the old and new to communicate modern Judaism. With diplomacy and skill he introduced "new old" traditions in worship such as including a well-trained part-time cantor. He wears a prayer shawl over his rabbinic robe, and does not object if congregants wear the traditional yarmulkes on their heads. Based on his classes in inter-faith dialog at Brite Divinity School, he said in a recent interview, "I think everybody (all denominations) is moving toward more ritual and traditional observances"[36] He hastened to add this did not mean Beth-El was embracing a Conservative stance, but rather adding richness to its services.

By an overwhelming vote in 1997, the congregation declared its willing-ness to relegate cherished memories of weddings and other rites to family

Congregation Beth-El 207 W. Broadway circa 1970. Courtesy Marty Stenzler

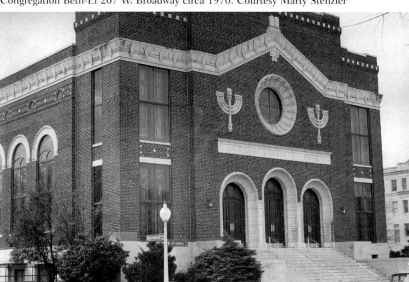

Congregation Beth-El 4900 Briarhaven, 2003. Courtesy Art Lederman

albums, and move to a new religious home. Once again women, this time Judie B. Greenman and Louise Appleman led the drive for a building fund.

In *Beth-El Congregation: Fort Worth, Texas 2000-5760*, Architect David Stanford explained ". . . my goal was to synthesize the history of Judaism with contemporary amenities and visions."[37] To conceptually develop the Temple site, he researched the design of King Solomon's Temple in Jerusalem. After much study and thought, he designed an edifice at 4900 Briarhaven Road that captures the aura of ancient Jerusalem and the utility of modern style. "Built of large, rough white limestone blocks, the complex features a series of walls, courtyards, and open space that become progressively smaller as worshipers approach the Holy of Holies,"[38] Weiner wrote. The colors are much like those of Jerusalem. Landscaped parking areas surround the building, creating a "walled" effect.

The architecture carries out the wishes of the congregation for a building that brings the outdoors in. Large plate glass windows in the sanctuary, which face east, symbolic of facing toward Jerusalem, give a feeling of light and openness. Stained glass windows on the east wall represent the symbols of Jewish worship and theology—creation, redemption and revelation. These features are "the new." Chairs, light fixtures, the two limestone Menorahs, and the scripture on the Rosenthal Meditation Garden wall (Give ear, O Lord, unto my prayer), "the old" were brought from the second temple. A part of the building houses the "Hall of Remembrance" where treasured items from the Broadway Avenue sanctuary are displayed. One memento is a tiny gold-plated shovel, a souvenir of rebuilding after the 1946 fire.

Not everything of value went to the new location. On November 26, 2000, Broadway Baptist Church dedicated a blue stained-glass medallion Star of David given by their former neighbors. The twelve-inch relic hangs in Broadway's reception area in a place of honor, facing east toward the temple. The inscription reads, "In recognition of 75 years of friendship, cooperation and respect. May the Lord bless you and keep you."

Despite the vividness of the new physical plant, Rabbi Mecklenburger declares it is the people that make the synagogue special. Although Beth-El has been home to many civic leaders, including Mayor Bayard Friedman and Congressman Martin Frost, he credits the cooperative spirit of all his congregants as making it a welcoming place to members and the community at large. "I found from the moment I got here that Beth-El was open to new ideas,"[39] he said. As he, and they, go forward he hopes to continue bringing Jewish values in a mix of traditional and modern elements of worship to an ever expanding flock.

Chapter Ten

THE LUTHERAN
CONGREGATIONS

William B. Williamson in *An Encyclopedia of Religions in the United States* described the Lutheran Church—Missouri Synod as ". . .one of the historic Christian churches frequently identified with evangelical denominations because of its evangelistic and missionary emphasis."[1] Their worship is liturgical and contemporary, and they underscore the authority of the Scriptures alone as God's truth for today. Rev. Walter Dorre, of Fort Worth's St. Paul Church explained, "The Lutheran Church is characterized by the simple Gospel message for the conservation and continuance of the unity of true faith."[2]

Lutherans hark back to Martin Luther, from whom they get their name. In the United States Dr. C. F. W. Walther is credited with organizing the Missouri Synod. He was the first president of Concordia Lutheran Seminary. The synod stresses both sacred and lay education. Parents are encouraged to send their children to Lutheran schools and instruction prior to membership is practiced.

■   ■   ■

St. Paul Lutheran Church—1896

God must have been watching over the roofers at 1801 W. Freeway because none fell off the steeply pitched roof of the striking contemporary designed church. Parishioners would argue that God has watched over St. Paul Lutheran Church since its inception as *Evangelisch Lutherische St. Paulus Gemeinde Zu* Fort Worth, Texas.

From a trickle of immigrants in the 1830s to a flood in the last half of the century, Germans of the Lutheran persuasion came to Texas seeking economic and political freedom. By 1890 they had moved from the Central to the North Texas area. At first missionaries from Dallas served the budding Fort Worth congregation, but in 1893 the synod assigned Johann C. Schulenberg as pastor. He covered his territory in a buggy and on horseback, serving preaching stations from Wichita Falls to Bridgeport to Bowie to Fort Worth. Although his pastorate included missions scattered over a 150 mile stretch of largely undeveloped areas to the north and west, most of his efforts went toward helping the Fort Worth church.

Chartered by the State of Texas in 1896 under its German name, and with money borrowed from the Missouri Synod, the flock built a simple wooden structure at the corner of Hemphill and Railroad (Vickery) for a total cost of $1,500. Legend has it the church was so narrow one usher, by using a yard stick with a box attached, could collect the offering with a single pass.

Schulenberg conducted services in German. This proved to be a problem when Swedish Lutherans sought to join the congregation. The next pastor, Paul Lehman preached in both English and German. To further attract parishioners, Lehman urged the purchase of bilingual hymnals, at a cost of fifteen cents each. Ill health caused Lehman to resign and Rev. Carl Baepler began his ministry in 1897. He left in 1900. The next pastor, Rev. L. J. Roehm, served from 1904 to 1908. He received a salary of $15.00 a month. Other expenses, recorded in 1906, revealed eighty-five cents for one month's electricity, and repair of hail storm damage in the amount of $4.10.

Worshipers numbered about seventy when Reverend H. Weinert ministered to the flock, 1909 to 1910. Rev. A. Bohot served the following six years, but internal difficulties marred his pastorate.

The congregation grew slowly until the 1917 arrival of Rev. W. C. Geisler. Under his guidance they built a new church and parsonage at May and Cannon Streets. During World War I the ruling board offered the use of the church basement to soldiers from Camp Bowie. Still, there was suspicion by some townsfolk of the German-speaking members' loyalty. In 1923 the congregation voted to change their name to St. Paul Evangelical Lutheran, but services were conducted in both English and German until 1933. "St. Paul experienced a setback when, after becoming ill while attending the synodical convention in St. Louis, Rev. Geisler was called home by the Lord on July 28, 1933,"[3] according to A Century of Grace.

The loss of their dynamic pastor, and the economic woes of the Depression era, brought to a close years of steady progress. Lutherans historically valued Christian education, yet the school Geisler worked so hard to establish and maintain, closed shortly after his death.

One of the school's teachers, Victor Behnken, pastored the church for the next thirteen years. Ordained and installed November 8, 1933, by his father, Rev. J. W. Behnken, vice-president of the Missouri Synod, the younger Behnken led the 300 members through the last days of the Depression and the World War II years. In 1943, at St. Paul's Golden Jubilee, the leadership unveiled plans for a $2,500 addition as soon as possible considering wartime shortages of men and materials. The congregation dedicated the new Sunday School building in July 1946. It contained six classrooms and two meeting rooms with space for 100 people.

Rev. Behnken resigned to accept a call to a church in California, and Rev. W. E. Dorre came to oversee many changes in the growing congregation. Chicago native Dorre graduated from Concordia College at Fort Wayne, Indiana in 1920 and received his pastoral training at Concordia Theological Seminary in St. Louis. He also held a degree in social science from the University of Houston. A member of the Air Force Reserves, he entered the service as a chaplain in 1941 and served until 1946.

At St. Paul he started publication of a newsletter, dubbed "Parish Paper," but he is best remembered as the pastor who moved the congregation into their new sanctuary on the West Freeway.

A *Star-Telegram* headline told the whole story—"St. Paul's (sic) Church, That of the Slanting Ridgepole, Should Be Seen From Inside,"[4] and indeed it is impossible to fully articulate in print the majesty of the building. Stained glass windows of modern design catch the morning sun and spread their softly diffused colors. The clerestory windows depict the life of St. Paul, for whom the church is named. The floor of the chancel is of Arkansas rough-cut marble. The seven steps leading to the altar represent the seven-fold unity of the Church, as seen in Ephesians 4:4-6. Forty-six nave pews seat 500 with additional seating in the choir loft and chapel. The north glass wall, away from the Freeway, looks out into the courtyard and a three-sided tower. Three hundred can be seated for dining in the Fellowship Hall.

Rev. Dorre left in 1959 for Sao Paulo, Brazil to become resident mission counselor for the Missouri Synod in South America. The saddened congregation bid him "Godspeed," and opened their hearts to Rev. E. E. Pipelow.

Pipelow's pithy sayings enlivened the church newsletter. He reminded his congregation of eternal truths with such admonitions as, "It does not make a person an angel to be eternally up in the air and harping on something," or "Keep your chin on the windowsill of Heaven.[5] In his four-year ministry the membership grew to 1202.

When Rev. Pipelow left for a church in Wisconsin, Rev. Gerald P. Otte succeeded him in 1963. Otte, a graduate of St. John's Lutheran College in Winfield, Kansas, and from Concordia Seminary, came to St. Paul from a pastorate in Houston. "Pastor Otte's appreciation for mission programs had been fostered by his first pastoral assignment. He was the founding pastor of Houston's St. Andrew Lutheran . . .where he started out with just five families."[6] Nine years later the church counted over 1,000 congregants. At St. Paul, like in Houston, his messages of evangelism and outreach resulted in rapid growth of the congregation. His 1979 death cut short Rev. Otte's ministry, but the congregation felt his impact long afterwards.

For two years Rev. Ken Hennings led the grieving flock. Previously associate minister, his move to senior status went smoothly. He kept the congregation focused until Rev. Jack Schneider became senior minister in 1982. Schneider had been associate minister and knew the congregation well. During the latter part of his ten year pastorate he prepared the congregation for their centennial celebration.

Reporter Paul Bourgeois wrote in September 1993, "St. Paul Church, one of the oldest Lutheran congregations in Fort Worth, is celebrating its 100th anniversary and looking forward to another century of service to the community."[7] Rev. Dr. John Messmann, pastor since June 1992, led the 2,000 members as they remembered their history and reflected on their progress over the years. One of those memories harked back to 1953. A widow in their congregation needed help. Her family, including twins, had outgrown their small home, but she had no money to buy a bigger house. Four carpenters, also members of the congregation, donated their time and materials and enlarged her house.

Frieda Lyle remembered riding the streetcar to church—the one at Hemphill and Railroad Avenue. Paul Brandt reminisced about his mother's playing the organ in the first two sanctuaries.

While it is pleasant to look back, Rev. Dr. John Messmann looks forward. He sees St. Paul as special because of its opportunity to have a widespread influence. "We send out a mailing to our members to over sixty zip codes, so we draw from Tarrant, Denton, Johnson, Parker and Dallas counties. Whatever God does here is multiplied among sixty zip codes," he said in a recent interview.[8]

In addition to its unique architecture, THE SIGN draws many comments. It came about in the 1960s when a member posed the question, "If companies advertise their products on signs and billboards, why don't we advertise God's

St. Paul Lutheran Church 1800 West Freeway.

promises?" And now they do. Each week different Bible verses, one for east bound motorists and one for west bound, are posted. One can only estimate how many thousands of passers-by, who never give thought to the church that sponsors it, are inspired by the verses. Rev. Messmann told of receiving letters from total strangers typically saying "I drove by in a moment of desperation in my life and felt God spoke to me." One writer said the sign "saved my life." "That's a blessing,"[9] he said.

While Lutherans traditionally came from Germany or northern European countries, Rev. Messmann explained that St. Paul's ministry now is representative of a wide ethnic mix. In 2002 a group of African immigrants, mostly Sudanese, once a month worship at St. Paul. Also, once a month immigrants from India worship there, and the church is reaching out to Hispanics. These efforts give St. Paul a decided international flavor, and that is another reason why Messmann, who grew up on a farm in Indiana, thanks God for his association with St. Paul.

Chapter Eleven

THE CONGREGATIONALISTS/ UNITED CHURCH OR CHRIST CONGREGATIONS

The United Church of Christ (UCC), not to be confused with the Church of Christ, was formed in 1957 by the union of the Congregational Christian Churches and the Evangelical and Reformed Church. These were themselves the result of unions. "The Congregational Churches of the English Reformation with the Puritan New England roots in America and the Christian Church with American frontier beginnings were both concerned for freedom of religious expression and local autonomy,"[1] Williamson wrote in *An Encyclopedia of Religions in the United States*. Tenets of the UCC are basically those of the several streams of its heritage, with emphasis given to unity in essentials, liberty in nonessentials, and charity in all things. These are combined with a strong emphasis on social justice.

Early Congregationalists promoted education as well as religion and founded Harvard, Yale, and Dartmouth colleges. The denomination counted among its members such noted theologians as the late Reinhold Niebuhr and Paul Tillich.

■   ■   ■

First Congregational Church—1903 ## *St. John's United Church of Christ—1881*

Fort Worth's claim to heritage from the Pilgrims who came over on the Mayflower is vested in the First Congregational Church, 4201 Trail Lake Drive. Very shortly after that historic ship landed, fifty-two passengers called a meeting, elected a leader, and formed a church. "They organized what was called a 'Civic Body Politic,' and promulgated a 'Declaration of Rights,' known as the Mayflower Compact, which became the organic law of the Congregational Church," Sioux Campbell wrote in an early *Fort Worth City Guide*. When the Pilgrims landed at Plymouth, the First Congregational Church in America was quickly established. "The parent church organization is still in existence at Plymouth, Mass.,"[2] Campbell wrote.

Reenacting their heritage even today, each Thanksgiving members of First Congregational don period costumes. At sunrise, while most Texans are still asleep, bustling figures in the church kitchen are preparing coffee, eggs, sausage, applesauce, and biscuits. "The women of the church, wearing the white hats and long gray dresses that covered the limbs of the modest Pilgrim women, have prepared the food. It's served to the hungry crowd by teenage girls, also garbed in traditional attire,"[3] according to an *ULTRA* article. They join others at long tables to ask God's blessing and partake of a bounteous breakfast before an early morning service. The celebration is so old none of the original worshipers are still living and no one remembers when the tradition began.

At 8:45 a.m. a male member raises a conch shell to his lips and summons the congregation to worship service. Men in black clothing with wide white collars and cuffs sit on one side of the sanctuary and women sit on the other side. The historic tithingman, for years played by the late long-time member Dr. William Skokan, raps the floor with a brass knocker on the end of a long stick: the signal for the preaching to begin. Because Pilgrim sermons tended to last two hours or more, the tithingman used the brass knob to tap the head of any male unlucky enough to drop off to sleep. The other end of the stick, equipped with a feather, he used to tickle sleepy women's noses. In addition to today's much briefer sermon, the service includes singing in the "lining" style since Pilgrims had no hymnals. The church welcomes guests to this observance.

The story of First Congregational is entwined with the boom days when Fort Worth was becoming a national livestock marketing center. On June 8, 1903 forty citizens signed a charter establishing the church under the leadership of Rev. George W. Ray, assigned here by the denomination's mission board.

First worshiping in a tent on Henderson Street, the group soon built a wooden meeting house nearby on Cannon Street. The *Fort Worth Record* noted, "It is a neat little structure, built at a cost of about $400 and will seat about 200 people."[4] Electric wiring for four lights cost $12.00 and a woodbox outside the front door held fuel for the heating stove. "One account states that 'a privy sat discreetly at the rear.'"[5]

Within a year the congregation made plans for a larger facility. They bought property at the corner of Pennsylvania and College Avenues and hired architects. "In addition to local building pledges, they were assisted with small grants and loans from the Congregational Building Society, and by a large gift from an unexpected source,"[6] Rev. Dave Barber said in a 2003 press release on the occasion of the church's one hundredth anniversary. The unexpected gift came from Battle Creek, Michigan. C. R. and Caroline Post were charter members of First Congregational. Their son C. W. Post headed the cereal company that made "Post Toasties." Letters in church's archives detail the arrangement. On Postum Cereal Co. Ltd. letterhead, dated 4/28/04 Charles wrote, "Dear Father, You can say to Reverend Ray that I have concluded to devote five thousand dollars ($5,000.00) to the Church enterprise somewhat along the lines he suggested."[7] The lines suggested involved the congregation raising $5,000 to match the gift. The letter is signed "Yours truly, Charles."

The July 1, 1906 issue of the *Telegram* described the new building. "A commodious auditorium, and deep rostrum, are surrounded by class rooms for the study of Bible lessons, and in the rear of the auditorium there is a handsome balcony."[8] Arranged as an amphitheater, the sanctuary had a seating capacity of 700. The article continued, "The high arched roof is finished in the natural color of the wood with which it is ceiled, and this effect being carried out through the entire building gives an impression of coolness that is strengthened by the perfect ventilation of the entire structure."[9]

Rev. Ray served until 1916, and William E. Jones pastored the flock until 1919, followed by J. E. Tedford and O. J. Read. In 1923, Rev. Samuel T. McKinney began a seventeen year ministry. After McKinney retired from active ministry in 1941, for years he led Bible classes in the homes of those who studied with him. In 1954 the group decided to establish a nondenominational church. It became known as McKinney Bible Church (see page 255).

Rev. D. D. Wilson comforted the First Congregational flock during World War II, with Glenn Utterback serving from 1945 until 1948. "In 1949, under the leadership of Dr. William C. Burton, the congregation decided to move to a new location in Westcliff,"[10] according to the 2003 press release. Not everyone supported the move. Those who did reasoned the old church had inadequate educational facilities, expansion would be difficult, and repairs expensive. Still, only eighty-two members made the move to the bald hill in a developing neighborhood.

Rev. Burton grew up in Everman when it was still a small community and Burton knew "just about everyone, including J. E. Foster," said volunteer archivists Carolyn Crowley and Helen Bernardez. Foster was developing Westcliff and Burton asked him for land on which to build a church. Foster agreed and after some negotiating, Burton secured the choice property.

The press release quoted, "A newspaper account of the new building said that the church 'was on one of the highest hilltops in the area,' which only a short time ago 'was a cow pasture.'"[11] Unlike the traditional Congregational little white-steepled church on the village green, this large church is Gothic in style and built of Crab Orchard sandstone. The sanctuary is lit with stained glass windows depicting Jesus, Abraham and Luke and traditional Christian symbols. The Gethsemane Window, the familiar image of Christ praying in the Garden, is the focal point of the sanctuary. The window was moved from the Pennsylvania Avenue church and reconfigured into a round design from the earlier square. The church is set in a dramatic panorama of expansive lawn and oak trees.

The congregation held the first service at the new location on March 5, 1950. The membership grew to almost 500. Pastors during this period included Clarence W. Baldwin and Rollin Russell.

Kansas native Ralph Nichols served from 1974 to May 1999. Dr. Nichols graduated from Andover Newton Seminary and received a Ph.D. from the University of Missouri. While leading First Congregational he participated in Allied Communities of Tarrant and the Tarrant Area Community of Churches. "He preached his sermon last Sunday, May 24th, 'Faith and Risk,'"[12] his obituary noted. The sermon was considered by many congregants to be not only timely, but one of outstanding and remembered deliverance. Nichols died of a stroke the following Tuesday.

In 1998 St. John's, a United Church of Christ, ceased operations. The membership deeded the property to First Congregational and many of the

First Congregational Church 4201 Trail Lake Dr. Courtesy First Congregational Church

congregation became active members there. The property, located at 908
Pennsylvania Avenue, was sold to Celebration Community Church.

St. John's had a rich history going back to 1881 when twelve families of
German descent began meeting in the H. Raab home with missionary Rev. F.
Werning. The next year the group secured a charter and Rev. A. H. Becker
became their first full-time minister. They paid John Peter Smith $300 for a
lot on Calhoun Street. "On that parcel of land was built a boxlike church with
five windows on each side for a cost of $800,"[13] according to archival records.
September 2, 1883 marked the date of the dedication service. A few years later
they moved the building to Texas and Taylor Streets and held the first service
in the new Evangelical Church.

St. John's seventy-fifth anniversary history noted, "The site of our church
on Pennsylvania was purchased in 1915. . . the church building was removed
to the new location. . . . The church was redecorated in 1935 at which time
stained glass windows were installed."[14] The congregation prospered and in
1951 a Gothic stone structure replaced the twice-moved frame building.

Early on, the first services were held in German, but phased out during
World War I. Still, the flavor of the German heritage was recaptured in tra-
ditional Christmas Eve services when the flock sang *Stille Nacht* just as
Joseph Mohr wrote it.

Despite the efforts of outstanding ministers, the latter half of the twentieth century was difficult for the church. The hospital district expanded into residential neighborhoods and as people moved away they moved their membership to churches closer to home. St. John's officially disbanded in 1998.

At First Congregational, following the unexpected death of Rev. Nichols, Rev. Jane McDonald served as interim pastor until the congregation called Rev. Dave Barber.

Some preachers *pray* for rain. Barber is more likely to *predict* rain based on his Ph.D. in meteorology from the University of Wisconsin. After college teaching the easygoing professor enrolled in Duke Divinity School to prepare for a second career. He "feels comfortable at First Congregational because he sees the members as very open and inclusive who espouse the values of the larger communion of the United Church of Christ,"[15] he said in a recent interview. One of his goals is to bring more people to an understanding of the church and thus bring more people into it. In 2003 the membership is around 215, but according to Rev. Barber, "Regardless of its size, this congregation has never wavered as a force for Christian leadership and justice in the world." He continued, "The church has always been an open, liberal, and caring church, welcoming people from many traditions, cultures and religious backgrounds, and with a solid commitment to benevolence—helping people in need at home and around the world."[16]

History supports his words. During World War II the church provided a day care center for mothers working in the war effort.

In addition to the traditional ways in which churches minister to the needy, First Congregational has sponsored five refugee families, starting with the Enrique Fernandez family from Cuba in 1963. Robert, who was six-years-old when they came to Fort Worth, is now a certified public accountant and has been Chair of the Board of Directors of the Hispanic Chamber of Commerce. The Tan and Oeur families immigrated from Cambodia in the early eighties, and the Hadzialic and Babic families from Bosnia arrived in the late nineties. All the families are now well established and are productive citizens.

These and other accomplishments bode well for the future of the "Pilgrim" church on the hill.

Chapter Twelve

THEY TOO MADE HISTORY

The criteria for inclusion in this book were that at least one church of the denomination must be one hundred years old or older, or if less than one hundred years, it must have made a significant impact on the community. This chapter profiles churches from a wide spectrum of theology, not yet one hundred years old, but important to the broader scope of Fort Worth congregations.

■ ■ ■

St. Demetrios Greek Orthodox Church—1910

Demetreos Anagnostakis, a native of Crete, arrived in Fort Worth in 1892. He dreamed of becoming a cowboy, but settled for a job as yard man in the cattle pens for the Fort Worth Trading Company. Six years later he was part-owner. In January 1910 he joined Vasilios Bouthounis (who Anglicized his name to Peter Booth), Demetrios Metaras, Peter Georgoulis and Nicholas Gavreil in organizing St. Demetrios Parish. They named the church in honor of Anagnostakis, J'Nelle Pate wrote in *North of the River*.[1] It was the first Greek Orthodox Parish not only in Texas, but in the entire Southwest. Fr. Athan Angelopulos of New Orleans held the first services one year later in rented second-floor quarters at Weatherford and Houston Streets.

As was the Greek custom, after the men established themselves they sent for their families, and the parish grew.

Almost a century later, St. Demetrios member Theodor Diakis summed up the ethos of his fellow Greeks. "Everywhere they go, they take with them the religion, the customs and everything. The church for us is not only the place we go to pray, it's the place we keep our customs, the place we keep our language. It's more than just the religion."[2]

During the council presidency of co-founder Peter Booth, the governing board bought a lot at the corner of Ross and N. W. 21st Streets in North Fort

Worth. In 1917 the cornerstone, still legible today, was laid. A special "Blessing of the Waters" ceremony by the Very Rev. Fr. Damianos Ermogenis, the first permanent priest, highlighted the occasion. Frs. Gerondias Coutouzis and Theoclitos Triantafilides also ministered to the congregation for short periods in its infancy. In 1916 Fr. Ermogenis came and led them into their second decade. Kirilos Papagrigoriou, Charalambos Marinos and Father S. Constantinidis served the parish during the 1920s according to the *75th Anniversary: 1910-1985* history.

As the cattle industry changed, many of the Greek families turned to truck farming and other small businesses, but the congregation remained vibrant. Firmly established now, the leaders started after-school Greek language classes for the children. A woman's organization and a church choir added richness to the ethnic fellowship.

"One of the outstanding pastors to serve the Greek community here," according to the *Star-Telegram,* "was Rev. Anastasios Vlamides, who was pastor . . . for nearly twenty years before his death in 1955."[3] In 1911, after graduating from high school in Constantinople, rather than be conscripted by the Turkish army, he boarded a French ship bound for the United States. Dressed in shirt sleeves and carrying a pad and pencil, he was mistaken by authorities for a dock clerk. "Once aboard, I was free of Turkish supervision,"[4] he explained.

Vlamides lived with an uncle in Galveston. When World War I broke out, he gained citizenship and enlisted in the United States Army as an infantryman. While in France, his skill in speaking English, French, Greek and Turkish led to promotion as an interpreter. Following the end of hostilities he returned to Galveston and was ordained into the priesthood. He founded the first Greek Orthodox church and from there he moved to Houston's Church of the Annunciation.

"In 1929 Father Vlamides came to Fort Worth to serve as pastor of St. Demetrios for the first time until 1935,"[5] the *Press* noted. That year the bishop transferred him to Little Rock, and later to Nashville.

The Rev. Fr. Germanos Stefopoulos served the flock from 1934 to 1939. During this time Mrs. Ourania Karadimetris organized the first choir and served as its director. With the help of their priest the women of the church formed the Athenia Society. Pete Dear, whose Greek name meant "to be beloved," started a youth group, the Sons of Pericles in 1937.

The church family mourned the accidental death of Father Stefopoulas who drowned while fishing at Lake Worth in May 1939. He is remembered for making sure every child in the parish received a Christmas gift, even in the depths of the Great Depression.

Rev. Fr. Evangelos Kontonikolaou ministered from 1939 to 1941. He and parishioner James G. Gavrel promoted the establishment of a church hall building fund. Their efforts bore fruit and in December 1940, Gus and Stella Barakis' wedding reception was the first held in the new hall. Father Evangelos is remembered for his leadership of the Tarrant County Greek War Relief work. Fr. Dimitrios Lolakas led the congregation from 1941 to 1942.

In 1943 Father Vlamides returned to St. Demetrios where he remained until his death in 1955. During this time he founded church educational centers at Wichita Falls and Waco, in addition to his local service. Vlamides also ministered to churches in Eastland and Breckenridge concurrently with his tenure in Fort Worth. The beloved priest died of cancer in August 1955. The congregation dedicated the seventy-fifth anniversary history to his memory.

Following Vlamides' death Rev. Fr. Germanos Tzoumanis served for two years, 1955-1957. He witnessed a dramatic change in the parish—the general assembly voted to allow women to serve on the Parish Council. The council elected Dr. Dorothy Patras president in 1972 and again in 1979. During her first term of office she was the first woman president in the whole Archdiocese of North and South America.

Other priests during the 1960s and 1970s were Dr. George Papademetriou, Gabriel Tsilakis and Paul Michaelides. Reverend John Contoravdis ministered to the group for sixteen years from 1976 to 1992.

An innovation occurred in the 1960s that changed the congregation in a major way. "Mrs. Artemis Smith . . . proposed an idea that grew and developed into a tradition that still delights more people than just the members of the North Side Greek Community. She suggested a fairly modest bread and pastry sale to acquaint the community with Greek baking and to help raise funds for the church."[6] Every November the aroma of baklava, karidopita, and spanakopita filled the North Side air. At first they set up in a small area behind the sanctuary, but in 1975 Father John suggested they expand the menu. The venture grew and the money raised funded the construction of the community center.

In November 1979 the communicants of St. Demetrios purchased three acres of land off the Jacksboro Highway near 21st Street to provide for future growth. A building committee developed plans for an all-purpose community center. They held ground breaking ceremonies, led by parishioner Rocky Barakis, July 18, 1982. Later phases included an educational wing and a new sanctuary.

Fr. John saw the building of the center, but he left to establish a congregation in British Columbia before the realization of his dream—a new sanctuary for St. Demetrios. During his long tenure, he enjoyed the devotion of his congregation. "One thing he did (was) he became a part of our community and families. He was everybody's friend,"[7] member Ann Diakis said.

Rev. Theodore Bita, who succeeded Contoravdis, did not fare as well. Within a year of his coming, the congregation fragmented. Some supported the priest, others denounced the Romanian-born cleric because he did not speak Greek beyond the required liturgy. St. Demetrios eventually healed, and the diocese appointed Rev. Robert Began to the parish. Poor health cut short his ministry.

Father George Bessinas took over the leadership of the now smaller congregation. Like Bita's, his tenure was arduous. The congregation asked the bishop to transfer him. "I did my best there, we just didn't get along,"[8] Bessinas told reporter Mark Lowery. In 1998 the priest went to a parish in Shreveport where he felt more comfortable.

Now without an ordained leader, the group continued to meet. Dr. Dorothy Patras spoke of this period in their history as a time of renewal. Although a proper service couldn't be held without a priest, members went every Sunday, lit candles, prayed and listened to a taped liturgy in Greek. This Patras found to be strengthening. Every other weekend Fr. Peter Murtos flew in from Raleigh, North Carolina to administer the sacraments. Described as a "really nice man," the seventy-eight-year-old cleric filled the void until 2000 when Father Nicholas Gamvas began his Fort Worth ministry.

With much pomp and ceremony, on Sunday, April 21, 2002 Gamvas and Rev. Nicholas Katinas of Dallas, led the marchers from their historic little

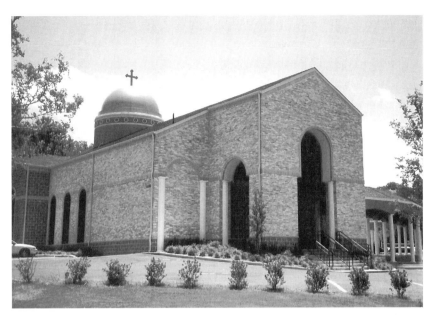

St. Demetrios Greek Orthodox Church 2020 NW 21st St. Courtesy St. Demetrious Church

church to the new one on the hill. Resplendent in their white, gold-trimmed robes, with ornate crosses hanging around their necks, the two were the picture of ecclesiastic elegance, except for Gamvas' cowboy boots peeking out from his vestment. "It is only a mile from the tiny brick sanctuary built in 1917 on Ross Avenue to the church's new home with the golden Byzantine dome overlooking Jacksboro Highway," reporter Mary Rogers wrote. "But every step took the oldest Greek Orthodox parish in Texas into the future."[9] Alcon Laboratories vice-president Nick Tsumpis walked in memory of his grandmother, Felio Tsumpis. She, in the 1920s, walked to the church every Saturday and cleaned candle wax from the carpet and dusted the icons and altar.

Father Gamvas went to a church in Hawaii in the summer of 2002, leaving the future in the capable hands of Fr. Michael Stearns.

Illinois native Stearns, following his graduation from Holy Cross Greek Orthodox School of Theology, served churches in Massachusetts. In Fort Worth he found the friendliness of the people, which he described as a mix of Greek and Texas hospitality, a welcoming combination. He was appreciative of the congregation's forward thrust as evidenced by the building of a new sanctuary. He spoke with pride of the new Hispanic Orthodox Mission.

This entity, a first of its kind, meets in the Ross Street sanctuary and serves the growing Hispanic population in the community. Barely into his pastorate, Fr. Michael wants to reach out to all members of his flock. And like all pastors, he dreams for the day when the mortgage is paid and St. Demetrios can be consecrated—another first. He sees a bright future for the church that has weathered so many storms, but now basks in the sunshine.

■   ■   ■

Christ Church Assembly of God—1925

Most new churches start out with a handful of members. Not so the First Assembly of God of Fort Worth. When the church organized on May 14, 1925, there were three hundred worshipers, many reluctant to formalize their fifteen-year-old congregation.

Back in the spring of 1910, Rev. Arch P. Collins and Rev. W. R. Potter began holding services in a mission on Fifteenth Street and thus the actual beginning of the church could be dated from that time. From the mission Collins led his flock to a camp meeting in Tyler's Lake Park. This park, just east of Hillside Park about midway to Sycamore, sat on land donated in the 1880s by the Tyler heirs. Around the turn of the twentieth century it was a favorite spot for picnics and family outings. Groups met at the pavilion, set in a grove of elms, oaks and willows, and near the lake. Later park officials drained the lake and renamed it Glenwood Park. But for Collins and his followers it housed fond memories. "Prayer and Praise services sometimes lasted all night. Truly the flame of Pentecost had been ignited in Fort Worth,"[10] according to a church history.

The 1910 "great camp meeting," and the sixth annual encampment of the Pentecostal people in the South, ". . . furnished the impetus for the organization of Assembly of God Churches in the city. . ."[11] according to Writers' Project data.

Mrs. W. C. Wilder, one of those in attendance at the camp meeting, felt the need to open her home for weekly prayer services. Historian Evelyn Newman wrote, "These . . . became a great source of strength for this new body of believers. The Wilders became strong leaders (and) it was through their leadership that a Sunday school was begun."[12]

From 1910 to 1925 the group of Pentecostal believers met in several locations. After the camp meeting they worshiped in a large tent at Daggett and South Main, then in rent free quarters on Main Street, and then Elizabeth and Bryan Streets. "The interest created. . . led to the creation of the first Assembly of God Church in Texas,"[13] the Writers Project historian noted. From Elizabeth Street the group moved to Clinton Street on the North Side. This proved an inconvenience for most parishioners and soon they were back on the South Side.

"At this time there was no formal organization within the body, in fact, there was considerable resistance to the idea of becoming organized, some feared that organization would quench the Holy Spirit,"[14] Pastor Darius Johnston wrote in "Taking A Look." Commercial banks would not make loans to loose-knit groups, so Pastors Hugh Cadwalder and O. H. Law convinced the members they needed to join the Pentecostal Assemblies of God. They did so and the bankers helped them purchase their first church property. They bought a lot at the corner of Hattie and Crawford and erected a building. Later they sold this property, worshipped again in a tent, then used the old Four Square Church on Annie Street. Plans to buy this building were scuttled and instead in the early 1930s they purchased the Presbyterian church on the corner of Jennings and Morphy.

Reverend W. W. Hall, Rev. F. D. Davis, and Rev. Stephen Vandemerwe led the congregation during this time. From 1941 to 1944 Reverend A. C. Bates served as pastor, and Rev. Charles N. Rice from 1944 to 1946.

Under the leadership of Reverend Leonard Norville, the congregation built a sanctuary at 1424 Hemphill Street. They undertook the $94,000 cost with a giant leap of faith. Dedicated in November 1946, the building housed the flock for twenty-three years. After Norville's tenure Rev. Charles Dobbins pastored the Hemphill Street church from 1951 to 1952. Other pastors during that decade were Ira Stanphill, Martin Davidson, and Tom Hollingsworth.

Reverend Eugene Perrault was minister in 1968 when the congregation bought property at 5051 Trail Lake Drive from the Pilgrim Holiness Church. In 1970, under the pastoral leadership of Jerry King the congregation was still raising funds to construct education and administration facilities.

Children's World bought the Hemphill Street property and took immediate possession. For seven months the flock worshiped at the old Central Methodist Church on Lipscomb Street. In 1971, with the first phase of construction finished, they worshiped in their new home. In six short years the congregation outgrew their quarters.

With the new building came a new name. In the 1970s, while keeping the Pentecostal message in their worship services, the congregation on Trail Lake wanted to broaden its base of appeal. They opted to change their name to Christ Church to attract people who were interested in a deeper walk with God, but were not comfortable within the traditional, and stereotypical, Pentecostal setting. The congregation remained under the umbrella of the Assemblies of God fellowship, but with their own constitution.

"In 1978 under the leadership of Pastor Jerry King, the property at 5401 Woodway was purchased from McKinney Memorial Church, for the sum of $400,000,"[15] historian Newman wrote. As need for space increased, the church found itself renting property in the strip shopping center across the street from the sanctuary. Pastor Darius Johnston would lead the flock to a new location in 1998.

Johnston's relationship with Christ Church dates back to a 1983 meeting with King. Johnston graduated from Fort Worth's Southwest High School, and from Southwestern Assemblies of God University in Waxahachie. The personable minister has seen membership grow from 250 to an average of over 900 in weekly worship attendance. Of his pastoral career he wrote, "It was an interesting turn of events that brought us to the (Christ) church. I told God when I started in evangelism that He would have to speak real clearly to me if He planned for me to stay an evangelist when children came along."[16]

As an itinerant minister, Johnston preached a weekend meeting at Christ Church for Jerry King, then he left for Tennessee to get married. He and bride, Cindy Brock, agreed he should continue in evangelism for five years, then they would start a family and he would take a church pastorate. A few months after the 1983 visit, the church called him to be their youth minister. Initially uncertain, Johnston promised to pray about it. "But one week after we (he and Mrs. Johnston) felt led of the Spirit to come to Christ Church we discovered

Cindy was pregnant—man were we shocked,"[17] he recalled. (Isn't there a verse in the Bible that says God moves in mysterious ways?)

More so than some congregations, Christ Church sees husband and wife as a team ministry. "During the two years that we served as youth pastors and then associate pastors, God regularly reminded us that we were not here by accident,"[18] he said. About the time he believed he should accept a position as senior pastor at another church, Jerry King revealed his plans to go into full-time missions/evangelism work. In March 1986 the Johnstons were elected senior pastors of Christ Church.

Typical of his preaching style was a sermon "Shut In to Shut Out," based on Matthew 6:5-13. He told his listeners that prayer was not "a fire escape, a game show, a talent show, or a wrestling match."[19] Concerning the use of humor in his sermons, he said, "I try to make it enjoyable. I think humor helps us to relax a bit, especially for visitors."[20] In the sermon he concluded by explaining that prayer is a lifestyle, a relationship, worship, and a partnership.

Johnston presented his vision, "Rejoice 2000!" to the congregation in late 1997. The $7.5 million project resulted in the purchase of twenty-one acres on Alta Mesa Blvd. and the building of ". . . 64,000 square feet of ministry

Christ Church Assembly of God 5301 Altamesa Blvd. Courtesy Christ Church Assembly of God

space," according to a 2002 brochure. Housed in a contemporary style plant, "The new ministry center includes 3,000 square feet of nursery space, a 1,350 seat sanctuary, a commercial kitchen and fellowship hall, a small auditorium that seats 250 people, and over 23 classrooms for small group and children's ministries,"[21] the brochure states. "We wanted a facility that was functional, practical, and user friendly, one that would be viewed more as a ministry center than simply a worship auditorium,"[22] the senior pastor said.

The future of the church is bright, according to Johnston, because the people take an active part in worship and service to the community, and both are the strengths of a congregation that went from camp meeting style of worship to contemporary form of worship.

■   ■   ■

First Jefferson Unitarian Universalist Church—1946

The mission statement of First Jefferson states, "We are a liberal religious community of diverse individuals. We nurture spiritual growth, encourage lifelong education, work for social justice, serve the larger community, and celebrate life's gifts together through meaningful worship. We welcome and support others in their expression of religious freedom."[23] This diversity includes the ordination of gays and lesbians, and the acceptance of humanists, pagans and Wiccans, as well as those of the more traditional Judeo-Christian leaning.

The term "Unitarian" designated a number of reform groups who pledged not to persecute one another while emphasizing the unity of oneness of God as distinct from the traditional Trinitarian formulation. "Universalist" also born in the post-reformation, defined those who opposed the doctrine that only the elect of mankind will be saved. "On the contrary, they said salvation was universal for the 'whole family of mankind.'"[24] The American Unitarian Association and the Universalist Church in American merged in 1961 to form the Unitarian Universalist Association.

Denton Limbaugh of Dallas recalled his father, Rev. Daniel C. Limbaugh, from 1902 to 1905 rode the interurban to Fort Worth to give lectures, but no church survived. In 1946, new Texans John and Ina Moore sought to unite with a Unitarian congregation, but still there was none. He asked Robert

Raible, minister of Dallas' First Unitarian Church how to start a church. Raible suggested he contact the national association's Lon Ray Call. Moore and Call placed an announcement inviting interested persons to a downtown hotel (sources differ on which hotel) for an organizational meeting. "So the new church was born in a room at the Worth/Blackstone Hotel on 7th St.,"[25] Dorothy M. Greninger wrote in *Unitarian Universalism in Fort Worth, Texas; 1946-1993.*

This witty account of their history is both informative and folksy. For example, in recounting their early adventures at establishing a church she asked, "Weren't we excited? And proud? Overachievers, we nearly worked ourselves to death." In those first years, congregants met in homes, or at the Women's Club on Pennsylvania Avenue. The group, with the assistance of Rev. Raible, formally organized on April 15, 1948. They called Rev. G. Richard Kuch as their first minister. He accepted ". . .so the new church had a minister, a mimeograph, people, and lots of spirit!"[26] Forty-seven men and women signed the Membership Book.

In March 1948 the congregation purchased a brick two-story house at 2912 Hemphill Street. "With a makeshift pulpit with an exotic scarf, the large living room that went across the front of the house became a good sanctuary,"[27] Greninger wrote. The dining room became a meeting room and the garage and upstairs apartment they converted to classrooms. Friday evenings they held book reviews and social events for the growing number of worshipers.

In addition to the problems inherent with getting a new church started, the liberal social views espoused by Unitarians led some citizens to equate them with communists. In the 1950s highly charged atmosphere of the Cold War, members sought to distinguish the difference between their philosophy and the totalitarianism going on in Europe. Consolidated Vultee (forerunner of Lockheed Martin) fired two church members, believing them to be security risks. Broadway Baptist's minister Guy Moore joined Kuch in their support. Other church leaders remained silent, but Texas Christian University asked Kuch to speak and clarify the Unitarian stance.

Member Harvey O'Connor made history when he sued Senator Joseph McCarthy. The Wisconsin senator's House Unamerican Activities Committee subpoenaed O'Connor and questioned him about his work as Public Relations

Director of the Oil Workers Union. O'Connor challenged the right of the committee to pry into the minds of citizens and won.

In 1950 Safeway Stores bought the Hemphill property and the church purchased two lots and a house on Forest Park Blvd., only to discover the seller did not have clear title. When the grocery chain insisted upon immediate occupancy, Temple Beth El rented the use of their chapel to the Unitarians. "At a special meeting on February 25, 1951, members voted to purchase Sycamore Heights Baptist Church at 2800 Purington St., in the Meadowbrook section. . . ."[28] Greninger recorded. Members donated time and talent to remodel the property, which looked more like the Alamo mission in San Antonio than a Fort Worth church. The tired, but happy congregation held the first service there in October 1951. The 139 seat sanctuary featured recessed lighting and a redwood paneled chancel.

Richard Kuch retired in 1952. His successor, Rev. Rex Aman pastored the church until 1955. The next minister, Don Jacobsen left in 1957 and the following year Todd J. Taylor came to lend stability to the congregation, which now numbered 160. After only four years he resigned to accept a position with the district office in Atlanta. By the late 1950s more mainstream parishioners joined the church and local citizens began to accept the congregation and appreciate their community services.

Rev. Walter W. Baese, Jr. came to the church in 1963. He held degrees from Marquette University, Milwaukee; Lakeland College, Sheboygan, Wisconsin; and Washington University, St. Louis. His graduate degrees were in philosophy and divinity. Prior to his Fort Worth pastorate, Rev. Baese led the First Unitarian Church in Philadelphia. He remained at First Jefferson for eleven years.

"Unitarianism's world history has been rich, interesting, and often controversy-filled. After formation of the American Unitarian Association in 1825," Greninger observed, "itself a rather controversial event, factions developed. Ralph Waldo Emerson left the Unitarian ministry partly because of objections to his exploration of Eastern religions."[29]

Local conflict arose in the mid 1960s. In September 1966, fifty members joined Jefferson Unitarian (for Deist Thomas Jefferson, drafter of the Declaration of Independence) and renamed the church and First Jefferson

First Jefferson Unitarian/Universalist Church 1959 Sandy Lane. Courtesy First Jefferson Unitarian/Universalist Church.

Unitarian Universalist. They called Robert Latham, 1973-1976, as their first official minister.

The congregation purchased land on Sandy Lane next to a public park in far east Fort Worth. In 1969 first they built what is now the Fellowship Hall and Religious Education Wing. Today a rustic native stone and wood sanctuary also sits among towering pines next to a meandering brook. A wooden bridge connects the rear parking area to the building. Inside, the sanctuary is of modern design in colors of rust and white. One wall of the conference room is glass. It looks out onto the garden area, bringing the outdoors in.

By 1976 First Jefferson was the largest of the Fort Worth Unitarian Universalist congregations. The church has become a social force in the community. In one early community project, fifteen out of fifty members volunteered to tutor adults as they prepared to take the General Equivalency Diploma test. The church has been in the forefront of the civil rights movement, including civil rights for gays and lesbians. Unitarians consider helping the needy a prime responsibility. In that regard, Pastor Craig Roshaven served two terms as president of the board of Eastside Ministries, a faith-based social service center.

Under the leadership of Marjorie Montgomery, who came in 1980, the church membership grew. Rev. Montgomery, raised a Lutheran in Buffalo, New York, earned a Master of Religious Education from Union Theological Seminary in 1959. Since Lutherans at the time did not ordain women, it never occurred to her to seek a preaching ministry. After moving to Arlington, Texas she joined a Unitarian church and discovered that denomination had ordained women as early as 1863. She attended Perkins School of Theology in Dallas for further training, then pastored a church in Belmont, Massachusetts for four years before returning to Texas. From 1980 until 1990 she led the First Jefferson congregation. Retired now, of her calling she said, "I loved being a minister."[30]

Rev. Craig Roshaven graduated from Starr King School of Ministry in Berkeley, California. The Cleveland, Ohio native, son of a Congregationalist minister, said First Jefferson is a perfect match for him. He appreciates the openness of the congregation to a wide spectrum of political and social views. "We are beyond tolerance to a welcoming congregation,"[31] he said in a recent interview. Rev. Roshaven's preaching style is informal as he shares deep theological concepts with a receptive congregation. "Religion should be about putting your whole self into it—full of singing and dancing and laughing and crying—and experiencing it, not just studying about it"[32] he explained.

His goals for the future? Rev. Roshaven wants to attract and serve families, and to expand the religious education program. Concerning education Greninger wrote, "We believe there is yet new truth to discover and more courageous ways to serve the fellowship of man. We cherish the prophetic voices of the past, but we would continue the search for new prophesy in our own time. . .and put into practice the religion we profess."[33]

A placard near the front entrance of First Jefferson Unitarian Universalist reads:

"Love is the doctrine of this church
The quest of truth is our sacrament
And service is our prayer."[34]

Pastor Roshaven and Pastor Emeritus Montgomery consider affirming these words to congregants and community their mission.

■   ■   ■

McKinney Memorial Bible Church—1954

Speaking of Bible churches, Rev. Gary L. Card, who pastored McKinney Memorial, said, "A Bible church is doctrinally conservative, evangelically oriented and denominationally unrelated. The church is self-governing, self-supporting and self-propagating."[35] Another minister, Paul Young, stressed that the congregation is "not anti-intellectual or a separatist or isolationist."[36]

Three areas of ministry—evangelism, preaching, and teaching—have shaped McKinney's purpose since its founding February 3, 1954. Handwritten notes by Mary Eitelman state, "On January 31, 1954, Sunday the first group of McKinney Memorial Church meets at the home of Mr. and Mrs. Guy T. Moore. The meeting is held at 7:30 P.M. and thirty-three attended. Mr. Frank Carter presides for testimonies and scripture."[37] Dr. McKinney was ill and did not attend, Mrs. Eitelman noted.

The history of the church cannot be told without recounting the life of Samuel T. McKinney. Born in Ohio February 2, 1867, he grew up in Plain Grove, Pennsylvania. There was no high school in the small town and after being tutored by Rev. James Parker, a Congregational Presbyterian minister, Samuel enrolled in college at age thirteen. Two years later, illness, (perhaps tuberculosis, records aren't clear) forced him to return home. He spent a year regaining his health, then entered New Wilmington College. Upon the death of his brother-in-law, young Samuel once more left school, this time to care for the family business. Again his education was delayed, until at age twenty-eight he began to study for the ministry at Chicago's Moody Bible Institute.

Shortly after his graduation he was ordained in Pilgrim Congregational Church, the largest Congregational church in St. Louis. "(He). . . held a pastorate in St. Louis, then one in Cripple Creek, Colorado, for 7 years, one in Denver for 14 years and one in Fort Worth for 18 years, retiring in 1941,"[38] according to an obituary in McKinney archival records. Dr. McKinney held only four pastorates in his long service of ministry.

After twenty years in the pulpit, Rev. McKinney attended a Bible Conference in Fort Worth and liked the city and the people. The one mentioned above who needed a pastor was First Congregational (see page 235) and he accepted the call. By 1941 McKinney, now in his seventies, felt the need to be relieved of the heavy duties attendant to ministering to a large church. After his retirement, McKinney moved his membership to Westminster Presbyterian Church (see page 83) and later to Calvary Presbyterian. (That church is now Calvary Bible Church in the Arlington Heights area.)

For years after his retirement Dr. McKinney held Bible studies in his home. As the classes enlarged, other groups formed and met in the homes of teachers or members. From this nucleus came the mega church on Arborlawn Drive.

Only one month after the establishment of the church, records show an attendance of sixty-six in Sunday School, with Mr. Claire Cardy listed as interim pastor. On February 21, 1954 the flock solicited names for their fold. They considered "Independent Presbyterian," and two others containing "Presbyterian" which reflected their heritage, but they are not affiliated with that denomination. "Grace Bible," "Church of the Open Door," and "Chafer Memorial" were also suggested before they settled on the name "McKinney Memorial Bible Church." They called Matt Prince to be their minister. Prince later was founder and president of NEW LIFE,INC, "A Christian mission whose only purpose is to make Jesus Christ known by the best means available,"[39] according to a church newsletter.

For four years the growing congregation conducted Sunday services in the Daughters of America Hall. Weekday prayer meetings were held in various homes. When Prince left to practice law in Tennessee, Dr. Howard Hendricks led the congregation during 1955 before he joined the faculty of the Dallas Theological Seminary. (Founded in 1924, this non-denominational institution educated several McKinney pastors.) Hendricks also became a well-known Bible Conference speaker.

In June 1956 Wendell G. Johnston began an eight-year ministry. Johnston, a native of Erie, Pennsylvania, earned a B.A. from Bob Jones University and a Master of Theology from the Dallas seminary. Before coming to McKinney he pastored a church in Cedar Lake, Indiana. He told a reporter, "The form of worship is essentially Presbyterian, centering around the preaching of the Word of God."[40] Under Johnston's guidance the congregation continued to fill a niche in the religious community.

A *Star-Telegram* feature, complete with photo, reported, "Rev. S. T. McKinney of 1019 S. Henderson celebrated his 91st birthday Sunday afternoon by breaking ground for McKinney Memorial Church at the corner of Trail Lake Dr. and Woodway Lane. . . ."[41] The new structure, located on a two-acre site in the Wedgewood community, was of masonry construction in contemporary design. The sanctuary provided seating for 200, and the Sunday School accommodated 175. "The first service in the new building on Woodway was a prayer meeting on July 30, 1958. The new Building (sic) was dedicated on August 17, 1958,"[42] according to a scrapbook in the church archives.

Rev. McKinney, until his death in 1960 at age ninety-three, taught an adult class at the church on Sunday mornings. He also conducted two weekday Bible classes in homes, a class for young married couples on Tuesday night and a class for women on Wednesday morning. He was an ardent supporter of missions and was honored as president emeritus of Central American Mission in 1951.

He became ill one Sunday after teaching his regular class. Diagnosed with "the flu" he died two days later. Funeral services were at McKinney Memorial.

In 1964 Rev. Johnston assumed duties as a dean of Washington Bible College in the nation's capital. Dr. Donald Campbell served as interim until the church called Rev. Gary L. Card in 1965.

Card, a native of Detroit, Michigan, received his education at Wheaton College Academy, Detroit Bible College, and the Dallas Theological Seminary. He preached (in English) for two years at the Russian Baptist Church in Detroit before coming to Texas. While a seminary student in Dallas, he frequently spoke at Baylor Hospital Chapel.

Rev. Paul Young preached at both the Wedgewood location and the sanctuary on Hulen Drive. *Star-Telegram* columnist George Dolan recalled a sermon the good reverend would probably just as soon forget. He wrote, "Young illustrated his message Sunday night with a flashlight. . . . He explained that a flashlight will not work without batteries and even WITH batteries, one must turn it on for the light to shine forth. A Christian, he said, like a flashlight, must be powered by God." He inserted batteries and instructed the congregation to order the flashlight to turn itself on, which of course it couldn't do. "He pointed out that Christians and flashlights must have their power turned on to work."

He switched on the flashlight—it didn't light. He rearranged the batteries—it still didn't light. "'It's a good thing God called me to be a minister,' he said, sighing, 'and not to work with complicated things like flashlights,'"[43] Dolan quoted him.

Young was himself a power in the pulpit as he led the estimated 1,000 congregants each Sunday. He grew up in Long Beach, graduated from the University of California at Fresno, and received his Masters Degree in Theology from Dallas Theological Seminary. Young served as youth minister at Clearwater Community Church in Florida and college minister at Cedar Avenue Baptist Church in Fresno.

During his pastorate at McKinney Memorial the members moved into the new sanctuary on Hulen Street. Dedication was held in December 1979. The split-level building featured an "in the round" rustic style auditorium with beamed ceilings and four skylights. Classrooms, a colorful nursery, and offices were on the lower level.

Dr. Dave Krentel became pastor of McKinney Memorial in January 1983. He was a gifted communicator with a passion for missions. During his tenure Ken Horton joined the staff as associate pastor.

Following his graduation from Auburn University, and service as an Air Force officer, Horton attended Dallas Theological Seminary, then served as youth minister in Greensboro, North Carolina. He joined McKinney as associate pastor in 1984. By 1987 when Dr. Krentel took a church in Illinois, Horton and the church leadership had developed a relationship that made it logical for him to assume senior pastor status. Horton still speaks with a slight twinge of Alabama when he recalls with reverence the history and people of McKinney Memorial.

He remembered Emma John Helm's nurturing him. "When I got here fifteen years ago," he told reporter Gustavo Reveles Acosta, "I was just a kid and didn't have clue what I was doing. Emma John reached out to me and helped me in so many ways." Mrs. Helm, a teacher in the children's department for forty-three years, and runner-up for the national 2002 Sunday School Teacher of the Year Award, considered him one of her own. Recognizing her at the award announcement, Horton revealed that the children's ministry center in the new church would be named in her honor. "'I wasn't going to cry,' Helm told Horton. 'But then you sneaked that one on me.'"[44]

Rev. Horton's major task has been maintaining the membership's focus on fruitful ministry, while building chairman Tom Magoffin and relocation administrator Brian Mills oversaw the building of a new and larger physical plant to house the ever-growing congregation. Dick McKinney, son of Rev. McKinney observed the May 2002 ground breaking. Gold-colored shovels and balloons cast a celebratory air to the occasion.

The earth-toned building of modern design on twenty acres at 4805 Arborlawn Drive, is neighbor to Ahavath Sholom and Beth-El Congregations, and Overton Park United Methodist Church. Rev. Horton pointed out in an interview that McKinney has excellent relations with denominational churches, without being part of a denomination. "We're grateful that Southcliff Baptist is having a great ministry and that St. Andrews Episcopal has a wonderful ministry."[45] Southcliff sent flowers for the new auditorium and another church offered to watch the children so nursery workers could attend the dedication.

With over 1,000 parking spaces available, McKinney Memorial serves congregants who drive from all over the county. "A covered 'porte-cochere' will

McKinney Memorial Bible Church 4805 Arborlawn Dr. Courtesy McKinney Memorial Bible Church

allow three lanes of traffic for dropping off people at the church,"[46] Jim Jones wrote. An extra large lobby will house coffee bars and can be used for church dinners and other meetings. The more than 97,000 square feet of floor space allows for seating 2100 in the sanctuary, plus classrooms, offices, fellowship facilities and a chapel that seats 150. An audio system and two giant video screens put worshipers in immediate range of the raised pulpit. A large cross on the back wall gives identity to the church. When asked the architectural style, Rev. Horton replied "inviting." In 2002, he hosted Rabbi Zeilicovich of Ahavath Sholom on a tour of the building in progress and the rabbi declared "Ken, this place says 'Come on in.'"[47]

Rev. Horton's goals are to invite people in, but also to encourage small group Bible study so that all may experience a closer relationship with God. Even in a huge sanctuary.

■   ■   ■

This work has been both laborious and inspiring. Laborious because at the onset I imagined no more than twenty or so congregations that would be considered "historic." Limitation of time and space forced me to profile only forty-four. There are so many others that could have been included.

In my visits, every congregation greeted me warmly. The inspiration I received from worshiping with them, knowing we all look to God, but perhaps through different rituals, strengthened me immeasurably. My prayer is that God will continue to pour out His richest blessings on all of the congregations of Fort Worth.

Endnotes

Introduction

1. Jan Batts, *Fort Worth Star-Telegram* (hereafter FWST) "Early Churches Result of Spiritual Pioneering." 2/25/1973, D4.

2. Robert S. Ellwood, *Many People, Many Faiths* (Englewood Cliffs, NJ: Prentice-Hall, Inc., 1982), 319.

3. Clyde A. Milner, II *et al*, *The Oxford History of the American West* (New York: Oxford University Press, 1994), 373.

4. Frank A. Driskill and Noel Grisham, *Historic Churches of Texas* (Austin, TX: Eakin Press, 1980), 1.

5. Driskill and Grisham, *op. cit.* 82.

6. Driskill and Grisham, *op. cit.* 204.

Chapter One: In the Beginning

1. Mrs. P. J. Brown, unpublished paper, Handley United Methodist Church archives.

2. Frederick J. Turner, *The Frontier in American History* (Malabou, FL: Robert E. Krieger Publishing Co, Inc., 1985), 165.

3. Encyclopedia Britannica Vol 18, "The European-Americans in Texas." (Chicago: University of Chicago, 15th Edition) 166.

4. Oliver Knight, *Fort Worth: Outpost on the Trinity* (Fort Worth: Texas Christian University Press, [hereafter TCU] 1990), 5.

5. Katie Casstevens *FWST*, "Religion Came Early to Fort Worth Churches, Now Aptly Called City of Churches," 7/18/1953, pm 5.

6. Julia Kathryn Garrett, *Fort Worth" A Frontier Triumph* (Fort Worth, TX: TCU Press, reprint 1996), 88.

7. Batts, *FWST*, *op. cit.* 2/25/1973, D4.

8. Charles A. Johnson, *The Frontier Camp Meeting* (Dallas: Southern Methodist University Press, 1955), 208.

9. J. C. Terrell, *Reminiscences of the Early Days* (TCU Press, reprint, 1999), 63.

10. Terrell, *op. cit.* 64.

11. Samuel E. Morrison and Henry S. Commanger, *Growth of the American Republic, Vol. II.* (New York: Oxford University Press,1980), 574.

12. Johnson, *op. cit.* 6.

13. W. Eugene Hollon, *The Southwest: Old and New* (New York: Alfred A. Knopf, 1961), 143.

14. *Federal Writer's Project*, (hereafter WP) microfiche #13643, quoting 8/19/1880 *Fort Worth Daily Democrat*.

15. Jo Ella Powell Exley, *Texas Tears and Texas Sunshine* (College Station, TX: Texas A & M University Press, 1985), 189.

16. Ibid

17. Warren Thomas Smith, *Harry Hosier: Circuit Rider* (Nashville: The Upper Room, 1981), 13.

18. Howard W. Peak, *FWST*, "Fort Worth's First Directory, Published 45 Years Ago, Was About Size of School Primer," 9/17/22, 11.

19. Ibid

20. Ibid

21. Milner, *et al*, *op. cit.* 370.

22. Peak, *op. cit.* 7/16/22

23. James M. Moudy, taped interview

24. Mack Williams, *In Old Fort Worth* "How They Lived 100 Years Ago" (Fort Worth: Mack and Madeline Williams, 1977) 42.

25. John M. Burns, *FWST* "Rural Churches, Long Desolate Marks of the Moods of Earlier Residents, Again Are Used for Worship" 7/21/1922, 1.

26. *Fort Worth Democrat*, "Churches," 2/22/1873, 2.

27. Marvin Garrett, *Fort Worth Press* (hereafter *Press*) "Early days weren't all whiskey and gunplay," 2/25/1973 F3.

28. Charles J. Swasey and W. M. Melton, Editors, *1878-1879 City Directory* (Fort Worth, Texas: printed at the Daily Democrat office), 15.

29. WP #13649 quoting 6/21/1887 *Fort Worth Gazette*.

30. Carol Roark, *Fort Worth's Legendary Landmarks* (Fort Worth: TCU Press, 1995), vi.

31. Hollace Weiner, *FWST*, "With modernity in mind," 12/1/2002, E6.

32. Mack Williams, *op. cit.* 19.

33. Terrell *op. cit.* 637.

34. Frances Edwards, *FWST*, "Fort Worth One of the 'Church-Goingest' Cities in the Nation," 5/3/52 pm, 7.

35. Brett Hoffman and Jeff Claaseen, *FWST*, "Survey enumerates faithful" 9/20/2002 B1, B5.

Chapter Two: The Christian Church (Disciples of Christ)

1. Lars Peterson Qualben, *A History of the Christian Denomination* (New York: Thomas Nelson & Sons, 1936), 566.

2. H. C. Armstrong, *The Disciples of Christ: Who Are They and Why Are They* (Baltimore: Association for the Promoting of Christian Unity, 1924), 6.

3. http//www.firstchristian-ftworth.org, July 2002, history of FCChtml 2.

4. J. C. Terrell, *Reminiscences of the Early Days* (TCU Press, 1999), 92.

5. Howard Peak *FWST*, "First Fort Worth Church Founded by Christians," 7/23/1922 (First Christian Church vertical files, Fort Worth Public Library, Local History Department)

6. Allan Carney, *Press* "Religion Rode into the City in Saddle Bags of a Circuit Minister Back in 1855" 3/32/1934 3.

7. Howard Peak, *op. cit.*

8. First Christian Church 115 Anniversary 1855-1970 booklet (6/21/1970), 1.

9. Oliver Knight, *Fort Worth: Outpost on the Trinity* (Fort Worth: TCU Press, 1990), 46.

10. Sanda L. Myers, Editor. *Force without Fanfare: The Autobiography of K. M. Van Zandt.* (Fort Worth: TCU Press, 1968; second printing 1995), 131.

11. WP #106138

12. Myers, *op. cit.* 132.

13. Myers, *op. cit.* 177.

14. George Stephens, taped interview

15. WP #13725

16. Stephens, taped interview

17. Carol E. Roark, *Fort Worth's Legendary Landmarks.* (Fort Worth: TCU Press, 1995) 98.

18. Stephens, taped interview

19. Roark, *op. cit.* 98.

20. Robert Wear, *FWST* "Rev. Mr. Anderson Marks 35 Years in First Christian Church Pulpit Today" 3/9/47 Section 1 p. 4.

21. *FWST* "First Christians Change Little," 3/12/55 pm 3.

22. *FWST* "Retiring Financial Secretary of Church Honored for Service 6/6/55 am, 2.

23. Jim Jones, *FWST* "First Christian's pastor leaves struggling flock," 6/1/91 G7.

24. Jim Jones, *FWST* "City's oldest gets new pastor," 7/1/2001, B1.

25. Janet Fowler, taped interview

26. History of Magnolia Avenue Christian Church booklet, 1.

27. Magnolia Christian Church (vertical file, Fort Worth Public Library, Local History Department)

28. Ibid

29. Imogene McCue, Magnolia Avenue History, 4.

30. McCue, *op. cit.* 5

31. McCue, *op. cit.* 10

32. Ibid

33. *Christian Church in the Southwest,* "Magnolia Ave. to Close Doors," June, 1983, 1.

34. Colby Hall, *The Early Years: University Christian Church* [Texas ? s.n. 1983?] 1.

35. *FWST* "University Christian Church Honors Dean Colby D. Hall at Celebration" 5/13/53 am

36. Colby Hall, typewritten 22 page booklet, vertical file, Fort Worth Public Library, 5.

37. Colby Hall, *The Early Years* 7.

38. Martha Youngdale, editor, *University Christian Church, Fort Worth, Texas* 1978 Pictorial Directory "A Brief History of University Christian Church," no page number.

39. Colby Hall, *The Early Years* 22.

40. Ibid 23.

41. *FWST* "Wide Recognition Gained by Church" 9/5/64, 3.

42. Jim Jones, *FWST* "New church leader seen as unlikely to stoke controversy" 11/16/91 pm B2.

43. Ibid.

44. Personal observation.

45. Charles Sanders taped interview.

46. Ibid.

47. Ibid.

48. *FWST* "University Christian to dedicate new addition" 9/6/02 B3.

49. Scott Colglazier taped interview.

50. Winifred E. Garrison and Alfred DeGroot. *The Disciple of Christ: A History.* (St. Louis: Christian Board of Publication, 1948), 468.

51. Mrs. H. V. Shanks, *Disciples All: A Study of the East Annie Christian Church* Fort Worth: E. Annie Church, 1.

52. Ibid.

53. Shanks, *op. cit.* 2.

54. Ibid.

55. Shanks, *op. cit.* 4.

56. Ibid.

57. Shanks, *op. cit.* 7.

58. Shanks, *op. cit.* 48.

59. Shanks, *op. cit.* 2.

60. "Community Christian Church: Homecoming-2002" 2.

61. Johnny Smith taped interview.

62. "Community Christian Church: Homecoming-1988" 2.

63. Bill Fairley, *FWST* "Lenora Rolla a fixture for half-century" 9/18/96 B5.

64. Lucy Fountain taped interview.

65. Max Morgan taped interview.

Chapter Three- The Catholic Congregations

1. *FWST* "St. Patrick's Is Mother Church" 4/9/55 pm 3.

2. Jean Andrus "Baroque Comes to St. Patrick's" 5.

3. *FWST* "Father Guyot Credited with Catholic Progress Here" 8/4/1904 4.

4. Carol E. Roark, *Fort Worth's Legendary Landmarks* 7.

5. Jean Wysatta, *Press* "Oldest Church Has Catacomb Crypts" 3/20/66 B16.

6. *Fort Worth Gazette* 7/11/1892, reprinted in "Given to God." University of Texas at Arlington Special Collections Library archives.

7. *Fort Worth Record* "Father Guyot Dies after Long Illness" 8/4/1907, 6.

8. William R. Hoover, *St. Patrick's: The First 100 Years*. (Fort Worth: St. Patrick Cathedral, 1988), 10.

9. Hoover, *op. cit.* 45

10. Andrus, *op. cit.* 8

11. Hoover, *op. cit.* 57

12. *North Texas Catholic* "Wolf To Observe Anniversary on June 9" 6/8/63, 10.

13. *FWST* "New Pastor at St. Patrick's—'Back Home' After 19 Years" 1/21/62, section 1, 23.

14. *The Handbook of Texas Online* DEFALCO, LAWRENCE MICHAEL 7/24/2003 printout, 1.

15. Hoover, *op. cit.* 80.

16. Hoover, *op. cit.* 82.

17. Hoover, *op. cit.* 91.

18. Jim Jones, *FWST* "Bishop of FW diocese ordained" 9/14/81 am 1.

19. Carlos E. Cuellar, *Stories from the Barrio: A History of Mexican Fort Worth*. (Fort Worth: TCU Press, 2003) 100.

20. "Brief Historical Sketch of All Saints Parish," All Saints archives, 11.

21. Taneya D. Gethers, *FWST* "Day of the Dead finds All Saints Catholic Church celebrating 100 years of growth and renewal," 11/2/2002 F3.

22. Ibid.

23. Cuellar, *op. cit.* 100.

24. Cuellar, *op. cit.* 102.

25. Cuellar, *op. cit.* 103

26. *A Celebration of 68 Years of Service of the Claretian Order to San Jose and All Saints Parishes: June 3, 1926 to June 30, 1994* Sponsored by All Saints Advisory Committee, Amado Guzman, Historical Consultant, All Saints archives, 13.

27. "History of San Jose Church," All Saints archives, 19.

28. Jim Jones, *op. cit.* F5.

29. Ibid.

30. *FWST* "Father Delgado leaving after four years," 7/1/94, 1.

31. Esteban Jasso taped interview.

32. Hope P. Ayala taped interview.

33. "History of San Jose Church," All Saints archives, 19.

34. Ibid

35. Jerry Thomas, *La Vida* "Our Mother of Mercy Catholic Church—We've Come This Far by Faith." 8/25/99, 1.

36. *2002 Directory* 8.

37. *2002 Directory* 3.

38. *2002 Directory* 2.

39. Pat Poundstone, *North Texas Catholic* "On Mission to America," 11/6/92, 16.

40. Poundstone, *op. cit.* 8.

41. Poundstone, *op. cit.* 16.

42. Michael Farrell taped interview.

43. Frank Staton taped interview.

44. Jerry Thomas *op. cit.*

Chapter Four— The Presbyterian Congregations

1. Allen Carney, *Press* "A Fearless Leadership and Years of Early Struggles Brought Progress to the Presbyterians." 3/23/1934, 15.

2. Park H. Miller, *Why I Am a Presbyterian* (New York: Thomas Nelson & Sons, 1956), 36.

3. Dorothy Iba, Rose Marie Jennings, Gail Barham and Dan E. Goldsmith, editors, *First Presbyterian Church: Our History*, (Fort Worth: First Presbyterian Church, 2000), 1.

4. Ibid.

5. Dan Goldsmith taped interview.

6. WP #13638.

7. Iba, *et al* 5.

8. *FWST* "Predict Prosperity for Taylor Church" 6/15/13 Section 2,48.

9. *FWST* "City's Only Carillon Has Interesting Story" 7/20/52, Section 2, 12.

10. Iba, *et al* 8.

11. Rev. French McKee, vertical files, Fort Worth Public Library, Local History Department.

12. Dan Goldsmith taped interview.

13. Iba, *et al* 9.

14. Valerie Fields, *FWST* "Fort Worth minister to receive award" 2/5/96, 20.

15. *First Presbyterian Church 1985 Directory.*

16. Juanita Cowan, *The History of St. Stephen* (Fort Worth: St. Stephen Presbyterian Church, April 22, 1997), 7.

17. Ibid.

18. Cowan, *op. cit.* 11.

19. Ibid.

20. Cowan, *op. cit.* 12.

21. Cowan, *op. cit.* 17.

22. *FWST* "FIERCE FIRE SWEEPS SOUTH SIDE; SEVEN ENTIRE BLOCKS BURN ; LOSS OVER $2,000,000" 4/4/09 Section 1, 1.

23. Cowan, *op. cit.* 18.

24. *FWST* "Wrecking Crew to Raze Old Broadway Church" 6/21/57 am 18.

25. Juanita Cowan taped interview.

26. Cowan, *op. cit.* 19.

27. Cowan, *op. cit.* 23.

28. Cowan, *op. cit.* 26.

29. *To The Glory of God: A Building for Worship* (Fort Worth: St. Stephen Presbyterian), 10.

30. Ibid.

31. *To The Glory of God: A Building for Worship* 11.

32. *op. cit.* 86.

33. Mark Scott taped interview.

34. Cowan, *op. cit.* 29.

35. Mark Scott taped interview.

36. Lois White Deaton, *A History of Hemphill Presbyterian Church, Fort Worth, Texas, 1891-1991,* (Fort Worth: Hemphill Presbyterian Church, 1991), 6.

37. Deaton, *op. cit.* 9.

38. Deaton, *op. cit.* 12.

39. Deaton, *op. cit.* 13.

40. Ibid.

41. Jim Jones, *FWST* "Windows to the Past" Hemphill Presbyterian Church vertical files, Fort Worth Public Library, Local History Department).

42. Deaton, *op. cit.* 14.

43. Deaton, *op. cit.* 15.

44. Deaton, *op. cit.* 16.

45. Centennial Celebration Committee, "Hemphill Presbyterian Church Time Line."

46. Deaton, *op. cit.* 18.

47. Personal correspondence.

48. *Time Line.*

49. Personal correspondence.

50. Robert J. Thomson taped interview.

51. Ibid.

52. Ibid.

53. Wilbur Klint, *et al*, editors *Westminster Presbyterian Church: Our Church History: 1888-1988* (Fort Worth: Westminster Presbyterian Church, 1988), 3.

54. "New Milestone in 62-Year History" Westminster Church archives.

55. Clifford Williams taped interview.

56. Klint, *op. cit.* 6.

57. Klint, *op. cit.* 7.

58. Klint, *op. cit.* 6.

59. Klint, *op. cit.* 8.

60. Klint, *op. cit.* 12.

61. Ibid.

62. Ibid.

63. *Press* "Westminster Presbyterian to Dedicate New Building Sunday" 5/20/60, 20.

64. email from Merle Scoggins to author 3/30/2003

65. Klint, *op. cit.* 16.

66. Klint, *op. cit.* 20.

67. Unpublished papers, Westminster archives.

68. Donald R. Hogg taped interview.

69. Ibid.

70. MEXICAN PRESBYTERIAN CHURCH, FORT WORTH, TEXAS: TEX-MEX PRESBYTERY, SYNOD OF TEXAS, ORGANIZED 1927, 1.

71. MEXICAN PRESBYTERIAN, 2.

73. MEXICAN PRESBYTERIAN, 3.

74. Cuellar, *op. cit.* 122.

75. Cuellar, *op. cit.* 121.

76. Cuellar, *op. cit.* 117.

77. "SOME THINGS ABOUT THE SOCIAL ACTION REPORT TO THE MOD-ERATOR FROM THE CLERK," unpublished document belonging to congregant Sam Frias, believed to be written about 1997.

Chapter Five—The Baptist Congregations

1. James Leo Garrett, Jr. *Living Stones: The Centennial History of Broadway Baptist Church* (Fort Worth: Broadway Baptist Church, 1984), 45.

2. Wortham, (no first name, no date, draft document of early Fort Worth churches) UTA Special Collections Library, 10.

3. Ann Arnold, *History of the Fort Worth Legal Community*, (Austin: Eakin Press, 2000), 129.

4. Lee Roy McGlone, "The Preaching of J. Frank Norris: An Apologia for Fundamentalism," dissertation, Southwestern Baptist Theological Seminary, 38.

5. Homer G. Ritchie, *The Life and Legend of J. Frank Norris: The Fighting Parson* (Fort Worth: H. G. Ritchie, 1991), 57.

6. Barry Hankins, *God's Rascal: J. Frank Norris & the Beginnings of Southern Fundamentalism* (Lexington, Ky:University Press of Kentucky, 1996), 118.

7. Gwin Morris, "Frank Norris: Rascal or Reformer?" *Baptist History and Heritage*, Vol 33, Aut. 1998, 27.

8. Leonard Sanders, *How Fort Worth Became the Texasmost City 1849-1920* (Fort Worth: The Amon Carter Museum, 1973), 90.

9. Sanders, *op. cit.* 91.

10. Ibid.

11. Sanders, *op. cit.* 94.

12. Garrett, *op. cit.* 148.

13. *FWST*, "Church Thinks All Bible God's Word," 6/11/55, 3.

14. E. Ray Tatum, "The J. Frank Norris Murder Trial of 1927," thesis, Southwestern Baptist Theological Seminary, 89.

15. Hankins, *op, cit,* 90.

16. Roy E. Falls, *A Biography of J. Frank Norris,* (S.I.:s.n., 1975, SWBTS) 98.

17. E. Ray Tatum, *Conquest or Failure?* (Dallas: Baptist Historical Foundation, 1966), 269.

18. Ritchie, *op. cit.* 180.

19. Ritchie, *op. cit.* 184.

20. Falls, *op. cit.* 96.

21. Falls, *op. cit.* 99.

22. Mark G. Toulouse, *Foundations,* Vol. 24, Ja-Mr, 1981, "A Case Study in Schism," 47.

23. Toulouse, *op. cit.,* 33.

24. Gwin Morris, *Baptist History and Heritage,* Fall 1998, "Frank Norris: Rascal or Reformer?" 21.

25. Homer Ritchie taped interview.

26. *FWST* "Church Thinks All Bible God's Word," 6/11/55, 3.

27. *FWST* "Church Starts on Building Plans," 1/1/58, 19.

28. *FWST* Evelyn Hernandez, "Baptist churches agree to merge," 10/12/81 am D1.

29. *A Brief Pictorial History of First Baptist Church, Fort Worth, Texas: 125th Anniversary* 12.

30. Don Wills taped interview.

31. Ibid.

32. *Handbook of Texas On Line: Mosier Valley, TX,* 5/10/2000, 1.

33. *FWST* Whit Canning, "A community being chipped away" 3/28/88, 6.

34. Texas State Historical Marker, 1983.

35. L. G. Austin taped interview.

36. Ibid.

37. *FWST* Valerie Fields, "Mosier Valley church celebrates 117 years of historical milestones." 6/9/91, Northeast Metro, E1.

38. *Through the Years: Mount Pisgah Missionary Baptist Church, 125th Anniversary* (Fort Worth: Mt. Pisgah 2000), 58.

39. Ibid.

40. Ibid.

41. *Mount Pisgah 125th Anniversary* 18.

42. *Mount Pisgah Baptist Church:1875-1975, 76 Memories* (Fort Worth: Mt. Pisgah, 1975), 18.

43. *Mount Pisgah 125th Anniversary,* 60.

44. *Mount Pisgah Baptist Church:1875-1975.* 19.

45. Nehemiah Davis taped interview.

46. Ibid.

47. *FWST,* Janette Rodrigues, "Davis maintains NAACP tone" 6/26/97 B6

48. Nehemiah Davis vita, unpublished.

49. *Mount Pisgah 125th Anniversary*, 5.

50. Lillian B. Horace, Edited by L. Venchael Booth. *Crowned with Glory and Honor: The Life of Rev. Lacy Kirk Williams* (Hicksville, NY: Exposition Press, 1978), 195.

51. Carol Roark, *Legendary Landmarks*, 94.

52. *FWST* "Mount Gilead, First Negro Baptist Church," 8/3/1913, A35.

53. Horace, *op. cit.* 112.

54. *Fort Worth Daily Gazette*, 5/13/1888 quoted by WP #13652.

55. Horace, *op. cit.* 112.

56. Horace, *op. cit.* 115.

57. Horace, *op. cit.* 117.

58. Boone, Theodore S., Ed. *Lord! Lord!: The Sermons of Dr.L. K. Williams* (Fort Worth, Texas: Historical Commission National Baptist Convention, U. S. A., Inc., 1942), 28.

59. WP #17482

60. Cedric D. Britt taped interview.

61. Ibid.

62. James L. Garrett, *Living Stones*, 26.

63. *FWST* "Woman Watches Growth of Church During Fifty Years, 9/17/33 am, 7.

64. *The Texas Baptist*, 8/7/1884, p.1, quoted by Garrett, *op. cit.*,40.

65. Garrett, *op. cit.* 82.

66. *FWST* Brett Younger, "In the valley of the shadow of football," 11/17/2002, B17.

67. Garrett, *op. cit.* 91.

68. Garrett, *op. cit.* 103.

69. *FWST* "FIERCE FIRE SWEEPS SOUTH SIDE; SEVEN ENTIRE BLOCKS BURN ; LOSS OVER $2,000,000" 4/4/09 Section 1, 1.

70. Garrett, *op. cit.* 167.

71. Garrett, *op. cit.* 192.

72. Garrett, *op. cit.* 266.

73. Garrett, *op. cit.* 319.

74. Garrett, *op. cit.* 447.

75. *FWST* Cullum Greene, "Broadway Baptists Thinking Only of Enjoying New $1,250,000 Building, 4/20/52, 16.

76. Garrett, *op. cit.* 483

77. *FWST* Cullum Greene, *op. cit.*

78. Garrett, *op. cit.* 652.

79. Personal correspondence.

80. *FWST* Jim Jones, "Tarrant church picks minister from Kentucky," 8/4/92, am, A12

81. Brett Younger taped interview.

82. *Why We Love Broadway: A Patchwork of Words*, Tiffany McClain, 23.

83. *Why We Love Broadway*, Billie Edwards, 13.

84. *Celebrating the Glory of God*, 1.

85. Shirley Abram, *et al Corinth Baptist Church: 1886-1986*, 2.

86. Abram, *op. cit.* 3.

87. Velina G. Willis, "Career Development Case Study of Rev. L. B. Adams," 4.

88. Willis, *op. cit.* 3.

89. *FWST* "Installation Set for New Minister," 11/14/1970, A3.

90. Willis, *op. cit.* 5.

91. *Fort Worth Record*, 5/22/1904, quoted by John Deets, *Century of Love* (Fort Worth: North Fort Worth Baptist Church 1990), 4.

92. Ibid.

93. Deets, *op. cit.* 8.

94. Deets, *op. cit.* 9.

95. *FWST*, "Church Stresses 3-Point Program." 10/24/64, 3.

96. Deets, *op. cit.* 43.

97. Y. C. Shamblee, *et al A Historical Narrative: Mount Zion Missionary Baptist Church*, 8.

98. Shamblee, *op. cit.* 1.

99. Shamblee, *op. cit.* 2.

100. Ibid.

101. Shamblee, *op. cit.* 5.

102. Reverend Louis Belvet George Biographical Sketch

103. "Mt. Zion Baptist Church, 108th Anniversary, 1894-2002," 6.

104. Personal observation.

105. Mt. Zion Baptist Church, 108th Anniversary, 6.

106. *100th Church Celebration: Greater Saint James Baptist Church*, 39.

107. *100th Church Celebration*, 8.

108. Kerven Carter, Jr. taped interview.

109. Ibid.

110. *FWST* Gracie Bonds Staples, "100 Years of Faith," 2/5/1995, A29.

111. Grimes Fortenberry, editor, *Mighty Works of Grace*, 1.

112. Fortenberry, *op. cit.* 57.

113. Fortenberry, *op. cit.* 159.

114. Fortenberry, *op. cit.* 187.

115. Fortenberry, *op. cit.* 199.

116. Fortenberry, *op. cit.* 218

117. Fortenberry, *op. cit.* 222.

118. Fortenberry, *op. cit.* 239.

119. Fortenberry, *op. cit.* 308.

120. Joel Gregory, *Too Great a Temptation* (Fort Worth: TX The Summit Group, 1994), 74.

121. Gregory, *op. cit.* 97.

122. Gregory, *op. cit.* 94.

123. Grimes Fortenberry taped interview.

Chapter Six—The Methodist Congregations

1. William B. Williamson, *An Encyclopedia of Religions in the United States*, 213.

2. W. Erskine Williams, "Sketch of History of Fort Worth Methodism," UTA Special Collections Library, no date, no page numbers.

3. WP #13765

4. J. D. F. Williams, *The First One Hundred and Twenty Years (1852-1972): A History of the First United Methodist Church, Fort Worth*, 6.

5. WP #13776

6. J. D. F. Williams, *op. cit.*, 11.

7. J. D. F. Williams, *op. cit.*, 13.

8. *FWST* "Magnificent New First Methodist Church Complete Is Opened Today," March 8, 1908, 13.

9. J. D. F. Williams, *op. cit.*, 20.

10. J. D. F. Williams, *op. cit.*, 21.

11. WP #22216

12. *FWST* 6/12/1931 "Tribute to Dr. Hawk." pm 16.

13. *FWST* "First Methodist Church to Get Rev. Gaston Foote as Pastor," 3/6/52, 4.

14. Frances Edwards, *FWST* "'Footnotes, Sidewalk Sermonettes' To Be Published as Book March 23," 3/17/56, 6.

15. J. D. F. Williams, *op. cit.*, 42.

16. Jim Jones, *FWST* "Senior Pastor at First Methodist Church to retire in June," 2/25/2003, B7.

17. Jim Jones and Brett Hoffman, *FWST* "Departing pastor cites tensions," 2/27/2003, B1.

18. Jim Jones, *op. cit, FWST* "Senior Pastor at First Methodist" 2/27/2003 B7.

19. John Gutierrez-Mier, *FWST* "Church ending TV broadcasts," 1/25/2003 B1.

20. Jim Jones, *op. cit, FWST* "Senior Pastor at First Methodist" 2/27/2003 B7.

21. Brett Hoffman and Jim Jones, *FWST* "First Methodist names pastor," 7/8/2003, B4.

22. Ibid.

23. Ibid.

24. Ibid.

25. J. D. F. Williams, *op. cit.*, 27.

26. Ibid.

27. J. D. F. Williams, *op. cit.*, 29.

28. *FWST* "RAZING WILL WRITE FINIS TO COLORFUL HISTORY OF CHURCH" (sic) 6/23/1938, 8.

29. Clyde McQueen, *Black Churches in Texas* (College Station, TX Texas A & M University Press, 2000), 184.

30. Joe Standifer, "History of Allen Chapel African Methodist Episcopal Church, Fort Worth, Texas, 1982, 13.

31. Standifer, *op. cit.* 15.

32. Ibid.

33. Bill Fairley, *FWST*, "Five ex-slaves established AME church," 2/6/2002, B6.

34. Standifer, *op. cit.* 20.

35. Standifer, *op. cit.* 21.

36. Standifer, *op. cit.* 19.

37. Standifer, *op. cit.* 14.

38. J. D. F. Williams, *op. cit.* 9.

39. "The C. M. E. Church Celebrates Its 115th Birthday"no author, 12/15/1985, p1, unpublished, church archives.

40. *Morning Chapel Christian Methodist Episcopal Church History: 1873-1977*, 8.

41. *Morning Chapel. . . History: 1873-1977*, 9.

42. *Morning Chapel. . . History: 1873-1977*, 25.

43. *Morning Chapel. . . History: 1873-1977*, 9.

44. Unpublished, handwritten historical account.

45. Charles Whittle, Unpublished, church archives.

46. Robert C. Warden, Unpublished, church archives.

47. Mrs. Billy Brown, Unpublished, church archives.

48. "The Church Bell," Unpublished, church archives.

49. Ibid.

50. *FWST* "'Responsibility' Is Handley Dual Role," 3/15/58, p, 3.

51. Betty Bryan taped interview.

52. Ibid.

53. Gus Guthrie taped interview

54. Ruth Reiter Stone, "ST. MARK UNITED METHODIST CHURCH" unpublished paper, United Methodist Records and Archives, Texas Wesleyan University West Library, 1. (Box 63.7).

55. Stone, *op. cit.*, 2.

56. Stone, *op. cit.*, 5.

57. Seth Kantor, *Press* "Church Had FW's Biggest Funeral . . . Now It's Empty," 6/26/1960, 10.

58. Vaughn Baker taped interview.

59. Anna Jo Johnson, Anniversary Chairperson, *St. Andrews United Methodist Church: Centennial Anniversary 1888-1988*, 3.

60. Carol Roark, *Legendary Landmarks*, 68.

61. Natalie Johnson, *History of St. Andrews United Methodist Church of Fort Worth*, 8.

62. Natalie Johnson, *op. cit.* 9.

63. Natalie Johnson, *op. cit.* 17.

64. Ibid.

65. Personal observation

66. William B. McClain, *Songs of Zion*, 73.

67. Ibid.

68. "Missouri Ave. Methodist Church," unpublished paper, United Methodist Records and Archives, Texas Wesleyan University West Library.

69. Monette Fugate, *Polytechnic United Methodist Church, 1892-1992: A History*, 6.

70. *The Church Visitor*, 1/8/1892, quoted by Fugate, 7.

71. JoAnn Jenkins, *A History of Polytechnic United Methodist Church*, 3.

72. Fugate, *op. cit.* 14.

73. Fugate, *op. cit.* 16.

74. Fugate, *op. cit.* 18.

75. Fugate, *op. cit.* 48.

76. Jenkins, *op. cit.* 5.

77. Georgia Allen taped interview.

78. Ibid.

79. Ibid.

80. Ibid.

Chapter Seven—The Episcopalian Congregations

1. Frank Driskill and Noel Grisham, *Historic Churches of Texas: The Land and the People*, 1980, 103.

2. Sioux Campbell, *Fort Worth City Guide* "St. Andrews Episcopal Church," WP #17493.

3. Mary Lou Herring. compiler, *St. Andrew's Episcopal Church: Fort Worth, Texas*, 1997, 25.

4. Jennifer Morrison, "The History of the Episcopal Church in Fort Worth: Controversy Amongst Tradition," 1997, 6.

5. Herring, *op. cit.* 8.

6. WP# 13638, quoting 4/17/1887 *Fort Worth Daily Democrat*.

7. Herring, *op. cit.* 6.

8. *Fort Worth Tribune*, St. Andrews Episcopal Church Edition, 12/29/1939, 1.

9. Herring, *op. cit.* 40.

10. Roark, Carol E. *Fort Worth's Legendary Landmarks* 84.

11. Herring, *op. cit.* 55

12. Herring, *op. cit.* 41.

13. FWST, "Picture Story of 62-Year-Old Episcopal Church," 12/29/39, 10.

14. Herring, *op. cit.* 48.

15. *Fort Worth Tribune, op. cit.* 12/29/1939, 1.

16. Herring, *op. cit.* 18.

17. Jim Jones, *FWST* "The Rev. John W. Hildebrand, retired rector of St. Andrew's" 2/6/2000, B9

18. Jim Jones, "St. Andrew rector accepts call to teach," 1/4/2000, B6.

19. Quintin Morrow taped interview.

20. Ibid.

21. Charles A. Watson, *Trinity Parish: 1893-1993*, *xi*

22. Mrs. C. K. Smullen, *The History of Trinity Church*, 10.

23. Watson, *op. cit.* 268.

24. Watson, *op. cit.* 95.

25. Watson, *op. cit.* 272.

26. Watson, *op. cit.* 185.

27. John H. Stanley taped interview.

28 J. Frederick Barber taped interview.

29. Ibid.

Chapter Eight—The Church of Christ Congregations

1. Allan Carney, *Press* "Church of Christ Started as Mission in 1892 at Jennings Ave. and Leuda St." 3/29/34, 8.

2. William B. Williamson. *An Encyclopedia of Religions in the United States: 100 Religious Groups Speak for Themselves.* New York: Crossroad Publishing Company, 1992, 77.

3. Wyatt Sawyer, *80 Years of Service 1892-1972*, 2.

4. Ibid

5. *History of . . . 1892-1992*, 4.

6. Dan Leaf taped interview.

7. L. G. Lacy taped interview.

8. *History of the Southside Church of Christ: 1892-1992*, 6.

9. *History. . .1892-1992*, 7.

10. Texas State Historical Marker, 1992.

11. *FWST* "12 Started Church in School Building" 5/19/1956, 2.

12. Personal observation.

13. *1973 Directory North Side Church of Christ*, 1.

14. John C. Goble taped interview.

Chapter Nine—The Jewish Congregations

1. Paula Oates, editor, *Celebrating 150 Years* (Landmark Publishing, Inc. 1999), 54.

2. Personal correspondence.

3. Ruthe Winegarten, and Cathy Schechter, *The Lives & Legends of Texas Jew* (Austin, TX: Eakin Press, 1990), 15.

4. *Congregation Ahavath Sholom: 100th Anniversary*, 4.

5. Alfred Cohen, *Dan/Den-Dunn Family Reunion* 11.

6. *FWST* "New Synagogue Monument to Activity of Shanblum, 8/31/52. Section 1, 10.

7. Personal correspondence.

8. *FWST* "Workmen Start Dismantling Old Ahavath Sholom Synagogue," 11/28/51 pm, 13.

9. Personal correspondence.

10. Jack Douglas, *FWST*, "Workers Tearing Down Synagogue Used 45 Years," 11/28/51, am 8.

11. Oates, *op. cit.*, 56.

12. *Congregation Ahavath Sholom: 100th Anniversary*, 96.

13. *FWST* "Rabbi Garsek Gets Honorary Degree," 5/16/60 am, 6.

14. *Congregation Ahavath Sholom: 100th Anniversary*, 23.

15. Leo Rosten, *Joys of Yiddish*, (New York: McGraw Hill, 1968) 239.

16. Oates, *op. cit.*, 24.

17. Jim Jones, *FWST*, "Garsek eulogy:'Our rabbi is no more," 9/28/85, am A24.

18. Jim Jones, *FWST*, "Rabbi called to heal divided congregation," 12/12/99 City Edition, B9.

19. Alberto Zeilicovich taped interview.

20. Ibid.

21. Hollace Weiner, *Beth-El Congregation Centennial* 1.

22. Winegarten and Schechter, *op. cit.*, 137.

23. Flora Schiff, *The Jewish Monitor*, 9/10/15, 6.

24. Hollace Weiner, *op. cit.* 31.

25. Winegarten and Schechter, *op. cit.* 118.

26. Hollace Weiner, *op. cit.* 32

27. *FWST* "Temple Beth-El Buys Property for $15,000 Buildin (sic) 2/28/1919, 8.

28. Hollace Weiner, *op. cit.* 35.

29. Hollace Weiner, *op. cit.* 40.

30. *FWST* "Fire Destroys Jewish Temple," 8/30/46 am, 4.

31. Hollace Weiner, *op. cit.* 41.

32. Ibid.

33. Personal correspondence.

34. Hollace Weiner, *op. cit.* 37.

35. Ibid.

36. Ralph D. Mecklenburger taped interview.

37. *Beth-El Congregation: Fort Worth, Texas 2000-5760*, 4.

38. Hollace Weiner, *op. cit.*, 46

39. Ralph D. Mecklenburger taped interview.

Chapter Ten—The Lutherans

1. William B. Williamson. *An Encyclopedia of Religions in the United States*, 203.

2. *FWST*, "St. Paul Lutheran Has New Building" 5/7/55 pm, 2.

3. *A Century of Grace, 1893-1993: St. Paul Lutheran Church*, 19.

4. *FWST*, "St. Paul's Church, That of the Slanting Ridgepole, Should Be Seen From Inside." 10/8/1954, 20.

5. *A Century of Grace,* 5.

6. *A Century of Grace,* 24.

7. Paul Bourgeois, *FWST*, "Lutheran Church marks century in community," 9/29/1993 am Tarrant Southwest edition, 2.

8. John Messmann taped interview.

9. Ibid.

Chapter Eleven—First Congregational/United Church of Christ

1. William B. Williamson. *An Encyclopedia of Religions in the United States*, 103.

2. Sioux Campbell, WP #17462.

3. *Ultra*, "Pilgrimage to Fort Worth," Nov. 1981, 60.

4. *Fort Worth Record*, "New Congregational Chapel" 7/5/1903, church archives.

5. Dave Barber, News Release, "100th Anniversary of First Congregational Church," 6/18/2003, Church archives 2.

6. Ibid.

7. C. W. Post, personal correspondence 4/28/1904, church archives.

8. *Fort Worth Telegram*, "Dedication New Church Building" 7/1/1906, 9.

9. Ibid.

10. Barber, *op. cit.*, 3.

11. Ibid.

12. *FWST* Dr. R. Ralph Nichols obituary, 5/27/99 am 8B.

13. *St. John's United Church of Christ 75th Anniversary: 1882-1957*, 2.

14. Ibid.

15. Dave Barber taped interview.

16. Ibid.

Chapter Twelve—They Too Made History

1. J'Nell Pate, *North of the River: A Brief History of North Fort Worth* (Fort Worth: TCU Press, reprint 1994), 63.

2. Mark Lowery, *Fort Worth Weekly*, Nov. 6-13, 1997, 5.

3. *FWST* "Orthodox Easter Dates Explained," 4/8/61, 3.

4. *FWST*, "Greek Orthodox Pastor, Rev. A. Vlamides," 8/11/55 am, 3.

5. *Press*, "Father A. Vlamides Dies in Home Here," 8/11/55, 3.

6. Pate, *op. cit.* 63.

7. Lowery, *op. cit.* 4.

8. Lowery, *op. cit.* 5.

9. Mary Rogers, *FWST*, "Taking change in stride," 4/22/2002, 1B.

10. Evelyn Newman, "A Historical Profile: Christ Church in Wedgewood," unpublished paper, 1.

11. WP #18213

12. Newman, *op. cit.* 1.

13. WP #18214.

14. Darius Johnston, "Taking A Look," unpublished, 1.

15. Newman, *op. cit.*, 15.

16. Darius Johnston, *op. cit.* 2.

17. Ibid.

18. Ibid.

19. Personal observation.

20. Darius Johnston taped interview.

21. Darius Johnston, "Rejoice 2000!" unpublished 2.

22. Darius Johnston taped interview.

23. "An Introduction to Unitarian Universalism," unpublished, 1.

24. "An Introduction to Unitarian Universalism." 2.

25. Dorothy Greninger, *Unitarian Universalism in Fort Worth, Texas: 1946-1993*, 4.

26. Greninger, *op. cit.* 6.

27. Greninger, *op. cit.* 9.

28. Greninger, *op. cit.* 14.

29. Greninger, *op. cit.* 22.

30. Marjorie Montgomery taped interview.

31. Craig Roshaven taped interview.

32. Ibid.

33. Greninger, *op. cit.*, 28.

34. Placard, First Jefferson Church.

35. *FWST*, "Ministry Pushed in Three Areas," 1/24/1970, 3A.

36. Jim Jones, *FWST*, "Church follows its membership to a new locale," 12/9/1979, 38A.

37. McKinney Memorial archives.

38. Ibid.

39. *PTL* Vol.1, no. 1, 1/20/74; church archives.

40. *FWST*, "congregation Is in $55,000 Property," 8/30/1958, pm 5.

41. *FWST*, "Minister, 91, Turns Earth on Birthday," church archives.

42. McKinney Memorial archives.

43. George Dolan, "Minister Fails to See the Light," archives.

44. Gustavo Reveles Acosta, *FWST*, "Sunday school teacher, 83, honored," 10/21/2002, B10.

45. Ken Horton taped interview.

46. Jim Jones, *FWST*, "Church launches new construction with a prayer," 5/27/2002, 10B.

47. Ken Horton taped interview.

Bibliography

Reference Works

Encyclopedia Britannica Vol. 18 "The Europeans-Americans in Texas." (Chicago: University of Chicago, 15th Edition) 166.

Federal Writers' Project. *Research Data, Fort Worth and Tarrant County, Texas* Microfiche. Fort Worth: Texas Writers' Project, 1941.

Books

Armstrong, H. C. *The Disciples of Christ: Who Are They and Why Are They.* Baltimore: Association for the Promoting of Christian Unity, 1924.

Arnold, Ann. *History of the Fort Worth Legal Community.* Austin: Eakin Press, 2000.

Brash, Sarah, Editor. *The American Story: Settling the West.*Alexandria, VA: Time-Life Books, 1996.

Boone, Theodore S., Editor. *Lord! Lord!: The Sermons of Dr.L. K. Williams.* Fort Worth, Texas: Historical Commission National Baptist Convention, U. S. A., Inc., 1942.

Bynum, E. B. *These Carried the Torch: Pioneers of Christian Education in Texas.* Dallas, TX: Walter F. Clark Co., printers, 1946.

Carpenter, Joel A. *Inside History of First Baptist Church, Fort Worth and Temple Baptist Church, Detroit: Life Story of Dr. J. Frank Norris.* New York: Garland Publishing, Inc., 1988.

Carter, James E. *Cowboys, Cowtown and Crosses: A Centennial History of the Tarrant Baptist Association.* Fort Worth, TX: Tarrant Baptist Association, 1986.

Cary, Reby. *Princes Shall Come Out of Egypt, Texas, and Fort Worth.* (Pittsburgh, PA: Dorrance Publishing Co., 2002.

Cuellar, Carlos E. *Stories from the Barrio: A History of Mexican Fort Worth.* Fort Worth, TX: Texas Christian University Press, 2003.

Deets, John. *Century of Love 1890-1990: The First One Hundred Years of the North Fort Worth Baptist Church.* Fort Worth, TX: s.n., 1990.

Driskill, Frank A. and Grisham, Noel. *Historic Churches of Texas: The Land and the People.* Austin, TX: Eakin Press, 1980.

Ellwood, Robert S. *Many People, Many Faiths: An Introduction to the Religious Life of Humankind.* Englewood Cliffs, NJ: Prentice-Hall, Inc. 1982.

Exley, Jo Ella Powell, Editor. *Texas Tears and Texas Sunshine: Voices of Frontier Women.* College Station, TX: Texas A & M University Press, 1985.

Falls, Roy Emerson. *A Biography of J. Frank Norris, 1877-1952.* [S.I.:s.n.], 1975.

Fortenberry, Grimes, Editor. *Mighty Works of Grace: A History of Travis Avenue Baptist Church.* Fort Worth, TX: Branch-Smith Printing Co., Inc., 1986.

Garrett, James Leo, Jr. *Living Stones: The Centennial History of Broadway Baptist Church* in two volumes. Fort Worth, TX: Branch-Smith Printing Co., Inc., 1984.

Garrett, Julia Kathryn. *Fort Worth" A Frontier Triumph*. Fort Worth, TX: Texas Christian University Press, 1996 reprint of The Encino Press, 1972.

Garrison, Winifred E. and DeGroot, Alfred. *The Disciple of Christ: A History*. St. Louis: Christian Board of Publication, 1948.

Gregory, Joel. *Too Great A Temptation: The Seductive Power of America's Super Church*. Fort Worth, TX: The Summit Group, 1994.

Colby Hall, *The Early Years: Fort Worth's University Christian Church* [Texas ? s.n. 1983?] 1.

Hankins, Barry. *God's Rascal: J. Frank Norris & the Beginnings of Southern Fundamentalism*. Lexington, Ky: University Press of Kentucky, 1996.

Herring, Mary Lou, Compiler, *Saint Andrew's Episcopal Church Fort Worth, Texas*. Fort Worth, Texas: St. Andrew's Church, 1997.

Hollon, W. Eugene. *The Southwest: Old and New*. New York: Alfred A. Knopf, 1961.

Hoover, William R. *St. Patrick's: The First 100 Years*. Fort Worth: St. Patrick's Cathedral, 1988.

Horace, Lillian B. Edited by L. Venchael Booth. *Crowned with Glory and Honor: The Life of Rev. Lacy Kirk Williams*. Hicksville, NY: Exposition Press, 1978.

Hudson, Winthrop S. *Religion in America*. New York: Charles Scribner's Sons, 1965.

Jenkins, JoAnn. *A History of Polytechnic United Methodist Church*. Fort Worth: Polytechnic United Methodist Church, 2000.

Johnson, Charles A. *The Frontier Camp Meeting: Religion's Harvest Time*. Dallas: Southern Methodist University Press, 1955.

Knight, Oliver. *Fort Worth: Outpost on the Trinity*. Fort Worth: Texas Christian University Press, (with new matter) 1990.

McClain, William B., Chairman of Hymnbook Project. *Songs of Zion*. Nashville: Abingdom Press, 1981.

McQueen, Clyde, *Black Churches in Texas: A Guide to Historic Congregations*. College Station, Texas: Texas A & M University Press, 2000.

Melton, J. Gordon, Editor. *Encyclopedia of American Religions*, Fifth Edition. New York: Gale Detroit Publishing, 1996.

Miller, Park Hays. *Why I Am a Presbyterian*. New York: Thomas Nelson & Sons, 1956.

Milner, Clyde A. II, O'Connor, Carol A., and Sandweiss, Martha A., Editors. *The Oxford History of the American West*. New York: Oxford University Press, 1994.

Morrill, Milo True. *A History of the Christian Denomination in American 1794-1911 AD*. Dayton, OH The Christian Publishing Co. 1912.

Morrison, Samuel E. and Commanger, Henry S. *Growth of the American Republic Vol. II* New York: Oxford University Press, 1980.

Myers, Sandra L., Editor. *Force without Fanfare: The Autobiography of K. M. Van Zandt*. Fort Worth: Texas Christian University Press, 1968; second printing 1995.

Neusner, Jacob, Editor. *World Religions in America: An Introduction*. Louisville, KY: Westminster/John Knox Press, 1944.

Oates, Paula, Editor. *Celebrating 150 Years: The Pictorial History of Fort Worth, Texas 1849-1999*. Fort Worth: Landmark Publishing, Inc., 1999.

Paddock, B. B. *History of Texas: Fort Worth and the Texas Northwest Edition*, Vol II. Chicago: The Lewis Publishing Company, 1922.

Pate, J'Nell. *North of the River: A Brief History of North Fort Worth*. Fort Worth: Texas Christian University Press, 1994 reprint.

Pellecchia, Michael. *Fort Worth: A Sesquicentennial Celebration*. Montgomery, AL: Community Communications, Inc, 1999.

Qualben, Lars Pederson. *A History of the Christian Church*. New York: Thomas Nelson & Sons, 1936.

Ritchie, Homer. *The Life and Legend of J. Frank Norris: The Fighting Parson*. Fort Worth: H. G. Ritchie, 1991.

Roark, Carol E. *Fort Worth's Legendary Landmarks*. (Photography by Byrd Williams) Fort Worth: Historic Preservation Council for Tarrant County, Texas, 1995.

Rosten, Leo. *The Joys of Yiddish*. New York: McGraw Hill, 1968.

Sanders, Leonard. *How Fort Worth Became the Texasmost City 849-1920*. Fort Worth: Texas Christian University Press, 1986.

Smith, Warren Thomas. *Harry Hosier: Circuit Rider*. Nashville, TN: The Upper Room, 1981.

Tatum, E. Ray. *Conquest or Failure: Biography of J. Frank Norris*. Dallas: Baptist Historical Foundation, 1966.

Terrell, J. C. *Reminiscences of the Early Days*. Fort Worth: Texas Printing Co., 1906. Reprinted by Texas Christian University Press in cooperation with Texas Wesleyan University on the occasion of Fort Worth's Sesquicentennial Celebrations, 1999.

Turner, Frederick Jackson. *The Frontier in American History*. Malabou, FL: Robert E. Krieger Publishing Co. Inc., 1920. Reprints New York: Holt, Rinehart and Winston, 1962, 1985.

Watson, Charles A. *Trinity Parish: Fort Worth, Texas 1893-1993*. Fort Worth: Trinity Episcopal Church, 1999.

Weiner, Hollace A. *Jewish Stars in Texas: Rabbis and their Work*. College Station, TX: Texas A & M University Press, 1999.

_____ *Beth-El Congregation Centennial, Fort Worth, Texas*. Fort Worth: Beth-El Temple, 2002.

J. D. F. Williams, *The First One Hundred and Twenty Years (1852-1972): A History of the First United Methodist Church, Fort Worth*

Winegarten, Ruthe and Schechter, Cathy. *The Lives & Legends of Texas Jews*. Austin, TX: Eakin Press, sponsored by the Texas Jewish Historical Society, 1990.

Williams, Mack. *In Old Fort Worth*. Fort Worth: Mack and Madeline Williams, 1977.

Williamson, William B. *An Encyclopedia of Religions in the United States: 100 Religious Groups Speak for Themselves*. New York: Crossroad Publishing Company, 1992.

Congregation Histories

(These records, some published, some available only in individual church archives; may or may not list authors or editors; may or may not be dated, and may or may not number pages. However, they are valuable sources of data.

Unless otherwise noted, they are housed in the individual churches or the Genealogy/Local History Department of the Fort Worth Public Library)

ALL SAINTS CATHOLIC

Amado Guzman, historical consultant. *A Celebration of 68 Years of Service of the Claretian Order to San Jose and All Saints Parishes: June 3, 1926 to June 30, 1994.* "Brief Historical Sketch of All Saints Parish."

"History of San Jose Church."

ALLEN CHAPEL AME

Joe Standifer. "History of Allen Chapel African Methodist Episcopal Church, Fort Worth, Texas, 1982.

AHAVATH SHOLOM

Congregation Ahavath Sholom: 100th Anniversary

BETH-EL

Beth-El Congregation Centennial: Fort Worth, Texas 2000-5760

BROADWAY BAPTIST

Garrett, James Leo, Jr. *Living Stones: The Centennial History of Broadway Baptist Church* in two volumes. Fort Worth, TX: Branch-Smith Printing Co., Inc., 1984.

Why We Love Broadway: A Patchwork of Words.

To the Glory of God: The Memorial Windows of Broadway Baptist Church.

CHRIST CHURCH ASSEMBLY OF GOD

Darius Johnston. "Taking A Look."

Evelyn Newman. "A Historical Profile: Christ Church in Wedgewood," unpublished paper.

CHRIST UNITED METHODIST

Ruth Reiter Stone, "ST. MARK UNITED METHODIST CHURCH" unpublished paper, United Methodist Records and Archives, Texas Wesleyan University West Library, 1. (Box 63.7).

COMMUNITY CHRISTIAN/EAST ANNIE ST.

Mrs. H. V. Shanks, *Disciples All: A Study of the East Annie Christian Church* Fort Worth: E. Annie Church.

"Community Christian Church: Homecoming-2002."

CORINTH BAPTIST

Shirley Abram, *et al. Corinth Baptist Church: 1886-1986.*

FIRST BAPTIST

A Brief Pictorial History of First Baptist Church, Fort Worth, Texas: 125th Anniversary. Arlington Baptist College archives.

FIRST CHRISTIAN

First Christian Church 115 Anniversary 1855-1970.

James B. Bradshaw. "History of the Christian Church in Fort Worth: A Term Theme. . . " TCU 1949.

FIRST CONGREGATIONAL/ST. JOHN

St. John's United Church of Christ 75th Anniversary: 1882-1957.

FIRST JEFFERSON

Dorothy Greninger. *Unitarian Universalism in Fort Worth, Texas: 1946-1993.*

"An Introduction to Unitarian Universalism."

FIRST PRESBYTERIAN

First Presbyterian Church 1985 Directory.

Dorothy Iba, Rose Marie Jennings, Gail Barham and Dan E. Goldsmith, editors, *First Presbyterian Church: Our History.* (Fort Worth: First Presbyterian Church, 2000)

FIRST UNITED METHODIST/ST. PAUL METHODIST EPISCOPAL

J. D. F. Williams. *The First One Hundred and Twenty Years (1852-1972): A History of the First United Methodist Church, Fort Worth.*

GREATER ST. JAMES BAPTIST

100th Church Celebration: Greater St. James Baptist Church.

HANDLEY UNITED METHODIST

Mrs. P. J. Brown. *Handley United Methodist Church.*

The Church in Action.

Charles Whittle, Unpublished, church archives

Robert C. Warden, Unpublished, church archives

Mrs. Billy Brown, Unpublished, church archives

"The Church Bell," Unpublished, church archives

HEMPHILL PRESBYTERIAN

Lois White Deaton, *A History of Hemphill Presbyterian Church, Fort Worth, Texas, 1891-1991* Fort Worth: Hemphill Presbyterian Church, 1991.

Centennial Celebration Committee, "Hemphill Presbyterian Church Time Line."

Iglesia Gethsame

"MEXICAN PRESBYTERIAN CHURCH, FORT WORTH, TEXAS: TEX-MEX PRESBYTERY, SYNOD OF TEXAS, ORGANIZED 1927." (sic)

"SOME THINGS ABOUT THE SOCIAL ACTION REPORT TO THE MODERATOR FROM THE CLERK," (sic) unpublished document belonging to congregant Sam Frias, believed to be written about 1997.

MAGNOLIA CHRISTIAN

History of Magnolia Avenue Christian Church.

Magnolia Christian Church vertical file, Fort Worth Public Library, Local History Department

MCKINNEY MEMORIAL

Archive scrapbooks, untitled.

MISSOURI AVE. METHODIST

"Missouri Ave. Methodist Church," Unpublished paper,United Methodist Records and Archives, Texas Wesleyan University West Library.

MORNING CHAPEL CME

Morning Chapel Christian Methodist Episcopal Church History: 1873-1977.

"The C. M. E. Church Celebrates Its 115th Birthday." 12/15/1985.

MT. GILEAD BAPTIST

"History of the Boone House,"

"A Tribute: Dr. L. Venchael Booth"

MT. PISGAH BAPTIST

Mount Pisgah Baptist Church: 1875-1975, 76 Memories. Fort Worth, 1975.

Through the Years: Mount Pisgah Missionary Baptist Church, 125th Anniversary. Fort Worth, Mt. Pisgah, 2000.

MT. ZION BAPTIST

Y. C. Shamblee, *et al. A Historical Narrative: Mount Zion Missionary Baptist Church.*

"Mt. Zion Baptist Church, 108th Anniversary, 1894-2002."

NORTH FORT WORTH BAPTIST

Deets, John. *Century of Love 1890-1990: The First One Hundred Years of the North Fort Worth Baptist Church.* Fort Worth, TX: s.n., 1990.

NORTH SIDE CHURCH OF CHRIST

1973 Directory, North Side Church of Christ

OUR MOTHER OF MERCY CATHOLIC

Our Mother of Mercy Directory, 2002.

POLYTECHNIC UNITED METHODIST

Monette Fugate. *Polytechnic United Methodist Church, 1892-1992: A History.*

JoAnn Jenkins. *A History of Polytechnic United Methodist Church.*

ST. ANDREW UNITED METHODIST

Anna Jo Johnson, anniversary chairperson. *St. Andrews United Methodist Church: Centennial Anniversary 1888-1988.*

Natalie Johnson. *History of St. Andrews United Methodist Church of Fort Worth,* unpublished paper, Missouri Ave. Methodist Church, United Methodist Records and Archives, Texas Wesleyan University West Library

ST. ANDREWS EPISCOPAL

Mary Lou Herring, compiler. *St. Andrew's Episcopal Church: Fort Worth, Texas,* 1997.

Jennifer Morrison. "The History of the Episcopal Church in Fort Worth: Controversy Amongst Tradition," 1997.

ST. DEMETRIOS GREEK ORTHODOX

St. Demetrios: 75th Anniversary 1910-1985

ST. PATRICK CATHOLIC CATHEDRAL

Jean Andrus. *"Baroque Comes to St. Patrick's."*

William R. Hoover. *St. Patrick's: The First 100 Years.*

Fort Worth: St. Patrick's Cathedral, 1988.

ST. PAUL LUTHERAN

A Century of Grace, 1893-1993: St. Paul Lutheran Church.

ST. STEPHEN PRESBYTERIAN

Juanita Cowan. *The History of St. Stephen.* Fort Worth: St. Stephen Presbyterian Church, April 22, 1997.

To the Glory of God: A Building for Worship.

SOUTHSIDE CHURCH OF CHRIST

Wyatt Sawyer. *80 Years of Service 1892-1972.*

History of the Southside Church of Christ: 1892-1992.

TRAVIS AVE. BAPTIST

Grimes Fortenberry, editor. *Mighty Works of Grace: A History of Travis Avenue Baptist Church 1911-1986*

TRINITY EPISCOPAL

Mrs. C. K. Smullen. *The History of Trinity Church.*

Charles A. Watson, *Trinity Parish 1893-1993*

UNIVERSITY CHRISTIAN

Martha Youngdale, editor, *University Christian Church, Fort Worth, Texas 1978 Pictorial Directory* "A Brief History of University Christian Church."

Hall, Colby D. *The Early Years: University Christian Church 1873-1941? 43?.* Typescript bound in TCU Library.

WESTMINSTER PRESBYTERIAN

Wilber Klint, *et al* editors. *Westminster Presbyterian Church: Our Church History: 1888-1988.* Fort Worth, Westminster Presbyterian Church, 1988.

"New Milestone in 62-Year History" Westminster Church archives.

Other Documents

Alfred Cohen, *Dan/Den-Dunn Family Reunion.* (Ahavath Sholom)

Fort Worth Gazette 7/11/1892, reprinted in "Given to God." University of Texas at Arlington Special Collections Library archives.

Lee Roy McGlone, "The Preaching of J. Frank Norris: An Apologia for Fundamentalism," dissertation, Southwestern Baptist Theological Seminary.

Rev. French McKee, vertical files, Fort Worth Public Library, Local History Department.

E. Ray Tatum, "The J. Frank Norris Murder Trial of 1927", thesis, Southwestern Baptist Theological Seminary.

W. Erskine Williams, "Sketch of History of Fort Worth Methodism," UTA Special Collections Library.

Wortham, (no first name, no date, draft document of early Fort Worth churches, UTA Special Collections Library.

Periodicals

North Texas Catholic

Baptist History and Heritage

Foundations

Baptist History and Heritage

The Texas Baptist

Ultra

Christian Church in the Southwest

Newspapers

Daily Democrat

Dallas Morning News

Fort Worth Daily Gazette

Fort Worth Democrat, weekly

Fort Worth Gazette

Fort Worth Press

Fort Worth Record

Fort Worth Star

Fort Worth Star-Telegram

Fort Worth Telegram

Fort Worth Tribune

Fort Worth Weekly

The Horned Frog, (TCU)

La Vida

Taped interviews

L. B. Adams

Georgia Allen

Hope P. Ayala

L. G. Austin

Vaughn Baker

Dave Barber

J. Frederick Barber

Cedric D. Britt

Betty Bryan

Kerven Carter, Jr.

Alfred Cohen

Scott Colglazier

Juanita Cowan

Nehemiah Davis

Michael Farrell

Grimes Fortenberry

Lucy Fountain

Janet Fowler

Sam Frias

John C. Goble

Dan Goldsmith

Gus Guthrie

Luther Henry

Mary Lou Herring

Donald R. Hogg

Ken Horton

Esteban Jasso

R. C. Johnson

Darius Johnston

Gregory H. Kimble

Wilber Klint

L. G. Lacy

Dan Leaf

Ralph Mecklenburger

John Messmann

Marjorie Montgomery

Max Morgan

Quinton Morrow

James M. Moudy

Dorothy Patras

Tom Plumbley

Homer Ritchie

Craig Roshaven

Charles Sanders

Mark Scott

Johnny Smith

John Stanley

Frank Staton

Michael Stearns

George Stephens

Robert J. Thomson

Elvie Walker

Clifford Williams

Donald Wills

Brett Younger

Alberto Zeilicovich

Other

Nehemiah Davis vita.

Reverend Louis Belvet George Biographical Sketch.

Msgr. Hubert J. Neu, telephone interview.

Velina G. Willis, "Career Development Case Study of Rev. L. B. Adams."

Texas State Historical Marker, 1992.

Texas State Historical Marker, 1983.

Index

Index of Congregations

General Index